Escaping Madness

Greenhill Books

Escaping Madness

EYEWITNESS ACCOUNTS FROM WORLD WAR II

Klaus G. Förg
Foreword by Roger Moorhouse

Greenhill Books

Escaping Madness: Eyewitness Accounts from World War II

Greenhill Books

First published by Greenhill Books, 2024
Greenhill Books, c/o Pen & Sword Books Ltd,
George House, Units 12 & 13
Beevor Street, Off Pontefract Road, Barnsley, South Yorkshire S71 1HN
For more information on our books, please visit
www.greenhillbooks.com, email contact@greenhillbooks.com
or write to us at the above address.

Roger Moorhouse foreword © Greenhill Books, 2024
Eva Burke English-language translation © Greenhill Books, 2024
Main text © 2022 Edition Förg GmbH, Rosenheim, Germany

The right of Klaus G. Förg to be identified as the author of this
Work has been asserted by him in accordance with the
Copyright, Designs and Patents Act 1988

Publishing History
Escaping Madness was first published in 2022 by Edition Förg GmBH,
Rosenheim, Germany, with the title *Dem Wahnsinn entkommen*.
This new English-language edition, translated by Eva Burke,
has additional material by Roger Moorhouse.

CIP data records for this title are available from the British Library

ISBN 978-1-80500-063-1

Typeset by JCS Publishing Services Ltd
Typeset in 11/15pt Adobe Caslon Pro
Printed and bound in Great Britain by CPI Group (UK) Ltd,
Croydon, CRO 4YY

Contents

Translator's Note

This is a collection of eyewitness accounts by soldiers and relatives of soldiers who fought in World War II. To retain the sense of the time which has elapsed between the narrators' past and their interviews, the past tense has been used.

Although written with hindsight, these memoirs carry a sense of real-time immediacy. They are based on interviews with Klaus G. Förg; written in the first person, the vividness of the memory and the personal voice of each narrator shine through. In a chapter where language can barely reflect the depth of human tragedy, we are thrust into the atrocities of the Warsaw Uprising. The chapter narrated by a prisoner of war in Russia makes for grim reading; it uses language still reverberating in reports from prisoners in forced labour camps operating around the world today. In another chapter, the language of an officer on a U-boat is more scientific; in stark contrast to the previous chapter, his report as a prisoner of war interned in America has, dare one say, a touristy appeal. But then, in the final chapter, the focus shifts and the reader now hears the female perspective in the sad voice of Rosa, daughter and sister of soldiers killed in the war.

From the protagonists' colourful depictions of nature and family life reflecting a charmed childhood in idyllic countryside, we move inexorably into the active war years. Here the language descends into dark descriptions of horror and deprivation. We do not hear of individual perpetrations of crimes or brutality by these soldiers, but the repetition of 'this image will stay with me forever' sounds an underlying tone of guilt. Most of the interviewees grew up on farms. Their vocabulary is witness to in-depth experience and knowledge of toiling on the land, of harvesting, forestry and husbandry. An exception is the chapter on the famous German U-234, with its own linguistic challenge and terminology specific to submarine warfare and radar technology. Throughout, the voices are of young people emphasising their own youth, their lack of insight and awareness. Listening to them, one senses that they felt plunged into a war for which they bore no responsibility. That, it seems, comes with old age; indeed, all the chapters end with a tone of introspection, realisation and hope spoken by these men and women at the end of their lives.

The German title, *Dem Wahnsinn entkommen*, has two components within the noun: 'Wahn' and 'Sinn'. Though 'Wahn' etymologically does not – as is commonly assumed – signify the noun 'Wahn' as in 'frenzy/mania/craze', it is derived from 'wahn', an adjective signifying 'empty/devoid'. We might look at both meanings. The war years as described by the protagonists were indeed senseless, devoid of meaning and understanding. And the 'mania' we hear about, when soldiers were observed acting in a frenzy while blindly obeying the orders of a madman, a 'Wahnsinniger', is woven through this entire dreadful period which was never meant to be repeated.

For the sake of clarity, I have referred to Polish, Ukrainian or Russian towns, rivers and cities by their official names as they are known today. For German cities and areas, I have maintained German spelling unless the place is particularly well known by its English equivalent (Bavaria, not Bayern, but Puchschlagen). Where I think it might be helpful for English-language readers to have a translation of German or Russian words, these are in round parentheses. Where the reader might benefit from an explanation or more information, I have added these in square brackets.

Eva Burke

Foreword

World War II is one of the most extensively examined and documented periods in human history. Yet, despite the huge volume of scholarship that chronicles the conflict, the experiences of German soldiers and civilians often occupy a rather liminal space in our collective memory. While the nefarious deeds of the Wehrmacht and SS are well known, their atrocities rightfully condemned, the personal stories of those individuals caught in the maelstrom – as perpetrators, bystanders or victims – are often pushed to the margins by the grander narratives of ideology or military strategy. This book, though rather modest in its scope, nonetheless foregrounds some of those first-hand accounts, and in the process provides a novel and nuanced German perspective on the war.

The five personal accounts presented here are the product of a series of interviews carried out in recent years by the author and publisher Klaus G. Förg. They provide an impressive spectrum of experiences, effectively spanning the European theatre of the war; from the brutal post-war captivity in the Soviet interior to the last gasp of the U-boat war, from the war in the air to the hardships of the German home front. The collective narrative that they present is a challenging and enlightening one: a tapestry woven with strands of triumph, of guilt, of suffering and of survival.

The account that stands out the most, perhaps, in its richness of detail at least, is that of Erich Menzel, whose seemingly charmed military career took him from the Reich Labour Service all the way to a prisoner of war camp in the United States, via flying for the Luftwaffe over the Soviet

Union and an improbable last-ditch U-boat mission to Japan. It is truly a remarkable story, and one which is told with such acuity and attention to detail that it carries considerable utility as a historical document.

Michael Strasser, meanwhile, was rather less fortunate. His service on the Eastern Front ended in Soviet captivity and a succession of prisoner of war camps in which he was obliged to perform hard labour, losing many of his comrades along the way. As an account of the harsh realities, and occasional tendernesses, of life in post-war Soviet captivity, his is a fascinating and enlightening story, all the more significant because of its rarity.

Heinz Polke's story and account of the Warsaw Uprising is certainly a fascinating one. It is almost Švejkian in character: that of an innocent who seems to sail unscathed through the maelstrom, shielded from events by serendipity and the petty kindnesses of others.

Taken together, all of these accounts – from the high-flier Menzel, to the rather humbler, rural life of Rosa Assböck – demonstrate the complexity and diversity of the German experience of World War II: the visceral thrill of combat, the shame of complicity with a criminal regime, or the numbing monotony of Soviet captivity. Amid the privations and horrors, there was often a complex interplay of other emotions: duty, fear and disillusionment, as the war dragged on and victory became increasingly elusive.

On the home front, meanwhile, the initial euphoria of quick, seemingly bloodless victories gave way to a grim new reality in which the Allied bombing campaign intensified and shortages of food and basic necessities vied for attention with the ever-present spectre of death. For many, life became a struggle for survival, marked by loss and suffering that transcended the front lines and left personal scars and societal trauma that would endure for decades.

Nonetheless, as these accounts show, there were also moments of good fortune, profound resilience and humanity; a kindly gesture by a superior, or a youthful friendship rekindled as post-war romance. They are a reminder that, for all the headline horrors of the war with which we are all so familiar, the atrocities and the moral complexities, it is still at heart a human story, one of ordinary people – with all their attendant virtues and faults – cast into extraordinary circumstances.

In highlighting the experiences of ordinary Germans – soldiers and civilians alike – this book aims to provide a rather more nuanced understanding of a nation caught in the very epicentre of one of history's darkest chapters. In much of the literature on the subject of the war, stale stereotypes and lazy binaries still abound; indeed they sometimes seem to multiply and proliferate as the events concerned recede beyond human memory. Yet, history is rarely so clear cut; grey areas, paradoxes and contradictions assail us at every turn. We must constantly remind ourselves of the cardinal virtues of the historian: objectivity, open-mindedness and a willingness to embrace the complexity. This book is a useful reminder of the necessity of those virtues. Through the voices of that generation of Germans who lived through the war – whether on the front lines or the home front – we gain an insight into the complex realities of human behaviour under extreme conditions; the resilience, the compromises, and the moral ambiguities that often result.

All of those whose life stories are reproduced here succeeded in, as the title puts it, 'Escaping Madness' of the war, in that they survived to tell their tale. Yet, for all of them, that survival was not a given, indeed in many cases it was merely happenstance or the intervention of some intangible providence: the product of a fickle fate, a fate which would fail to smile on so many of their fellows. 'Madness' indeed.

Roger Moorhouse
2024

Preface

For several years I have been meeting up with soldiers who served for the Wehrmacht in World War II, spending many hours listening to their experiences during the Third Reich. I must have carried out forty-eight conversations with my interviewees, all the while being acutely aware that we were running out of time, seeing that these men were fast approaching their hundredth birthdays.

Listening to the veterans recounting one horrendous and traumatic event after another, I was rather surprised that these men were both physically and mentally in good shape, though admittedly many years had passed since the end of the war. For some of them it was the very first time they had dipped into their past and the reasons for that could be manifold. Perhaps it was shame that had held them back from openly speaking about their memories for so many years. Or perhaps their silence stemmed from sensing that people in Germany and Austria shied away from being reminded of this terrible period. Many obviously felt shame at being German as it was our nation that had caused this mad war, a war that turned out to be the biggest catastrophe in the history of humankind to date. While other peoples were in a position to take pride in their own nation, in my opinion this only happened in Germany when the football world championship took place. That event, branded a *Sommermärchen* (a summer fairytale), was when country could once again feel proud and hoist the nation's flag. It has taken the Germans sixty-one years.

'All Germans were perpetrators', a student of history once countered in a conversation I had with her. In the first few years after the war much energy was spent both in scientific research and in publications to differentiate meticulously between the guilty political organisations and the morally clean Wehrmacht. But as the years went on, it became increasingly obvious that the German army was also involved in the crimes committed by the Nazi regime. Nonetheless, I am unable to agree with the conclusion made by this student. After carrying out many conversations with ex-soldiers, I conclude that millions of young men were driven into this war by a brutal regime which did not allow for refusal or disagreement. The young lads were never really convinced that it was justified or indeed necessary.

My interviewees all came from normal families. Many had grown up on farms where they had laboured in the stables or on the fields belonging to their fathers. Or they had been apprentices, students who never had the urge to leave home, to leave their familiar environment to join a war without knowing whether they would ever return to their families. Refusal was not an option and would have only led to severe punishment or even death.

In Germany, much like in other totalitarian regimes, many men had failed to succeed in their civilian lives which, in the face of the global economic crisis at the time, wasn't entirely their own fault. By becoming a member of the NSDAP and joining the SA and the SS, its paramilitary organisation, they hoped to gain professional success as well as social standing. It was precisely these political careerists who acted with exceptional barbarism and cruelty initially against their own political adversaries in Germany, and then later, during the war, unleashed their brutality on the alleged enemies of race and ideology. Ultimately it was these 'partymen' and the ruthless followers of Adolf Hitler who carried the responsibility for the crimes committed in the name of Germany, and not the countless simple soldiers who somehow had to manoeuvre themselves through these difficult years. It is quite understandable that only a few of them managed to remain unaffected by the incessant indoctrination and ideological brainwashing. Essentially, they were just hoping they would survive.

In our conversations, all these people were open and honest about what they had experienced, what went through their minds at the time and what feelings they might have had. Overcome by the impact of their

Heinz Polke recounts his wartime experiences.

traumatic memories, some burst into tears. They were able to remember the most minute details of those dark years. They had never been able to push away or forget those dreadful experiences, which continued to have an impact on them later on, as they became older. At the same time these eyewitnesses were conscious of how fortunate they had been to survive and return to normal life. I didn't meet a single person amongst those I interviewed who would glorify the war. Instead, they all insisted that this event must never happen again. Despite the horrendous atrocities which they recounted, these conversations remain the most impressive and memorable experiences I have had in my life.

With my books I strive to impart the horrors of dictatorship to a new generation untouched by them, to teach people that history must not be forgotten, nor must it be allowed to repeat itself. I am losing hope that we can do this. At the time of putting the finishing touches to this book yet another megalomanic despot in Europe is attempting to redraw existing and agreed-upon national boundaries by using military force. His sole purpose is to turn his imperialist visions into reality. The Russian attack on Ukraine markedly resembles a story plucked from the past; current events echo a time of rulers we thought we had put behind us. Yet, here we are with Ukraine – the country most profoundly affected by Stalin's brutal force of power and by Hitler's heinous crimes – suffering yet again violence and injustice. Once more our world seems to be staring into an abyss. At this hour I can only express the hope that when you hold this book in your hands this awful war has also become history.

Klaus G. Förg

The Horrors of the Warsaw Uprising

AN EYEWITNESS ACCOUNT BY HEINZ POLKE

My childhood in Dresden was short lived. I was born on 14 August in the Saxonian capital, but soon after my birth my mother gave me away to be looked after by strangers. My grandfather must have somehow heard about this as he started investigating my whereabouts. He found out where I lived and brought me into his home in Mainaschaff, a district in Lower Franconia. It was therefore a rather bumpy start to life, seeing as my parents wanted nothing to do with me. Rumour has it that Mother was poor and that my parents weren't good people. My grandmother had already raised five children back in Russia and obviously now decided to take in a sixth. To me, Grandmother was like a loving mother – unlike my grandfather, who was incredibly strict. Nonetheless, I have fond childhood memories.

When Grandmother was asked her reasons for having shown such generosity, she used to answer: 'You don't understand. This child is looking for his mother. I simply had to take Heinz in and trust that I can raise him properly.'

She did all she could for me, caring for me and looking after my well-being. My own mother most certainly couldn't have given me anything close to such a home, and I was happy growing up there. My first day at school approached and I was not looking forward at all to holding my *Schultüte* [a paper cone filled with sweets, a German tradition for the first day of school], which was usually warmly welcomed by children. Instead, I burst out crying, not wanting to step into the school building. Grandma agreed to walk me into the classroom and sat next to me for the entire day. She accompanied me again the next day, but at that point the teacher felt Grandma should leave me to it and return at the end of the school day to pick me up. From then on, Grandma picked me up every single day.

The years of my childhood went by without me ever truly becoming especially aware of any political changes. The war broke out when I turned fourteen. I was fearful and discussed this with Grandma, but she was actually quite calm about it and wasn't particularly concerned.

'No need to be frightened, boy. Mark my words, before they call you into the army the war will be over.'

Meanwhile I had started an electrical apprenticeship. By that time our National Socialist state had seeped through all areas of life. Hitler was venerated by most, and when the order for hoisting flags was issued, most houses were decorated with a swastika flag. If someone was unwilling, people would stare at them and frown – though, quite possibly, even worse could befall that person.

I eventually completed my apprenticeship in Aschaffenburg under my master electrician, a truly fine human being who along with his wife often invited me upstairs into their flat for a meal. They both did their very best not to let the other apprentices realise that on some level they treated me as a son, seeing that I didn't have any parents. My master took me along on all his calls and I remember quite vividly visiting an elegant lady living in a villa in Platanenallee who requested from my master that he bring along 'the small dark-haired boy'.

One day I was asked to do some repair work in that villa. The lady went out to do some shopping, leaving me behind on my own. She obviously had full confidence in me. Upon her return and as a form of remuneration she served me a delicious meal and gave me a tip as well before sending me on my way. The following day my boss's wife asked me how it had been for me.

'It actually went all right,' I answered, at which she simply shook her head in disbelief, saying how surprised she was that the lady had placed such trust in me.

While Grandma was relatively indifferent towards the Nazi regime, Grandpa was slightly more enthusiastic about the military successes achieved by the Wehrmacht. August von Mackensen had made a particular impression on him. Grandpa worshipped this man, a Prussian field marshal who had chalked up impressive results while fighting on the Eastern Front during World War I [During World War II Mackensen expressed concern about the atrocities committed by the Wehrmacht in Poland]. Grandpa had spent many years in Russia, posted to the middle section of the front, where he had been charged with the stockpiling of tree trunks from which pulp was extracted and earmarked for a firm in Pirna. Even after the war, he'd continue his forays into the woods, where he would mark trees due for felling. On his route he'd often drop by at our place in Mainaschaff, invariably bringing me a small trinket or food he wanted to surprise me with. Fortunately, because this time round he was too old, he wasn't called up for military service.

The war was moving along, with the end of my apprenticeship fast approaching. Just a few days ahead of the trade exams my master had an inkling of what was lying ahead: 'I know full well that you'll be called up soon.' And he was right. In 1942 I was called up to report to the Reichsarbeitsdienst (RAD) in Irlbach [the Reich Labour Service, a paramilitary organisation in Nazi Germany].

Our main task was to excavate a large area in order to create an ice pond for a brewery. The ice would be hacked out in the winter, then cut into chunks and stored for the summer in barrels to cool the beer. This type of labour entailed digging like mad, day in and day out. Totally exhausted by the end of the day, we collapsed onto our mattresses.

Honestly, those days were unbelievably hard. We had to do the digging without the help of any machines, as we'd only been given simple shovels to work with. We lugged the earth onto trolleys and it was down to us alone to move them – pushing against them with our bodyweight, leaning and shoving with all our might. Somehow, we managed despite the lack of trains to help us. Every day was brutal, the torturous labour and the drill exercises that brought us to the brink of collapse. We filed past our superiors shouldering spades, blades pointing upwards like guns – it was harsh.

When we were about to complete our service, they came to recruit for the Waffen-SS. We would, so they promised, receive better food and even be offered a crate of oranges. It's quite incredible that they tried to convince us young soldiers to join the SS by tempting us in with some oranges.

'Wouldn't you want to come and join the Waffen-SS?' I was asked. But I resisted all their attempts to recruit me. 'No, I don't, and thank you for your understanding.'

I truly had to muster up all my courage to utter these words; the uniformed officer was really quite intimidating, and any disagreement seemed near impossible. So I just continued serving for the RAD and despite my refusal I didn't suffer any repercussions.

*

A call-up letter arrived – this must have been around the beginning of 1943 – ordering me to report for military training in Gelnhausen near Frankfurt with Battalion 87 of the 25th Panzer Division, under the leadership of Lieutenant General Adolf von Schell, an officer to be reckoned with. I even had to drive him at one point, and it was pretty nerve wracking as I absolutely did not want to make any mistakes.

'How are you, son? Happy here? Is everything all right?' he asked, his tone genial.

'Yes, sir, Lieutenant General!'

The military training in Gelnhausen was short but extremely hard. Part of the course included wading through mud, then immediately getting our soggy uniforms dry and presentable, ready to report within just ten minutes. Anyone who failed in this task was severely punished with a harsh drill and ordered to crawl through the sludge a second time.

The order came from a sergeant who was tough as nails – a hellish sort of a guy who once ordered a comrade in my barracks to get fully undressed, then don a gas mask and a steel helmet.

At that very moment an officer entered the room and had a go at my comrade: 'What on earth do you think you're doing?' he barked. 'Get into your clothes immediately!'

The incident, of course, did not go unreported. The sergeant's actions had consequences and he was promptly demoted. He was one of the first in our unit to be killed in service.

The training lasted approximately half a year, after which we were posted to Norway, somewhere in the vicinity of Oslo. We boarded the ship in Friedrichstadt, sailed up the Skagerrak and got a glimpse of the top of ships' masts, a reminder of the ships that sank there during World War I. As for me, I was so seasick that frankly I couldn't do any 'sight-seeing' and, in fact, I could never be bothered about these relics in any event. After we disembarked, we were transported to the army training grounds, a busy place with a lot of comings and goings. Fortunately, my boss, Senior Lieutenant Knudsen, was a decent fellow. Once, marching past us as we were lined up and standing to attention, he inspected us top to bottom, seemed to reflect for a moment before turning to me and stating: 'You're going to be my driver.'

'Sir, but I don't have a driver's licence,' I said.

'Pass it. And once done, report back to me. Understood?'

'There are car mechanics among the comrades. Why not give the job to one of them?' I continued.

'But I want *you* to be my driver.'

'Yes, sir.'

That's how I came to be his chauffeur. He too wanted 'the small dark one'. I remained in this post until the end of the war, and throughout my service he never failed to be very kind towards me. Once, when food rations were short, I was about to serve him a meal, but he simply pushed the dishes aside, towards me: 'You take it, you need it … you're still so young.'

We remained in Norway for only a brief period, after which we were posted to Denmark for our group to get replenished. First to Aalborg, then to Aarhus. One day I was ordered by my senior lieutenant to fetch some secret documents and I was meant to go on my own, without him. I got myself to division headquarters, picked up the documents, and on my return chanced upon a lovely army café. I stepped in and committed the crucial mistake of leaving the secret documents in the car. Sipping my coffee, I thoroughly enjoyed the lovely day I was having, gawking at pretty girls around me. I had barely left the café when I nearly had a heart attack, suddenly seeing that my car had gone – with the documents inside it.

Luckily, I remained calm and stood nonchalantly near the café entrance, waiting to see what was would happen. Would the car maybe turn up? And, would you believe it: after a few moments had ticked by, my stomach still churning, my car suddenly came round the corner with a sergeant sitting inside. He got out, slammed the door shut and entered the café. Sweating bullets, I forced myself to keep my composure. I approached the car slowly, got inside, and casually drove off. Some officers were lolling around nearby but didn't pay me the slightest attention. I drove for some 3 km and only then did I dare pull over to the side, stop the engine and open the glove compartment. My relief was huge, needless to say, when I saw that the envelope was there, with the secret documents still inside.

Upon my return, the boss asked me whether everything had gone smoothly. 'All good,' I replied, 'and all messages have now been dispatched.'

My heart gradually stopped thumping. If this had gone belly-up, it would easily have spelled my death. The Wehrmacht knew no pardon when it came to such serious misconduct.

Eventually we boarded a freight ship, loaded our sixty-four tanks and set course for Poland. From the Polish coast we headed towards Warsaw, putting hundreds of kilometres behind us as we crossed the country, winding our way through woods, across fields and past villages, where the inhabitants tended to hide behind doors and windows upon hearing our approach.

Throughout this I would be driving our senior lieutenant in a Tatra, a car similar to a VW where one could fully unhinge the doors. Our journey through Poland lasted several days and was relatively uneventful, with only the sound of roaring tanks easily reaching the village folk from afar and putting the fear of God into them. We rumbled through once-populated areas, the streets now deserted, no one in sight.

*

We set up camp in a forest near Radom, some hundred kilometres south of the capital. The Russians had evidently caught wind of our movements and had decided to pelt us with grenades that promptly exploded when they hit tree trunks. Even now the bangs of the detonations reverberate in my ears – I'll never forget it. After each blast flying splinters filled the air and you could be blown up at any moment.

The pounding continued for several days, we didn't dare leave the forest and spent our nights crouched inside our tanks – there was no let-up even when it was pitch dark. I vividly remember turning to God at those times and praying fervently for him to save me. 'Dear God, please, please protect me, I'm still so very young. Please let me survive, let me live.'

This was the first time I cried in that war. Fortunately, however, what with the deafening inferno of detonations and the mayhem all around us, nobody seemed to notice. This, mind you, was the first time I had lived through an attack. Catching any sleep with us lot squeezed in the tight quarters of the tank was utterly impossible. Shaking like a leaf, I was frightened to the core. Thoughts of home, memories of my grandma, of my master and all those dear to me came popping up in my head – but I knew that not a single one of them was able to offer me any protection. Not here.

Time and time again the Russians would attack us with their small planes dropping phosphorus-filled bombs. They'd literally shovel them out of their aircraft, the bombs exploding in mid-air and the deadly phosphorus trickling down on us. During one of these raids, a comrade was hit directly, and a thick layer of phosphorus covered his entire body.

Petrified, incredulous actually, I stood by and watched this young man's body crumple up. Within a few moments he had burnt to death. I'll never forget him. He had stood only a very short distance away from me, a few metres maybe … This grisly image will stay with me forever.

Dawn was breaking and my comrades in the tanks began to stir. By decree of the military administration the milking of cows in the nearby village had been forbidden and the sound of distressed cows mooing at a high pitch was so unsettling to my boss that he turned around and ordered us to milk them immediately so that children of the village could once again be provided with milk. Delighted women farmers embraced us, grateful that their livelihood had been saved.

After a second night stuck in our tanks, we received the order to decamp and were briefed on what was to follow. Rumour had it that there had been an uprising in Warsaw. We, so ran the order, were called upon to crush it, immediately, urgently and with the utmost brutality.

Our path was leading directly towards Warsaw, to the entrance of the city. I had no idea what lay in store for me and could only hope to emerge alive. I was a young lad, only nineteen years old, without a clue of what fighting an uprising involved. I was full of trepidation, tense, fearing death at any moment.

We arrived at the line held by the insurgents and were greeted by massive resistance. With the insurgents shooting at us from windows and out of cellars, they initially succeeded in preventing us from getting in. Three of our tanks went on the attack, shelling high-rises with their 7.5-cm PaK cannon, but, with their strong defences, they withstood the onslaught. The sturdy buildings were constructed like bunkers and there was a sophisticated underground tunnel network that allowed the insurgents to move around undetected. They fought with whatever they could lay their hands on – this didn't just involve small arms but also bottles filled with flammable liquid as well, the so-called Molotov cocktails, that caused us to lose several tanks. Our tanks! Despite their primitive weapons, the fighters succeeded in setting even these on fire. The sound of explosions and screams filled the air, streets were covered in blood, strewn with heaps of rubble and shattered glass, the sky was thick with smoke, ash and dust – it was a veritable inferno. Our tanks rumbled through, there was shooting, but to no visible effect. We had even requested the monstrous 15-cm railway gun but none of the buildings I could see crumbled, withstanding the relentless onslaught.

There was no way for us to push forward. Holed up in their fortified houses, cellars and underground sewers, the insurgents launched their ferocious attacks, firing at us and hitting our tanks with a barrage of Molotov cocktails. It looked as if they'd even been able to avail themselves of anti-tank rockets, which succeeded in disabling several of our tanks and blowing many of them up, their crews burnt to death by the flames.

My senior lieutenant and I remained under cover – sitting in our Tatra at some distance from these horrific scenes. Indeed, in this respect we were lucky, managing to stay away from death and destruction even if it was only a stone's throw away. But we could certainly follow every move and every explosion through our binoculars, which was crucial as my boss was the one charged with leading this operation.

Night fell and I sought shelter inside a tank – the safest place to be in those dark hours. There was no way I could go to sleep, firstly because we were too shaken up, but also because the inside of a tank is not exactly the most comfortable of places. Either we were tightly squeezed against each other or crushed into a corner.

Police units and the SS arrived the next morning, a formidable force slamming their way into the area. 'Don't take any prisoners!' was the cruel and murderous order as throngs of residents of all ages, arms raised above their heads, emerged from the buildings. They were killed instantly – there was no pity. Having to watch this was the most horrendous event in my life. Wasn't it just a a couple of years ago that I'd worked as an electrician's apprentice? The chaos I was tossed into was brutal and barbaric.

Bloodied dead bodies were strewn all over the street, mostly unarmed civilians who had put up a bitter fight, never able to make sense of the cruel fate that had befallen them. Forced to escape from the explosions and fumes into the open, they might have desperately clung to some hope – but, in the end, it was all in vain.

A man emerged from a house with his arms raised. We asked him why he kept turning his head right and left. 'If I turn right, I'll be fired at by the others, if I turn left, then it'll be by you. We're condemned either way. Our only option is to defend ourselves to our very last breath.'

'Stop!' This order for our group to cease firing should have put an end to this slaughter. But the last shot was yet to ring out. The assignment from hell was to be accomplished without mercy, without escape, without any humanity. Innocent civilians were killed, women and children were shot in cold blood. Heaps of contorted bodies, disintegrating corpses piled high and growing in numbers with an unbearable stench filling the streets. Helpless, I watched.

Movement was impossible. We couldn't break through the lines; our tanks were unable to smash the buildings where the fighters had holed themselves in, so we radioed for aerial support, which promptly arrived, the Stukas diving down and dropping their 250-kg beast, together with other massive bombs that pulverised the buildings with perfect precision. In preparation for their arrival, we spread marking panels across the tanks with painted swastikas indicating to the pilots the line to where we had pushed through. Otherwise, of course, it would be us who'd have become the targets.

The resistance collapsed after the Stukas had done their job, striking from above and pounding every street and every building. Any resistance fighters who had survived clambered over rubble to emerge out of the ruins, arms stretched upwards in a sign of capitulation. They were instantly shot dead.

My head throbbed as I looked around me at these dreadful scenes of devastation and death. Let me survive all of this – that hope kept going through my mind. And still I did not lose my nerve, nor did I go mad. I thought of my grandma, who had been utterly convinced that the war would end at the time when I had been called up. And now, look at this mess! The horrors of the war had kept up with me, but my will to come through it intact remained as strong as ever.

With the buildings now lying destroyed, we were finally able to penetrate deeper into the city. En route – my job was still to be the driver of my boss's Tatra – I threw a glance down a narrow lane along which a tank was moving, towards the other end. The lane was indeed so narrow that the tank barely scraped through. Then suddenly a woman came running out of a doorway, pushing a pram and … the tank jerked forward, its tracks crushing the hapless woman, together with the pram and the baby inside. A mother and her child, flattened to pulp.

Our tanks were ordered to move forward as we didn't want to run the risk of having them pelted by the Molotov cocktails that would have been hurled at them from behind where some fighters were still sheltering. At that moment my eyes fell on what only seconds before had been human beings. Instead, all that remained were heaps of disfigured corpses, piles of bodies, black puddles running into the sewers next to them. The sight of this sickening execution has had a most profound impact on my whole life. I can never forget it.

And yet, this wasn't to remain the only atrocity to which I bore witness. We drove on in the direction of the market square and pulled up on one side of the square. A thick layer of rapidly decomposing bodies carpeted the entire cobbled square, the area engulfed by an eerie silence.

A tall, slim woman burst out of a house with five little children by her side. They probably intended to escape, somewhere, anywhere, with the woman herself no doubt at a loss as to where else to turn. I knew, of course, that all she wanted to do was flee and save her children. An SS man came bounding across the square, holding his machine gun at the ready. 'Stop!' he screamed. The woman, who had gathered the smallest of the children into her arms, leaving two on either side of her, stared at the soldier panic-stricken.

Impassively, the soldier cocked his machine gun and fired a spray of bullets. The mother and her children lay prostrate in the middle of the market square. They lay side by side, united, as they had been in life. Some of the children must still have been alive – I saw their small arms moving, and their whimpering was clearly audible from where we were. The SS guy drew closer. One more bullet into the heads of the children finished them off. Job done, he calmly strode away as if nothing out of the ordinary had just happened. He seemed to be emotionless, acting like an automaton.

This is what my boss and I witnessed from where we sat in our car. He remained silent, and I didn't utter a word – both of us were stunned, aghast, in complete shock. My boss kept glancing across to me, probably wanting to get a sense of how I was registering these appalling events, but he himself didn't say anything, not a word. He remained calm on the outside with only the corners of his mouth twitching ever so slightly. Deep down, he was troubled.

Instantly every detail of this horrific scene etched itself into my memory. The soldier was a monster. I still see the SS insignia of his helmet in front of my eyes.

Somehow, I managed to deal with these events, and quietly turned to God, praying that he allow me to survive the insanity.

There are only two options when coming to terms with experiences such as these. One is to get used to them, to develop a thick skin, so to speak, by simply getting through. The other option is to wait until you just go mad. This is what happened to one of our gunners. He suddenly swivelled the gun of his tank, directed it against our own men and yelled something incomprehensible, his face all contorted. But before he could cause any harm some squad members dragged him out of the tank and had him transported home. In fact, there were quite a few soldiers who went crazy, even towards the end when the war was nearly over. They would hold a grenade by their head and end their lives with words that said something like this: 'One last shot before I fall into Russian hands.' And that was that.

Just a short while after this gruesome and murderous scene had unfolded before our very eyes, a lieutenant returning to his troop crossed the market square. A careless act, as it turned out. The night was still, not a sound to be heard. Cautiously, obviously sensing danger, he crossed the square. Nobody was there, save the heaps of putrefying corpses still littering the ground, covered by a thick layer of congealed blood. A shot from the direction of a cellar interrupted the calm and the soldier before us sank to the ground, screaming out in anguish. He was mortally wounded, his body shredded to pieces, intestines spilling out. Shocked, we swiftly retreated, anticipating further attacks.

In the final analysis it was, of course, an uprising of the doomed, with no one standing a chance. A group of people were desperately fighting for their lives, but the SS executed them with ruthless brutality. Everyone in their sight was shot; there was not a moment's hesitation. The square was piled high with grime, oil, torn belongings, debris and a mass of dead bodies – it was a bloodbath. Many had been flattened by the tanks whether dead or alive – none were spared. There had been no respect for life.

The air was still – the only sound had been the single shot that whipped across the square before fading away. Mouths open, we stared ahead, not knowing what would happen next. My boss still did not utter a word, I could only hear him breathing heavily. It all reminded me of a staged horror scene in a bad film. But this here was real; it was gruesome, stark reality.

Dusk was falling as we sat in our parked Tatra. Only one radio was working at that time, with all the others having been shut down as per our orders. Slowly the darkness settled in and with it, this horrific day that had cost the lives of so many came to an end.

We withdrew into our tanks, where we felt safe. Nobody could sleep as firstly it was much too tight inside the tank and secondly, we were all deeply disturbed by what had happened. The following hours seemed endless and while waiting for dawn to break we slipped in and out of a light slumber. One person would be whispering something quietly while the other was lost in thought, thoughts about home, about family, about their own guilt and above all, thoughts of how to survive. The chaotic and catastrophic situation we found ourselves in could hardly have been worse. Here we were, in the middle of a city, surrounded by people who were prepared to kill us instantly if they were only given the opportunity. And us? We murdered everyone who crossed our path, even women and children – this was likely the worst part for me to come to terms with. Is there anything more dreadful, more shocking, than to witness innocent people simply shot dead without a care?

We had completed our assignment and began our retreat the next morning, leaving behind us a place engulfed in deathly silence. We progressed slowly with only the droning noise of our engines accompanying us. The firing from cellars, houses and sewers had ceased. Most of the fighters who were still alive were resigned to defeat, having run out of ammunition and no longer able to put up any meaningful resistance. There were only a very few of them left, truth be told, as most had been wiped out by the Stukas.

Gradually our tanks rumbled through Warsaw and continued onwards, leaving the city behind as if nothing had happened, their wheels crushing the corpses strewn across the ground as if they were but rubble or rubbish. Nobody even thought of stepping out to collect the dead bodies, since you couldn't rule out that a sniper would fire at us. Only the thunderous rumbling of the tank tracks filled the air. You couldn't even hear the chirping of the birds, and not a single word was spoken. It was silent.

Every single one of us understood that something tragic, something awful, had taken place over those past hours, that so many people had lost their lives, that so many women and children had been brutally murdered. The shock of such horrendous crimes having been committed above all by the police and the SS units had a profound impact on our spirits. Somehow, however, we had to deal with what had happened, and with our own guilt. Put simply, anything that moved was gunned down. Leaving the city felt like leaving a cemetery, a haunted field of death. I tried thinking of my grandparents, of my old master, of home; I just hoped I would survive. Survival was everything.

It was during this operation that I first encountered anti-Semitism – I was still only nineteen years old. It hadn't ever been on my mind when as a youngster since during my apprenticeship I was often called out to a private Jewish home to fix something. I was always treated in a friendly manner and would get a tip. For me, Jews represented people who held a different faith, that was about it. Why Jews would now be persecuted and murdered was a mystery to me, indeed quite incomprehensible. I reflected on these questions while driving out of Warsaw, it was puzzling to me, but leaving Warsaw in our car with my boss sitting next to me in silence, I couldn't find any answers.

*

We moved south in the direction of Bohemia and Moravia – away from this landscape of horror and death. My boss and I were travelling in our car closely following the tanks as it was us who commanded the unit. Unaware of what was to befall us in the next few months, we were lulled into a deceptive calm, winding our way through fields and meadows, past quiet villages with empty streets. The inhabitants remained in their homes, relieved to see us roll by without stopping. But with the Russians hot on our heels, this tranquillity was short lived.

Towards evening on each day we had to stop over in a village and find quarters for the night, and one of my duties was to organise somewhere suitable for my boss. Certainly, here and there it might well have happened that a woman was raped, but I only came close to witnessing such an assault once. I entered a house and at the same time two sergeants walked in, with one of them intending to rape a woman even though, hard to believe, she had her children with her. His comrade was having none of it. *'That's* what you want to do with her?! Scram!' he yelled and slapped him hard around the face.

The sergeant slunk away, and I asked the woman whether she would be prepared to have someone spend the night in her house. She agreed, so this is where my boss stayed while I went on the lookout to find something for myself.

In the meantime, the Russians had succeeded in penetrating the front, which meant that we immediately had to withdraw even further and more rapidly. We sped through the landscape, past open farmland, fields and hamlets, but we couldn't get rid of the Russians on our back. They shot at us daily, resulting in enormous explosions, some of which set fire to quite a few tanks and their crews. Those losses were dreadful, and we just weren't able to put up any meaningful defence – the Russians were simply far superior.

We passed Łódź and attempted to continue towards Wrocław. In the late afternoon we would often find an empty house where we could spend the night, but failing that we slept in our *Kübelwagen* [light military vehicle with bucket seats]. Not the most comfortable night's rest, but better that than lying dead or seriously injured in no man's land. We had run extremely low on food and with hardly any provisions left, we ransacked the empty houses for anything we could find, in particular flour and sugar. Fortunately, we still had enough fuel left.

Lieutenant Knudsen barely said a word, knowing full well that our circumstances were dire. His only objective was to bring his troops to safety somehow. But how? What was he meant to do? The only thing happening was us being hounded across the land without having the wherewithal to put up any resistance.

We travelled from Wrocław to Lubań, then north to Cottbus – the Russians were on our tail, firing at us from their tanks with *Stalinorgeln* [lit. 'Stalin's organs', a rocket that made a terrifying howling sound]. Our troop numbers were now visibly thinned, but we didn't even have enough time to bury our comrades and were forced to leave them lying where they had dropped dead.

I can barely describe what went through my mind at the time. I was alive, yes, but somehow this didn't mean much to me any more, and my only concern was that when death did come it would not be too painful. En route, we often picked up lost comrades who were scattered around and we did our best to integrate them into our company. With all of us now gripped by despair, we could only put our hope into our senior lieutenant and trusted that he would bring us home alive. Hope, it is said, springs eternal – what an apt, yet, given our dismal situation, not very encouraging expression.

We were heading towards Frankfurt an der Oder but I had the distinct feeling that something awful was about to befall us.

'The Russians are planning a full-blown attack,' I hazarded behind the steering wheel.

'What makes you think that?' countered the senior lieutenant. 'What's with you?'

'Just look at the sky, all those red-green lights, masses of them, signal lights indicating targets. I'm telling you,' I insisted, 'the Russians are about to break through – and with great force!'

'Have you gone mad?'

'Just wait and see, this is what's going to happen, for sure.'

Both of us cocked our ears and there was no denying it: the faint rumble of tanks and gunshots were ominous. I simply had this gut feeling and it stemmed from previously having observed Russian attacks and the sky turning different colours. For a while we just sat there, my senior lieutenant suddenly silent. He knew of course that I was right and he was deliberating our next move. Turning to me, he mumbled quietly: 'You know what? I'll report sick … We'll head off to the quarters of the general of the tank division, and I'll report sick. I'll make sure that you'll get out of here.'

And indeed, the following morning, we headed to the command post, where we requested a meeting with the general.

'What's the matter, Senior Lieutenant?'

'I wish to report sick, General. I'm no longer able to lead my unit. I suffer from dizziness and on top of that I am plagued by dysentery.'

'Fine, then return home. Report to the hospital. Forty kilometres from the front line.'

'Can I take my driver along?'

'You can. Once you've recovered, report back.'

'Yes, General, sir.'

And that was that.

We departed but kept one eye on how the situation evolved on the ground, albeit from far away. Unfortunately, my suspicions proved correct and what I had predicted soon became a reality. A terrible reality. The large-sweep Russian operation was launched only a few hours later, with their soldiers breaking through the lines, our positions collapsing and our men fleeing in all directions. We must have lost half of our division. From our sixty-four tanks I would never see a single one of them again. I never got to find out what had happened to our comrades – they had quite simply disappeared from the face of the earth, extinguished for ever, and this barbaric war was to blame.

As for me, I was extremely lucky – good fortune seemed to be part of my life. However, in terms of provisions we didn't have much, so we just doggedly travelled onwards, either southwards or westwards in hope of shaking off our pursuers.

As we were able to maintain ongoing radio contact with Brigadier Oskar Audörsch, commander of the 25th Panzer Division, or whatever was left of it, we were guided towards Frankfurt an der Oder. Audörsch, it has to be said, never left his men's sides. With a flask of cognac tucked away in his pocket for when he felt a comrade needed cheering up in moments where it was particularly hard going, he would encourage and reassure them.

'Chin up, boys,' he'd say. 'There you go, have a sip!'

We travelled through the region, just the two of us in the *Kübelwagen* for several days, eyes peeled, desperate to reach our destination. The entire landscape with its villages, the odd farm and fields seemed to be sunk in a coma and I had the strange sensation that even inanimate objects around us, from doors to lampposts, were taking cover. We decided to sleep in the car at night and occasionally managed to obtain some food. People were scared and distrusted us deeply, and they were visibly relieved once we moved on.

Trying to cross the Oder proved tricky as the bridge across it had been blown up. Meanwhile, with the Soviet advance gaining considerable speed and Russian troops drawing ever nearer, we fled west towards Berlin. Approaching Fürstenwalde I was startled by a strange smell and remember turning to Senior Lieutenant Knudsen to tell him I thought the area smelled like a crematorium [Fürstenwalde was the location of a subcamp of the Sachsenhausen concentration camp].

'Come off it, Heinz, you're wrong. And besides, how should I know what's being burnt around here? Don't give it another thought.'

I didn't continue the conversation but in my mind I was certain that they were incinerating corpses. Knudsen, of course, knew precisely what was happening but was reluctant to share any information. Perhaps he wanted me to remain ignorant of the truth and not be horrified. The command post where we were supposed to report was in Fürstenwalde. We arrived and found the place completely deserted – not a single person who might have given us any orders could be found.

With the Russians still pursuing us we decided to travel south towards Moravia while continually being sprayed by the bullets they rained down on us. Our best bet, we thought, was to circumvent cities and villages and instead cut across the area, bypassing Cottbus and Dresden.

Prague was going to be our next destination since joining our division was out of the question, with their sorry remainder withdrawing towards Lower Bavaria. What a mess awaited us there! The city was teeming with Russian soldiers enlisted with the Vlasov Army who had fought on Hitler's side against Stalin but now, to save their own skin, had switched to the other side. [Andrei Vlasov was a former Red Army general who collaborated with Nazi Germany.] The Czechs, it goes without saying, harboured a deep hatred towards us. As for us? We'd been provided with neither ammunition nor food. That was it, then: we had no other option than to force our way into the homes and scramble about for anything edible that we could put our grubby hands on. Stepping out from behind the buildings, out of windows and cellars, the inhabitants attacked us from all sides. Guns blazed as fierce fighting took place in passages and alleyways, and it was in these tight quarters that we suffered our heaviest losses as our comrades lacked protection. Dead bodies covered the pavements, pillars of smoke and dust filled the air, and what with the deafening noise of gunshots and explosions engulfing us, the situation was unbearable. Bullets whined over our heads and their continuous hissing spelled further destruction and disaster. All we cared about was getting out of this bloodbath alive … and we did. Miraculously, neither my boss nor I were injured. 'Let's get out of here!' was the phrase at the forefront of our minds. Meanwhile, many of our comrades were killed and several tanks set on fire. We had suffered a huge loss in this city.

We had no idea about our destination other than the fact that we had to move onwards and to the south. Left with nothing – no food, no ammunition – all we could fortunately rely on was sufficient fuel. Once, as we were fast asleep in the car, Russians ambushed us from both sides and bullets grazed the chassis. I started the car, pressed on the accelerator, and we made a dash for it. Our Tatra certainly was the worse for wear, with many bullet holes in its body, but it kept chugging along with a seemingly intact engine. I had a small injury on my hand but it didn't bother me much.

In Gronau, Moravia, we chanced upon an abandoned castle, where we spent a few days before continuing on towards České Budějovice. We had been ordered to meet up on Hill 119 in order to report on the Russian approach.

En route, I suddenly felt extremely uneasy. It had become eerily still. Not a sound to be heard.

'Senior Lieutenant, sir, this feels strange … my sense is that we're in no man's land.'

'Are you frightened? What's the matter with you? There's nothing untoward!'

Suddenly, I spot a distant Russian light armoured reconnaissance vehicle advancing towards us, its Soviet star clearly visible. We both turned pale. Dry-mouthed, we didn't utter a word, knowing full well that this could spell the end of a long journey. Until that moment we had managed to stay alive – but what was in store for us? A man, standing upright in his tank with his headphones on, was approaching fast. Squinting, we heaved a sigh of relief as we recognised Major Witte of Panzergrenadierregiment 146, camouflaged as a Russian soldier.

'Blimey! What the hell are you doing here?' he yelled. 'Turn back instantly, you'll be dead meat before you can say boo! The Russians are having their meal and I managed to watch them without being discovered. I know their strength and I know their timing. Go back to where you came from and leave the counterattack to me.'

'Senior Lieutenant, sir, what do you suggest we do?' I asked my superior.

'I can't see anything, but we'll turn around.'

So we did. And not a minute too soon, as the Russians launched their attack right then and there. With an accurate and precise plan to hand, they deployed their men in strategic positions and led their tanks into battle. True to his word, Major Witte indeed attempted to take control and stop the counterattack, all the while monitoring the situation. Standing erect in his vehicle, he tried his utmost, but he didn't have a chance in hell. All he had at his disposal was a motley crew of soldiers who were no match for the Russian tanks wedging them in. As for armaments – well, the Russians' equipment was far superior to ours, and the same held true for their personnel, including many women amongst them. *Panje* carts [Panje horses are small robust Russian horses] were loaded with barrels filled with fuel – whereas by now our good selves barely had any fuel left.

With the horrendous lack of resources on our side, I always tried my very best just to keep afloat. One day my senior lieutenant remarked out loud that our food situation was dire – we had to get our hands on some food.

'Leave it to me, Senior Lieutenant, sir,' I calmed him down, trying to sound optimistic. 'I'll definitely think of something.'

I entered a small kiosk which ordinarily was supposed to serve only members of the SS, who were easily recognisable by the *Totenkopf* [death's head] insignia on their caps or collars – but as it happens, we Wehrmacht soldiers enlisted with the tank squads also wore them. Marching into the store, head high and confident, I casually pointed to the emblem, and it proved enough to get me a few sausages, a bit of cheese and some bread.

When it came to fuel, the overall situation was much more favourable, and though we had entered the final phase of the war, there seemed to be no shortage. So when we ran low during our journeys, I'd reach into the back of the car for my small suction tube, generally used for wine bottles. Here it came in handy for drawing fuel from battered vehicles abandoned by the roadside. A crate, originally designed to hold three grenades, served as our food basket, and thus equipped, we were off. In short, that's how I managed to struggle through; otherwise I wouldn't be here.

It was the beginning of May, and we had arrived just short of Budweis when we caught up with the news: Germany had capitulated – the war had ended. Happy shouts of joy erupted from everywhere, as all of us were utterly worn out and exhausted. Demoralised and broken, none of us felt any commitment to carrying on that war. Rommel, the motorcyclist who had been charged to convey the message to us, didn't waste a second and zoomed off at breakneck speed to cover the area, yelling at the top of his voice: 'The war is over, the war is over!' But, in his exuberance, he crashed into a parked tank and was killed instantly. Stunned at tragedy hitting at this late hour, my heart went out to this wonderful young chap who so deserved to see his home again.

Driving towards České Budějovice we passed a long stretch of shapeless refugees trudging along forlornly, their carts piled with belongings. I got chatting to a distraught woman who related to us her desperate experience. During the ice-cold winter of 1944/5, after the Russians had overrun her hometown, she, her three children and their grandfather set out towards the west. One night the temperatures dropped so dangerously low that the children froze to death and the grandfather suffered such severe frostbite that his legs were no longer able to support him. Not knowing what to do, the distressed woman settled the children's bodies into a ditch, covered them with snow with only their heads still visible. Seeing that the Russians were hot on their heels, she shuffled onwards – a woman half-dead amidst a grey column of listless people.

Given that Germany had capitulated, we had no option but to concede defeat. We entered České Budějovice, which was now under American, Russian and French control, parked our Tatra and surrendered. This was the end. Our hosts certainly didn't welcome us with open arms, with the Czechs taking our car and our weapons off us and one of the guys pressing the muzzle of his pistol with such force against my temple that you can still see the mark today.

One Russian stomped up to me, gruffly tore my watch along with its chain out of my pocket – it was a gift from my grandfather. 'Urr, Urr,' he barked into my ear [Uhr is 'watch' in German].

Some of my comrades couldn't bear the thought of ending up in a Russian prisoner of war camp so much that they committed suicide instead.

Though I too often pondered what might be in store for me and what choices I had, suicide was out of the question. 'You've come so far, Heinz,' I said to myself, 'and you're so close to the finishing line, are you really going to give up?' 'No,' I convinced myself, 'stiff upper lip and carry on.'

With the aim of humiliating us, the Russians assembled an army orchestra and instructed them to play German march music. Gathering themselves in groups, they then forced us to file past in rows of twelve. I'll never ever forget the smirks on their faces. At that point we were tired, dirty and starving, not having had any food for several days. It was rumoured that the general was keen to test our endurance.

Finally, we were transported to a prisoner camp near České Budějovice located in a vast area surrounded by woods. We spent another few days there without food or water and were left to fend for ourselves. Another part of the prisoner camp held refugees, along with their carts and wagons. The terrifying screams of women being gang raped haunted us night after night. It was horrendous. Prostrate on the damp ground we listened helplessly. Sleep was out of the question.

After several days we were given permission to fell trees and build cabins for ourselves to protect us from the elements. One day, rounded up on a square, we were informed which of the Allied powers we would be under. Some ended up with the Russians, others with the Americans, or the British, or the French.

I was unlucky and landed in a Russian POW camp which was heavily guarded and any attempts to escape would have surely ended in death. None of us would have known where to escape to. By then, hunger and thirst had also taken their toll and we were extremely weak.

*

The camp was a mess. The Russians and the Czechs had never considered that prisoners would arrive here in such large numbers. They resorted to slaughtering the horses that had belonged to the refugees just so that they could provide us with something to eat. But first, so that the meat wouldn't rot, we were ordered to dig ditches and attach hooks to the sides, from which the slabs of meat were hung.

The camp was entered through a large, tightly guarded gate. Thanks to my aunt, who was Russian, I had picked up some Russian from her and formed a plan. Turning to my boss, I advised him that we needed some wood to make a fire. 'And how do you suggest that we get out of here to do that? Totally impossible,' he retorted.

'Watch me!' My spirit hadn't yet been completely quashed and giving up just like that wasn't my style. 'Let me go and you'll see.'

I organised a cart, found a horse, harnessed it and approached the guard posted at the entrance.

'Where are you going?'

'I must collect wood to make a fire.'

'Go – if you don't return, you know what'll happen.'

I drove through the gate, went about searching for wood, planks, anything that could burn, and loaded my cart. Returning to the camp, the gate was opened to let me through. Open-mouthed, my comrades couldn't believe what had just taken place – the upshot was that we were able to make a fire, though there still wasn't any food for us other than the horse meat. Everyone's favourite bit was the horse liver and there was quite a scramble for that. Every man for himself, if not, he would die.

One day we were loaded onto cattle trucks. Evacuation. Some thirty to forty men were crammed into each wagon; we sat tightly huddled together on the bare floor with a hole in the middle attached to a funnel – for us to relieve ourselves.

Everything we owned had been confiscated, including the knives, of course, and all we were allowed to keep was a spoon. The wagon door slammed shut and was sealed off, which also meant that no food or water would be distributed to us. Slowly the train rumbled along with none of us having any idea of our whereabouts or destination. Sometimes, a few scraps of information filtered through the slits of our wagons and the language spoken gave us a clue of where we were – traversing Hungary or Romania. When the train came to a halt and no guard was in place, locals who were keen to be helpful crawled beneath the wagons and handed us some food through the funnels. We were immensely grateful. Some wagons remained without food and water, and many died from thirst and exhaustion. The Russians used the next stop to drag dead corpses outside and, just like rubbish, dumped them behind the embankment. Our lives hung by a thin thread.

The journey took us to Odessa, by the Black Sea. By then the comrades were at an all-time low, stripped of all willpower. After having suffered for days and nights that ran into each other, enduring thirst and hunger and having been confined to such a dark space, we found ourselves unable to think properly. And yet it's quite unbelievable what men can endure, and most of our lot managed to survive the trip.

Upon our arrival in Odessa, we were taken off the vehicles and transferred to the port, where we boarded a freighter. Like cattle, we stood shoulder to shoulder, hardly able to breathe. With no opportunity to relieve ourselves, we ended up having to do our business where we stood and in our clothes. The stench on the boat was ghastly and the journey lasted until we reached Sevastopol on the Crimean peninsula. Back on land, we trudged past some onlookers whose hateful eyes bore down on us miserable survivors, bedraggled men who shuffled along fearing stones that might be hurled at us. We tried to protect ourselves with our arms stretched above our heads – nobody else was going to do this for us.

Trucks were standing by and, once shoved onto their loading bays, we were driven to Feodosia, a different Crimean city where, for the first time, a bit of food was handed out. My senior lieutenant hadn't ever left my side until that point, and together we had gone through this long and hellish journey. But this now came to an end as we were allocated to different camps, with me transported to the vicinity of Kerch, a seaport city in the eastern part of Crimea. The camp, as such, hadn't yet been constructed, so we were herded into an open field which was tightly guarded all around. Ordered to build our own barracks, we collected bricks and stones from houses demolished by the war and with sand and cement built makeshift huts for us to live in. The entire camp with its 1,200 inmates had only one single water tap.

Truly barbaric conditions, but, once again I used my Russian-language skills and looked to communicate with the guards. One had to be careful to approach the right sort of guy, and I knew that the Mongolians were a tough lot, merciless and strict, so I sought out a Ukrainian soldier. However, he couldn't help me either and simply growled back that I needed to deal with the situation as best I could.

At least we were regularly provided with food: a thin soup with some peas floating around, a lump of kasha, which was a buckwheat porridge, along with some wet bread. Four to five slices were allocated per person; this had to last us the entire day.

During the first year of our internment some fifty men died every single day, with the Russians always passing the camp and asking how many prisoners had gone 'kaputt'. We put the bodies of our dead comrades into carts, which the Russians then moved away. Only later did we find out that the corpses were dumped into mass graves and covered with rubble and mud.

During my internment I first got jaundice and then, because we were so tightly crowded together, I contracted abdominal typhus – a very common disease in the prisoner of war camps and caused by the horrendous situation without even the most basic hygiene. While most didn't survive the infection, what with being generally run down and weakened, I was admitted to the camp hospital and recovered. Those who had been infected were quarantined for six weeks and assigned to a room with some fifty comrades – all men who had been visibly ravaged by the illness, emaciated, literally starved and too weak even to move. Some had swollen heads, much like balloons, though their legs were stick-thin. A cloud of death hung over them and by then nobody even bothered giving them any food. The bigger guys died first, the slimmer ones lasted a while longer. One lad, his eyes pleading, leaned forward towards me and whispered: 'Could you get me some water?' This I did, and carefully taking a sip he threw me one of the saddest looks I've ever seen; it will stay with me forever.

Our daily ration consisted of three heavily salted fish. During one meal, I remember being spooked out when I realised that what I held in my hand was a mouse. Sick to my stomach, I never touched these so-called fish again. At some point I realised that all my teeth were loose and when I told a Russian soldier, he suggested I take an onion and rub it into my gums. Though I didn't trust him I followed his advice, and much to my surprise my gums improved. A dentist at the clinic explained that loose teeth were a result of vitamin deficiency. 'Eat those fish again,' she told me, and I learnt something important that day.

This doctor treated me with kindness and professionalism, but one day she disappeared. A Russian guard divulged that she had been arrested for not having dealt with the German POWs with sufficient strictness.

Another incident with medical staff involved a young female doctor who approached me with a hefty book in her hand and summoned me to accompany her to the ward. There, stretched out on a bench, lay a dead man covered by a blanket which the doctor swiftly removed. She proceeded to dissect his head using a scalpel, uncovering both the cerebellum and the cerebrum, with blood gushing out and dripping to the floor. Spending some time studying the inside of this corpse's head, she then ordered me to mop up the blood. This was obviously the reason why she had ordered me to accompany her.

After many months in the camps, we underwent a selection where ten prisoners were picked to excavate the half-decaying corpses of comrades who had succumbed to disease and hunger. It obviously didn't sit quite right with the Russians that they were buried on the campsite, so they needed to be transported away, likely to the Black Sea, where they were probably thrown into the water. Back at the camp, we were ordered to fill the holes where our comrades had lain with cement, and to build foundations there for future houses.

The required stones for the construction of the foundations and walls had to be carted in from the nearby quarry, known for its shell limestone. The comrades enlisted for that job had to descend some 100 metres down the pit in a wooden crate attached to a pulley but then climb back up via a ladder. Steel saws were used to carve out the stone blocks from the rock. At the sharp sound of hissing blades, one had to instantly jump aside, as it meant that the rock surface had become loose. Many comrades lost their lives, crushed by the tumbling rocks before they had time to move away. The extracted blocks then had to be cut to precise measurements. The labourers were forced to reach the set quotas, otherwise their food rations were reduced, and they'd be penalised with additional work such as weeding between rows of barbed wire.

My job was lugging the mortar for the construction work on the houses, which meant that I had to carry huge pails around, all on an empty stomach. By evening I was utterly exhausted, though this was still far preferable to digging out the corpses from mass graves. That was a horrific task which nobody will ever be able to put behind them. On a daily basis a ten-man squad was selected for this horrendous job, but luckily, I was never one of them.

I soon learnt from skilled plasterers how to use a trowel and apply the mortar and even got a compliment from a guard watching me: 'You!

Expert!' Right then and there I'd become an expert and was therefore called upon to finish the plastering of some fifty houses. On top of that, I was even summoned, along with some other comrades, to decorate ceilings with stucco work. We were in such demand that we were ordered to build a theatre. Though we only ever really had the most basic materials and equipment at our disposal, we came up with impressive results – more impressive than Russian labourers could offer. Not surprisingly, but much to our disappointment, we were told that we'd stay put until the whole site was properly built up. Disheartened, I knew the score. We had been sentenced to hard labour and there was no way out – our return home would be delayed, if indeed it would ever even come to pass.

Once, when I made my way into the theatre, I found the entire floor covered in sunflower seeds. 'That's quite normal around here,' explained a Russian, 'when we go to the theatre, we like to chew on sunflower kernels. We bite into them, eat the inside and then spit out the shells. Someone will eventually sweep up the mess.'

Building homes was only part of our chores. We were then enlisted to help construct factories. Trains loaded with machinery from Germany would arrive quite frequently; they were unloaded and their contents carelessly thrown into the sand. Watching on, I couldn't help thinking that this sloppy handling of the machinery would surely render it useless. But I was wrong. The Russians carefully took the equipment apart and then reassembled them, which put an end to our work at the factories.

Women too were part of the teams, especially when it came to technical stuff. 'How come you know so much about these things?' I asked a young Russian woman. 'I studied it,' she replied. 'Mind you, here in Russia, our university studies don't take as long as yours do in Germany,' she continued, 'we mostly learn on the job, perfect our skills in practice and do much less theory.'

This is how time passed. Months turned into years, and it was now 1949. Gradually the camp was emptied, with prisoners being sent home group by group. One day, my labour brigade was ordered to start on a construction project in Simferopol, building military housing for high-ranking officers. On my journey there I felt despondent. Will I ever get to return home? I asked myself wistfully. What with being considered an 'expert' again and again, will that really ever happen?

Upon our arrival at the site in the evening, a Russian warden barked his orders. 'Five man experts, two handyman – off with you.'

'*Nyet*,' I retorted. 'Six man experts, one man forced labourer.'

'Let me go back,' I murmured to my comrades.

'They only want five experts,' they countered.

'But I'm not going to play this game any more,' I remained firm.

'You!' bellowed the warden, 'Get off your backside or I'll slap you with twenty-five years' forced labour in Siberia!'

'Go ahead then,' I screamed with the despair of the powerless.

Fuming, yet intimidated by my insolence, the warden spat at my feet. 'Go to hell! Back on that lorry!'

Returning to the camp where the comrades had already started clearing up, ready to leave, the gates were open to let us in. Worried stiff as to what would befall me, I wondered whether my name was going to be on the list of those chosen to return. Or was I slated for forced labour? In the end I was lucky and was listed as one of the returnees, had some clothes and a towel flung at me, and then ordered to get myself onto the cargo wagon of the train travelling to Kerch. From there, another train would take us to the west in the direction of our home. Though overjoyed, each one of us on that journey was deep in thought. What awaited us? Was our family still there? Was everyone alive? Was our house still standing? Would I be able to find work to keep myself afloat?

After a few days we reached Leipzig and then it was off to Hof, to the Americans. We had cottoned on that the Allies had meanwhile turned into bitter enemies, with the interrogating American officers very keen to find out how we had fared in the Russian POW camps and what our observations had been. In return for us supplying them with what we knew, we were even offered compensation of twenty German marks. In my mind, this clearly smacked of a trap and, convinced that they would try and catch me out, I prepared myself. When an American then asked me what my experiences had been in Russia, what kind of labour I'd been forced to do, I just answered that I didn't want to talk about that kind of stuff. Indeed, many of my comrades provided similar answers, while others were tempted by the reward and yielded.

We were handed our discharge papers and I boarded a train that took me to Aschaffenburg, and then onto Mainaschaff where my grandparents lived. Their house was locked, however, and their neighbours informed me that my grandparents were no longer alive. I knocked on the door of the neighbour further along where my Russian aunt had her place, and there it transpired that another uncle had taken possession of my grandparents' home, which meant I didn't have access to my room.

'Can't take you in,' he immediately informed me in a gruff tone, 'we've got our own two children to look after.'

Turning again to my Russian aunt, she showed me more kindness, assuring me I'd have a roof over my head. All she'd ask me to do was to reclaim my mattress from my grandparents' house.

Walking back to my grandparents' house, now owned by this uncle and his wife, I knocked on the door. The wife answered, knife in hand. 'Every knock on my door is someone wanting something,' she snapped. I was clearly floundering, but instantly understood that the house I had grown up in would remain shut to me forever. With no other option I yet again resorted to the Russian aunt, who was thankfully supportive. 'Don't worry ... I'll find a mattress for you,' she said, and somehow it all worked out.

I was particularly concerned as to what might have happened to my erstwhile boss, Senior Lieutenant Knudsen. We had gone our different ways back in the POW camp in Feodosia, as simple soldiers and officers would end up being interned in different camps. The last time we'd been together, I remember him asking me for a cigarette and I was more than happy to oblige, handing over my last one. I didn't smoke, so it made no difference to me. He mumbled under his breath that the two of us 'are now nothing but a pair of losers'. He seemed resigned but added: 'One can only hope that we'll survive this whole thing. And when you get home, make sure to call on me – I'll always be there to help you.'

Those were his last words, and I vividly recall him looking deep into my eyes before the Russians herded him onto a wagon taking him God knows where. I tried to find out his whereabouts through the Red Cross repeatedly but failed. He never returned to his home in Hamburg, with his wife and children being reported missing as well. He evidently did not survive his imprisonment, and his family was probably killed. I still think about him today – he was truly a fine human being.

My Long and Arduous Road

AN EYEWITNESS ACCOUNT BY MICHAEL STRASSER

I quite enjoy thinking back to the years I spent as a child and youngster in Puchschlagen, a small rural village situated in the district of Dachau, north-west of Munich. With its 150 inhabitants, Puchschlagen was by far the smallest community in that area at the time.

My father had inherited the family farm called Zum Baumer, which he had taken over shortly after the end of World War I, in 1919. In that same year he married Maria Lochner, whose family also owned a farm in Puchschlagen; the two of them had known each other since childhood.

Taking over the farm proved difficult for my father not just because of the economic crisis reigning in Germany at the time, but because Grandfather had always chosen to give his attention to running the restaurant part of the farm at the cost of working the land. My aunt would often grumble about how Grandfather kept moaning about not being able to get a decent pint seeing as the war years dictated that people had to make do with 'Dünnbier' [a thin/light beer with an alcohol content of less than 2 per cent]. As it happens, he'd never get to enjoy his longed-for 'decent pint of beer' since he died one year after handing over the farm to my father. This, in turn, meant that I'd never get to know him.

From my father I knew that the farmers in the village had already made moves to parcel off our 'Baumerhof', probably because they reckoned that the family would be forced to sell it off, being in dire straits. But my parents refused to let the pressure get to them. They rose to the challenge and built up the farm, which grew and developed into a healthy business. The farmers' scheme fell through and the farm remained in our hands. It was during those hectic years that I was born, my parents' third and youngest child, on 27 September 1927.

Times were difficult, with inflation and the buckling economy draining Germany and even impacting on our modest farm. Josef Loder, a farmer living nearby, was forced to sell his handsome estate, Zum Scharl. As it happens, his father was the inspiration for the eponymous tragic figure of Andreas Vöst in Ludwig Thomas's novel [Ludwig Thomas was a nineteenth- and twentieth-century author who wrote about everyday life in Bavaria].

Vast areas of agricultural land and properties were offered for sale or traded, a common practice at the time. What happened when farmers swapped estates amongst themselves was that smaller and rather badly farmed plots were joined together, much like today when land is re-parcelled and consolidated, but on a voluntary basis. My father, however, was a dab hand at running his estate and managed to purchase seventeen additional *Tagwerke* [1 *Tagwerk* equals approx. 3,000 m²], an impressive achievement given that the years between 1926 and 1930 were exceptionally grim. After this acquisition, our family farm owned an uninterrupted stretch of meadows and farmland.

It was quite a different story for the Scharlhof, where everything kept going downhill, even under its new owner Josef Thurner, who simply mismanaged the place and finally, towards the end of 1930, recognised that he couldn't hold onto it any longer. The cattle trade demanded a good deal of savviness, which Thurner never claimed to have, and as a result he lost a lot of money. For example, a farmer might sell him a scrawny cow for a premium price, or might give him it to him in exchange for a fat cow, and he would only come to realise his mistake once it was too late, and he'd be saddled with a cow of little value. On top of that, Josef Thurner was likely heavily in debt to the banks, with the size of his farm now significantly reduced. By spring 1930 it was clear that he would need to sell his homestead, having been hit particularly hard by the economic slump, and my father seized the opportunity. He swiftly made the necessary arrangement to exchange our smaller Zum Baumer farm with Thurner's Scharlhof. One fine evening in June 1930 the deal was cut over a glass of wine and without any prolonged negotiations. On that day, so ran father's account later in his life, he simply returned home from the pub and announced that he'd 'traded in our farm in exchange for the Scharlhof'.

You can well imagine the shock on Mother's and Grandmother's face. But that was just the beginning of what would then develop into quite

The Strasser family in front of the family farm in Puchschlagen.

a frenzy of deals involving the purchasing and trading-in of farms in Puchschlagen. My family moved out of the farm where I'd been born and set up home in the Scharlhof, while another neighbour, the owner of the Pechlerhof farm, now took over the farm we'd just vacated, and the Geretshauser family who used to own the Schneiderhof in turn bought up the now available Pechlerhof estate. The small Schneiderhof farm remained empty. This kind of property market flourished, what with the various farmers' appetite to wheel and deal in it.

But this mad carousel of buying, selling and trading soon stopped, with the 1930s not showing any signs of an economic upturn. Indeed, the crisis especially impacted those who ran into debt as a result of trading in their properties. Years later, when remembering with glee what had happened, my father would regale us with his stories. 'Invariably these three guys trading in their properties couldn't keep up with the interest payments' is how the story usually ended.

My parents managed not to get caught up in the whirlwind and remained on the straight and narrow, keeping a tight grip on their affairs. The years passed without any upheavals that would threaten to disrupt our lives. Until, that is, Adolf Hitler came to power. Suddenly, the atmosphere was laden with anxiety as change was afoot. Today, Adolf Hitler is condemned as the biggest criminal in history, but at the time many considered him to be a saviour as the country's situation improved, with everyone suddenly finding work again. There was a general feeling that Germany's fortunes were on the up and up and the farmers, mired in debt, were now able to recover.

I started primary school after the Easter holidays of 1931 in the nearby village of Kreuzholzhausen. The school year started in spring, not in September as it does today, and it took us some two and a half hours to get there, with more than half of the path gently winding its way uphill through the forest. We walked all the way as nobody owned a bicycle, let alone a car, and there weren't any buses either. If in winter there was a particularly strong snowfall, some farmers took their horse and cart and the thrilling trip to school at top speed was the highlight of the day. Anyone too late to hop on before the carriage took off had to leg it.

All seven year groups shared a single classroom: that's forty children taught by one teacher, whose name was Andrä. We kids loved it and especially enjoyed our lunch hour as we had the run of the village. Eventually, in 1938, there was a separate year 8 but I, who was still in year 7, had to stay put. Farm children had to enrol in the *Feiertagsschule* (holiday school), a sort of agricultural training centre. It initially took place on a Sunday, but then changed to being open on weekdays. I left school in 1939 but attended the *Feiertagsschule* for another two years.

I was fifteen when the war broke out in 1939. My dream was to train as a mechanic specialising in agricultural machinery, but it turned out not to be an option at the time and I had no choice but to work on my parents' farm.

At the time the war still had little impact on us back on our small farm in the Dachau hinterland, yet I was curious about what was happening in the world and read everything I could get my hands on. Soon enough, however, the war caught up with us as well. I still remember the day when our family was affected right at its heart: the postman delivered the call-up letter requesting my older brother Josef to report for the army, and that's when it all started.

Soon thereafter he was ordered to travel to the Verdun barracks in Munich-Freimann and was enlisted with the artillery corps. First posted to Lille in northern France, he served as of April 1941 with troops massed into assembly areas along the Bug river, which forms the border between Poland and Russia. Nobody knew what was going on as Germany and the Soviet Union had agreed on a non-aggression pact. On 22 June 1941 at 0200 hours it was, however, terminated, the minute Germany launched Operation *Barbarossa* and attacked Russia. The invasion would take my brother Josef to Lviv, Smolensk, to participate in the Yelnya offensive and then move further to Mozhaysk and Gshask until he ended up 17 km short of Moscow. The much-dreaded Russian winter, often called 'General Frost', put a halt to the German invasion with rain, sleet and the cold, causing it to fail miserably. My brother would later tell us gruesome stories about the ensuing protracted and horrendous trench warfare.

He served with the 7th Infantry Division where armaments were transported by horse-drawn carriages. A massive accident happened in August 1942 when his horses suddenly bolted, tore loose from the carriage, overturned it and galloped away in a blind frenzy. My brother got caught underneath the carriage, suffered a concussion and other injuries and was transported from Smolensk to the army hospital in Munich, passing through Kiedrich and Eltville. Unfit for service, he was dismissed from the Wehrmacht on 15 December 1942.

The accident likely saved my brother's life, as many of his comrades from the same unit would not return from the war, but as fate would have it, he was later killed in another accident much like his first.

Back at home, our family was very busy working on our farm, in particular since my grandmother was no longer alive, my mother was near-blind, and one brother was far away in Russia, fighting for Germany. Being desperate for help, we were given a man called German [sic], a French prisoner of war. Another French prisoner of war by the name of Gordie worked on the neighbour's farm, but sometime during 1942 – it was August, I think – they both escaped, and we never found out what happened to them. The incident was of course reported, and it didn't take long for us to be given some other forced labourers. The way this came about was that Herr Reindl, our mayor, would drive by horse and cart to Dachau's Dulag camp, a transit camp for prisoners of war, and return with three of them [Dulag is a contraction of *Durchgangslager*, transit camps where prisoners of war were processed and interrogated].

One of them was a young fellow by the name of Ivan and he was the one allocated to our farm. He'd been deported from the Ukraine, from somewhere near Kryvyi Rih, and having been born in 1925, he was therefore just one year younger than me. Ivan's young life was marked by unbelievable suffering. One harrowing ordeal after another. After being taken prisoner, he was first transported to Vienna, then managed to escape but was recaptured and ended up in the Penzberg colliery. From there he once again attempted to escape but failed, and his ordeal continued with his deportation to Dachau, and from there he was brought to us.

He was a tall guy with a round shaven head; I'd be reminded of him later when I myself was in Russia, surrounded by men looking much the same. The day he arrived at our farm, we had noodles made of rye flour and deep-fried in lard along with a piece of bread soaked in milk – that was our supper, and Ivan joined us. The guy was completely starved and, realising that he could help himself to as much as he wanted since he was sitting at our table, he stuffed himself to such a degree that he ended up doubling over in pain later that evening suffering from severe stomach cramps. It was so bad that Father hauled him onto his horse cart and drove him to the hospital in Dachau. The day before we had loaded up the carriage with sacks of potatoes that were meant to be delivered to an industrial plant in Mossach, and Dachau was on the way. It turned out that the doctors couldn't help Ivan and they told him his pain would just subside without any intervention. Nonetheless Ivan spent the day there and Father picked him up on his return.

Ivan quickly settled in, worked alongside us and ate at our table – just like the rest of us. I shared my bedroom with him, which was located in the barn and generally referred to as the 'men's den'. On my return from Russia I was informed that Ivan had remained at our farm until the end of the war, never once attempting to escape. He obviously much preferred his stay with us to the horrendous experience he had to endure as a prisoner of war in a camp.

Meanwhile my year group of men born in 1924 was called up for army service. I was ordered to report on 7 December 1942, meaning that I sadly was going to miss my brother's return home, which only took place on 15 December. Enlisted with the 199th Infantry Regiment in Brannenburg near Rosenheim, I was quite excited to leave the parochialism of my village behind me. Army service began with a training period, during the course of which we would have to make known any particular skills, and when one day our instructor asked whether any of us had a driver's licence, I volunteered. Though we didn't actually own a vehicle back home, I had passed a driver's test level 4 and in our small village this was quite an achievement. But it didn't turn out quite as expected, and us lot who claimed to possess such a licence drew the shorter of the straws: we had to report early on Sunday mornings to then be assigned to another detail with none of us knowing which detail this would be. Were we going to be enlisted in the Wehrmacht's motor transport service? No siree, Bob! All this licence afforded us was a stint in the kitchen, where we'd peel potatoes. Then came a Sunday when, in closed formation, we were dispatched to the other side of the Inn river, but not before a visit to the church. After that we had to report in the open square of the barracks, preparing for defence.

The foundation course was extremely brief and saw us boarding a train to France as early as 20 December. Taking advantage of a short stop at a freight station, officers, some older privates and also some experienced soldiers accompanying the transport took themselves to the nearby city and returned laden with liqueur. Naturally, us lads had fun enjoying the drink, though the liqueur tasted like sweet oil. Before we knew it the lot of us were totally drunk and found ourselves toppling over, ending up lying underneath and on top of each other on the floor of the carriages. It was a right mess.

After several days of travel, we finally arrived in Lons-le-Saunier, where we were taken to our lodgings, a row of army barracks. First off, we had to clean the toilets – filthy standing loos lined up back-to-back, some six or eight of them on either side, each with a few steps leading up to its own separate wooden door. They were downright disgusting.

Lons-le-Saunier was situated in the French part of the country governed by the Vichy regime, which meant it lay behind the demarcation line as defined by the Armistice. Once Vichy itself was also occupied and the French soldiers forced to withdraw, they obviously made quite sure that we'd inherit this repulsive 'cultural relic' they called toilets. On top of this, the food was awful. Once we were served roasted horse meat, but strangely enough and much to our surprise it didn't even taste all that bad. Another time, we had been given permission to go on leave, we passed a butcher selling pork and purchased a huge quantity of thick slices. There was no way we could eat it all that same evening, so we stored the leftovers in the tin lid of our mess kits, ready to gobble it up the next morning. To our great disappointment we woke up to find nothing but a few dry bits, everything else had dissolved and turned to water.

That stint in the army all went to plan, with field exercises and a cross-country run every morning leading us to Montaigu, located 5 km away from the barracks and on a slight elevation, in the foothills of the Jura and only some 80 km away from the Swiss border.

It was rough, with orders and instructions hollered at us every single hour – day and night – and so-called slovenliness resulting in fierce punishments. If we happened not to be in tune when singing on our marches, the instructor bellowed, 'Tanks from the right!' which in fact meant taking full cover and immediately throwing ourselves into the roadside ditches. Barely had we scrambled back onto the road than he'd shout 'Low-flying attack from the left', and the whole rigamarole would start all over again.

The date of 15 January 1943 will stick in my mind for ever. The minute we left our barracks, it was the same spectacle as always. Sergeant Klein, replacing the company commander on that day, was the only one in charge. Such was his displeasure with our performance that he decided to mete out a slew of gruelling punishments such as crawling on our stomachs through the mud to the point of exhaustion. When it was finally time to return to the barracks for lunch we were covered from head to toe in filth, but it meant that we'd be allowed to stay behind in the afternoon to clean up. What looked like a reprieve turned into sheer hell, however, with us being ordered to remove from our uniforms every single fleck of clay which stubbornly remained stuck to the fabric no matter how fiercely we scrubbed at it. This incident didn't go unnoticed by the superiors and Sergeant Klein got his comeuppance when he was penalised. Ordered to serve with 4th Company, he was forced to perform strenuous labour on gun carriages.

One morning after finishing off a night exercise, we were ordered to gather at the outskirts of the city, where we were greeted by the army band, who played alongside us. This admittedly made such hour-long marches much more bearable.

Our instructors seemed to be particularly nit-picky about what to us appeared to be utterly insignificant matters, such as how to arrange our lockers or how to make our beds. Strict rule-books dictated everything. When we arrived in the courtyard of the barracks and the chief sergeant requested squad leaders or the room chiefs to be present, we'd immediately know that it boded ill: the state of our barracks had been found lacking and we'd get a dressing-down. As a punishment for what they deemed the slightest infringement of the rules the inspectors would litter our barracks with all sorts of shit. They'd tip over the coal scuttle, tear apart the bedding and knock over our backpacks – there seemed no end to their spiteful harassment. *Bettenbauen* [making the beds] was my particular bane as I invariably made a mistake. But then came 1300 hours and, strutting up and down, they'd check that all was spick and span. Then, once again, we'd be driven back to the exercise grounds and have further rounds of training on heavy guns and live shooting. So much for our time in France.

Towards the end of March 1943 our training came to an end and we were transferred to Holland. Here, the 376th Division had to be restructured – it had been completely destroyed in Stalingrad – and newly formed regiments 672, 673 and 767 were included. Our journey took us to Leiden, where we dismounted to then travel to Zöetermeer. Sectioned off into companies, I ended up in the nearby village called Benthuitzen.

This time they allocated a school building for our lodgings and every day we'd set out to the training grounds. Part of the course were the lessons teaching us how to cross rivers because the country was full of large canals and trenches, and our feet got routinely soaked. After several weeks we were dispatched to Zaandam, located 8 km from Amsterdam on the North Sea Canal. Once again, our lodgings were set up in a school building.

To carry out our service we were provided with bikes, since the main part of our training took place in the dunes surrounding Scheveningen and Wassernar reaching as far as Haarlem. Our most brutal enemy turned out to be the sand that literally found its way into even the tiniest crevice of a gun. Worst of all, deadly in fact, was when it got buried inside its lock. The weapon would jam as a result and we were then forced to take it fully apart to clean it thoroughly.

As to be expected when posted with the infantry, there was a lot of marching across the countryside. Once a week we were allowed to visit the local swimming pool, where I finally learnt to swim – well, at least to the extent that I wouldn't drown. Swimming wasn't an opportunity I had had back in Puchschlagen. The teaching methods in the army were, however, cruel, with those not knowing how to swim simply being pushed into the water by the instructors. If a guy didn't come to the surface, three lifeguards would jump in and haul him out. One instructor felt the urge to shove one of our lads, who came from somewhere in the mountains, into the water, and we only realised much later that he never emerged. When he was finally dragged out, he had turned blue. Paramedics saved him at the last minute. This traditional practice of pushing someone into the water was eventually stopped.

Dutch children would often run alongside our marching columns and join us in our songs. When we'd come up with a new tune, they'd have learnt it by heart after two or three days while also sharing with us their own songs, one of which I remember:

> The first was a boy, the second a girl
> The third didn't want to come, the fourth had no time.
> The fifth was too thin, the sixth was too fat,
> The seventh had pocketed the legs of the eighth
> Yuppe yee, Yuppe yee.

The months spent in Holland were quite jolly for us lads, it has to be said. It allowed us to explore the world a bit more and experience some exciting adventures, starkly contrasting with our days at home, which were filled with tedious chores like feeding the animals, milking the cows or clearing out the stables. It was generally monotonous. Here we got to frequent restaurants with menus featuring unusual foods such as mussels – quite an extraordinary dish for us simple folks who'd never even seen something like this. The thought of a vacation also crossed our minds, and it wouldn't have been such an outlandish idea, seeing as we served in the army. But in view of the dangerous situation in the west, Senior Commander West wouldn't hear of it, neither did Field Marshal von Rundstedt, and they both blocked all requests for leave. Instead, in September 1943 we were ordered to report to Breda, near the Belgian border. Yet again we would be restructured and regrouped.

Inside Ukraine, Followed by the Eastern Front

No sooner had we been stationed in Breda than were we ordered to board a freight train heading for Russia. Three battalions for each regiment travelled to Russia with the rest dispatched to France. Our train crossed Germany and Poland in the direction of Zhytomyr, a main railway junction located just before Kyiv, where a sudden Russian advance resulted in the carriage with our luggage in being cut off. It was carrying our supplies, and we were therefore left with nothing more than what we were already wearing, including our weapons. The rest was gone: our backpacks, our vehicles and other stuff – never to be seen again. We continued further south and unexpectedly chanced upon the front line at Kryvyi Rih.

Passing through Saksahan and Oleksandriia, Russian ground-attack planes strafed and bombed us at will. And despite instantly taking cover, we had to mourn several dead comrades. The war with its deadly claws had all of a sudden gripped hold of us youngsters, forcing us to confront the stark reality: life can be cut short in one instant.

With the air attack behind us, we positioned ourselves up a slight incline and looked down on a small river winding its way through the rocky landscape. Two piles of straw, heaped up high, served as the company's provisional command post – but this too was short lived. The Russians, well aware of our location, had dug themselves in on an incline smack opposite us and relentlessly fired tracer ammunition across, setting the heaps of straw alight.

Much of the night was spent digging ourselves in further up the hill, to a depth of some 2 metres, where the soil was still wet and soft. Though these foxholes weren't ideal, they at least offered us a degree of protection. During the day we had to remain under cover and well out of sight from the vast fruit orchards covering the hillside opposite, where we could just about make out the main road leading to Kryvyi Rih.

The order to launch the attack on the Russians came on the third day, with the objective being to draw closer to the highway. It turned out to be fairly easy. We crossed the river and set up camp at the edge of a fruit plantation where, once again, we dug trenches, much larger ones this time, which we then covered with tree trunks and mounds of earth. While the previous pits accommodated only one gunner, these had space for three and offered proper shelter for us lads, who now had a clear view over the main road behind which the Russians had built their own pits, with brief but intense skirmishes then breaking out between the two sides.

To find out more about our enemy's movements we formed spy groups, and this is how the days dragged on, taking us to mid-November, intermittently dropping shells to inflict as much damage on the Russians as possible while we ducked for cover when particularly heavy Russian projectiles whistled past our heads. These were known to inflict unusually serious injuries.

When I Was Wounded

In mid-November the Russian attacks became so heavy and frequent that one day, during lunch, we had to leave our trenches behind and retreat. Once we had reached the command post I realised to my horror that my gun was unloaded. I had mistakenly left the ammunition behind and was immediately ordered to return to our original position and fetch it. Approaching the trenches, I suddenly felt a dull thud against my left shoulder and warm liquid poured into my glove. Taking it off, I saw my hand drenched in blood. Without further thought, I turned on my heels and, racing past the river, I could hear the horrible shouts of the Russians, 'Urhhh, urhh', as they stormed out from behind the plantations. Petrified, I along with a few other stragglers fought our way through to the crossing. It was tough. It was there that the Russian advance was to be blocked.

The only ones permitted to cross the river over a narrow bridge were the wounded, with an officer at one end, his pistol at the ready. My wound was plain for anyone to see, and with blood dripping out of my coat sleeve I certainly didn't encounter any difficulties. The wounded – there were five of us – were ferried back to Saksahan, where we were fortunate to be looked after by a medic who immediately bandaged us up.

On 14 November 1943 our unit lost comrade Sepp Schöttel, a fine fellow hailing from Bavaria, just like me, and I was sad to have to continue without him. The following day the wounded were transported by vehicle to the field hospital located in Kryvyi Rih. Severely wounded soldiers on stretchers lay writhing and moaning in pain and were filling the halls of the building, with doctors rushing around them, their aprons splattered with blood. I had suffered a clean shot into my shoulder which only required a proper bandage and the arm to be stabilised. On the second day after this incident, a transport consisting of all us injured soldiers was bundled off, and it was back to the front line. With a detour that was necessary due to the Russians having captured the railway junction in Zhytomyr, west of Kyiv, the train travelled via Odessa to Lviv.

The journey lasted several days, taking us into the first week of December, and my bandage, now riddled with lice, caused unbearable itching. Transferred to the Lviv army hospital, I broke out into a fever, which rose to 41 degrees, and because my wound had become inflamed the medics decided I required surgery. Once they had cut it open and properly drained it, I gradually recovered.

Towards the end of December 1943 I was ordered to board a hospital train heading towards Reichenbach, which was situated in the Góry Sowie, the Polish mountain range. Today it is called Dzierzoniów, located in Lower Silesia. Our stay there only lasted for three weeks before we were sent to nearby Ulbrichshöh, situated on a hill, overlooking a gentle valley. Here we were to spend a relatively calm winter, seeing as it was pretty much unaffected by the turmoil of the war. By the end of December my wound had healed up nicely, and on top of that I was granted four weeks' leave, my first since having been enlisted on 7 December 1942. Dismissed from hospital by the end of March 1944, I was transferred to recuperate with the convalescent company in Giebelbach, near Lindau, close to the Bodensee. Meanwhile, bombs were dropped on Friedrichshafen, targeting in particular the Maybach factory which manufactured the engines for the German tanks. A further four weeks' leave would allow me to have a breather, away from the war.

Operation in Romania

Unfortunately, the situation began to heat up mid-June 1944. Transferred to a replacement company, I was first stationed in the Silbersdorf barracks, near Bregenz. Given one day of leave, I took a hike up to the Pfänder, savouring the splendid view over the mouth of the Rhine where it leads into the Bodensee. But these carefree days soon came to an abrupt end, and we were ordered to travel from Silbersdorf to Kempten, from where a transport was organised to take us to Bessarabia in Romania. Pulling in to Munich's train station on 29 June 1944, we were given a few days' leave to visit relatives living nearby and though I had an uncle and an aunt in Munich, their home was on the other side of the city in Sendling, and too far away for me.

We then travelled by train to Vienna and from there on to Bruck, situated on the Leitha river, where we spent two days. To deal with the logistics of coping with the steep ascent ahead of us we required no less than four locomotives, with two of them pushing and the other two pulling. Once at the top, the locomotives that had pushed us up were uncoupled, with the other two transporting us to Hungary. At our first stop, we could easily identify the Hungarian railway workers wearing their distinctly embroidered shirts.

At the beginning of July, we reached Iași in the eastern part of Romania, from where our companies marched along the Prut river towards the south, passing Costuleni and heading towards Măcărești, a small village situated on the left-hand bank of the Prut river. After being divided into groups we were directed to our lodgings: private homes with thatched roofs and the customary clay floors that, much to our disgust, were heaving with lice. Vast corn fields bordered the banks of the Prut, providing the locals and us too with some basic foodstuffs. Cornmeal was mixed with water and boiled to a thick porridge that, once cooled down, would be turned over like a pudding. Known as *mamaliga*, the only added ingredients were water and salt, but alongside it we would also get a very spicy fish soup.

Further south the farmers grew vines and grain; once harvested, these would be threshed in the farms, not out on the fields. Houses were built with courtyards where the door leading to the road could be bolted, quite similar to the historical Bavarian farmsteads. The cut grain would be arranged in a large circle, all round the concrete floor, which had been swept clean prior to the threshing. Two farmers on their horses would then ride their animals around the yard several times and trample the crop for as long as it took for their hooves to loosen the edible part from the straw to which it was attached. A third person would stand by with a basket and collect the horse droppings that were invariably mixed in with the grains. The straw would then be cleared away, the grain heaped onto a vehicle and driven off towards the Prut. In the vast expanse flanking the river the farmers had spread flat sheets made of a hard material, onto which the grains including the chaff would be unloaded. A good wind then carried away the chaff while the grain fell back on the ground.

As I mentioned before, every house had its own door leading to the road. On our evenings off duty, we'd spot a small group of goats gathering in front of a bolted gate, which made us curious. For what reason where they doing this? We'd soon find out that each goat would wait its turn to be let into the courtyard to be milked. That milk was then turned into the famous goat's cheese!

During our stay in this part of Hungary we kept busy by refining our combat practice, and as the Romanians were our allies and seeing that the 4th Romanian Mountain Division was very close by, they'd be regularly treated to our assault patrols' display, where we showed off different manoeuvres and combat methods. Their officers, assembled on the hilltop, would look on. This particular Romanian division had been equipped entirely with German weapons, but what with the Romanians switching allegiance to the Allied forces on 23 August 1944, we'd ironically then be attacked by our erstwhile allies who were now using our very own guns.

During one of our training sessions down in the valley, we heard about the failed assassination attempt on Hitler. It was 20 July 1944, and from then on the *Deutsche Gruss* [Nazi salute], which involved extending the right arm from the shoulder into the air with a straightened hand, was introduced into the Wehrmacht rule-book, as until then it had been mandatory only for civilians [the so-called *Volksgenossen*, people's comrades].

The nearest town to Măcărești, where we were positioned at the time, was Iași, situated in the north-west and some 35 km from us. The surrounding area with its 'black gold' was highly desirable for mining, and for this reason we Germans tried to keep it in our hands as long as possible. Even then, fuel was a crucial commodity when waging war. But in the middle of August the enemy air raids commenced, and with Americans jettisoning their bombs on this area, we were forced to terminate the extraction.

On 19 August 1944 trucks took us towards Iași, which was already facing heavy Russian attacks that forced us to withdraw to Costuleni. After hastily digging ourselves into the undergrowth on a hill along the Prut, we attempted to withstand the continuous shelling until it was no longer possible. We couldn't hold on and withdrew further. Behind us, the new crossing over the Prut near Costuleni was blown up, but I'm not sure who was behind the operation. On 21 August 1944 we had what would be our last warm meal served in the field kitchen – a date one doesn't easily forget.

With a clear view across the Prut, we had a good grip on what the strategic situation was and of how far the Russians had advanced. Our aim was to reach Huși, close to the only crossing over the Prut still intact. Meanwhile, however, the Romanian king had toppled Marshal Ion Antonescu's government in Bucharest, which had been allied to the German Nazi regime. The newly formed Romanian government immediately signed an armistice with the Western powers and declared war on Nazi Germany. With Romania switching sides we'd become easy game for the Russians as the front had been divided in such a way that every German division was immediately positioned next to a Romanian one, which of course meant that the Russians were able to break through at every other front section.

Quite frankly, while I cannot recall precisely what took place and on which date, I clearly remember that once we reached Huși, we faced a huge crowd of soldiers covering a vast space. The place had become one big military camp, and everyone was clamouring to cross the bridge leading to the west. Teeming with retreating soldiers, the western side had largely got out of hand – no control whatsoever. There were no units in any sort of formation to be found – ready prey for the Russians, who swooped down with their fighter bombers and low-flying planes. Heaps of dead soldiers carpeted the battlefields, and strewn around lay the cadavers of the horses that had died in huge numbers as a result of wounds, exhaustion, starvation or exposure to the elements, their stomachs now bloated and decaying because of the extreme heat. All the support groups were assembled at this site, causing additional confusion, congestion and low morale. But in order to reach the west there was no alternative but to cross the river, seeing as the Russians were also rapidly approaching from the south and were fully engaged to push forward.

I was lucky. One of the fortunate ones to reach the west by being able to cross the bridge, I then watched on as attempts were made to collect soldiers who were by then scattered all over the place. With there being no way for previous units to be rebuilt, soldiers were shifted around to form new and smaller units. The only thought on every soldier's mind was to get the hell out and escape this particular section of the front where twenty-one German divisions were facing annihilation. We were literally surrounded by the enemy and attempts to escape – they'd take place at least twice or three times a day – were quashed with an iron fist. In the end, all escapees were chased back.

Once, it was towards the end of August, we were ordered to mount an assault gun and decamp. Descending a steep slope, we ended up in soggy marshland covering a wide expanse, with the assault guns sinking deep into the mud and getting hopelessly stuck. We had no other choice than to stomp through the sludge on foot with our groups steadily losing men. By the end it was only the six of us trudging up and downhill, and only during night-time, as by then the Russians had occupied villages and roads down below in the valley. During the day we would dig ourselves in, either atop a mountain or behind hedges where we were well out of sight and reach. During the night, inching our way forward, we'd prowl for bread or anything edible but whenever we'd come close to a hamlet or a cluster of cottages the dogs would start barking, which naturally put us in danger of being caught. We had no option but to approach the odd house at the edge of a village and beg for something to eat.

In the early morning of 4 September, while it was still dark outside, we reached the Seret river. Realising that the place was teeming with Russians, we turned fast on our heels. En route, we chanced upon what we thought was a field of tomatoes, but discovered, much to our horror, that what was growing there were hot peppers. At the edge of the village, we could finally lay our hands on some bread and were even offered a bundle of hay in some farmer's loft to sleep on. The night passed quickly, with the farmer returning at 0900 hours and asking us to leave as otherwise, he added, the Russians were bound to shoot him if they noticed that he had sheltered German soldiers.

Russian Captivity

What other choice did we have than to obey? The alternative would have meant being taken prisoner by the Russians or being killed by them. We scarpered but made quite sure to take apart our pistols and we frantically tossed the parts in all directions. Passing an orchard with plum trees further along, we didn't miss the opportunity to pick some – for us lads, the war had ended and nothing seemed to matter any more. Would we get caught stealing? Nobody said a word, everyone was petrified. I don't really want to recall or describe what went through our minds at the time – it simply was dreadful. Turning a corner, we were spotted by four Russian soldiers. '*Stoi, stoi*,' they yelled. '*Ruki Verkh*'. 'Stop. Hands up!' We stopped in our tracks. No point in doing anything else!

'*Urr, jest*', they bellowed as they approached us [*Uhr jetzt* – Watch, now]. Hardly had the words been spat out than one of the Russians ripped off my watch. It was no different for my comrades. The plundering continued before they shoved their guns into our backs and pushed us along in front of them until we arrived, as was to be expected, at the yard where they had assembled all those they'd captured. The march commenced, lasting the entire day until we reached the river, just where we had camped out the day before. We were some twenty-five men by then. Stripped naked, forced to carry our clothes on our heads, we

51

crossed at a ford and miraculously, despite a strong current, made it to the other side. It was late at night when we were herded ashore and locked up in the cellar of a small house, guarded by the Russians. Huddled tightly together because of the narrow space, we spent the night with the Russians sleeping above us.

Onwards towards the city of Bakan the next day, where, for the first time the Russians distributed some food to us: a cup of millet gruel. Our lodgings were the Bakan barracks, where we'd spend two or three days provided with only one slice of bread per day. In the meantime, the number of prisoners of war had swollen to something like 2,000, divided into groups of 100 prisoners. Flanked on both sides by Russian guards, we marched towards Roman. Desperately hungry and thirsty and surrounded by a lush landscape, we cast our eyes longingly towards the enticing fields bordering the road. Occasionally, a lad would break away to grab a melon or perhaps a corncob. Bang! Without warning, a short sharp burst of fire had struck him down. We were on a death march and trudging along in line with my exhausted and famished comrades was pure hell. With every shot that rang out, our bedraggled bodies flinched, and shuffling or stumbling past a dead man spread out in the dirt, we were simply grateful it wasn't us.

The following night we were pushed into a deep pit with the Russians standing guard at the top. How could anyone have a chance to escape?

The march continued to Roman and once we entered, the inhabitants mercilessly lashed out at us with flailing sticks and heavy clubs. Russian Cossacks on horses stared down at our sorry lot impassively. Each one of us desperately sought a spot in the middle of the line to avoid being beaten. Until our column reached the barracks, where we were allowed to remain for a while, it seemed we were running the gauntlet.

With our uniforms by now in tatters, and most of us having been stripped even of our mess kits, we gathered some tin from the tops of roofs and shaped it into containers to hold the lunchtime stodge. At home it would only have been fit for a dog – if at all. For me, it reflected what had become of us. Barely human, emaciated silhouettes who meant nothing. The latrine consisted of a wooden beam with a sump behind it to collect the faeces.

One day we were all called to report and ordered to march to the river, where we were supposed to wash. Staggering towards our destination, we suddenly realised how many of us prisoners of war there actually were. When the front line had reached the hilltop overlooking the river, the last ones were only about to leave the barracks.

After some time had gone by, I suffered a painful itch in my pubic hair, and it grew so painful that I overcame my embarrassment and enquired of an older and more experienced comrade whether he could advise. 'I'm dying of pain in the lower region,' I confided. 'Gosh, my lad', he responded in the broad accent of the German region where he came from. 'You've been infested by lice,' he said drily, 'and their eggs are nestling in the hair.' Somehow, I must have become infected but luckily one of the comrades miraculously still owned a pair of scissors and I cut my hair as best I could. I had turned twenty years old by then but had never experienced suffering from a lice infestation. This was just the beginning.

Transport to the POW Camp

A few days after my twentieth birthday, 28 September 1944, a large convoy of prisoners was herded into a freight train with each wagon holding 120 men. The last wagon, however, wasn't filled to the brim. The Russians didn't shove many men into the last wagon – they just selected four Romanians whom they took along with them. They were to be allocated the best spots in the camp later on and lord it over us Germans.

The train set off with each one of us squeezed in between the legs of the guy crouching behind us. If someone had to get up to go to the loo, he had to clamber over the rest of us to reach the middle of the wagon where a hole had been cut into the door through which two slabs of wood shaped into Vs had been fixed – and that was our latrine, whether you had to pee or poo. Cursing and swearing, the men would yell at the guy shoving himself through the packed pile to reach the hole – but what choice did he have? The food we received was sparse, a slice of dry bread and a mug of tea, sometimes a handful of millet gruel.

On the fourth or fifth day, we were handed a piece of salt herring which made us even more thirsty. When the door was pushed open on the eighth day as the train came to a stop, the guard's first question was about how many dead bodies lay inside. *'Sgolko kaput?'* (How many kaput?)

On 15 October 1944 we arrived at the Mozhaysk train station, where we were rounded up and then taken to a pond where the guards gave us permission to wash; some just drank the water instead. Then it was off to the camp situated some 2 km outside the town and probably constructed by the Wehrmacht. Our lodgings, defined as bunkers, were large spaces dug halfway into the ground, filled with soil that we now had to excavate. Mozhaysk is located 80 km south-west of Moscow, on the postal route to Smolensk.

Mozhaysk: The POW Camp

In the bunkers, on either side of the corridor were two levels of wooden bunkbeds with mattresses of poplar trunks that had been sliced to measure some 30 cm across and just put side by side. And that was it. The trunks, of course, were so uneven and rough that we ached lying down. We slept in our clothes, which meant wearing the same stuff day and night. In addition, we were squeezed so tightly against each other that if one guy turned over, the rest of us had to follow suit and irritated comrades would further poison the atmosphere with their complaints.

Each of us prisoners was registered and everyone's 'cards' were held in the commander's office: our surname, forename, father's name and unit was written in ink on a piece of poplar wood with mine reading: 'Strasser, Michael Kaspar, Div. 376, Reg. 767'.

In the mornings we lined up for the roll-call in rows of ten, which made it easier for the Russians, who seemed to find counting to be a difficult process. Once they had gathered together the last lines, the first ones had already moved away due to the frost and wind. The constant repetition of this process felt endless. The year 1944 was notorious for the early arrival of a bitter winter, with an ice-cold wind blowing sharply across the landscape and temperatures dropping to 30 degrees below freezing. Once the men had lined up on the frozen ground, it turned out that one or two prisoners had gone missing, with the Russians then scouring the infirmary to see whether they were perhaps among the dead. Every once in a while, a comrade also died of sheer exhaustion or due to sickness, his dead body lying somewhere in a bunker.

We lined up every day, early in the morning before work and in the evening when we returned, and it was only then that we were permitted to go to the so-called dining room which had been sunk halfway into the ground and then filled up. Each of our three daily meals consisted of 750 grams of soup, and the lucky ones would find a piece of carrot floating around. At lunch time, 250 grams of kasha were added, a typical Russian buckwheat porridge, and once a day we also received 750 grams of bread, 'chleb' as they called it, a very moist bread that cannot even be compared to the kind of bread we were used to from back home.

If someone hadn't eaten his bread but wanted to take it to where he was detailed to work, he lost out. Because of the cold, that 'chleb' would freeze and likely cause diarrhoea or, even worse, result in dysentery. I never bothered even trying this and always ate my bread along with my soup.

Our work entailed labouring the whole day out in the forests, felling trees, loading up the chopped firewood onto sledges and then dragging it into the camp. The sledge, fitted with an iron bar across the front, was moved by four men pulling a rope slung over their shoulders, with some other prisoners at the rear of the vehicle, steering or braking. Sometimes we'd transport entire tree trunks, which were then sawn into planks. A hefty trunk was heaved into a specially constructed metal structure with one man on top of the trunk and one below. The two men would take it in turns to pull a crosscut saw and produce a certain number of cut planks. Here too, based on the socialist industrialisation plan, prisoners had to meet a quota, and in our camp it amounted to a daily output of planks measuring a total of 40 metres. If the men worked well together with smooth cooperation between them, they could go well above the predetermined quota and receive extra rations, such as a supplement of soup or even a piece of ordinary bread.

Washing and delousing took place once every four weeks. We hung our threadbare clothing on an iron ring which then entered a large chamber heated to 70 degrees, which got rid of the lice. During that time, we could wash ourselves, with each one of us receiving a bit of soap and a small bowl filled with warm water. But before this, all our body parts covered in thick hair growth were shaven – again, to kill off any hidden lice.

Finally, we were allowed to pick up our garments on the other side of the hot chamber. It felt good to slip into the still warm clothing, a brief comfort against the bitter cold that plagued us throughout. Unfortunately, however, this whole process only killed off the lice, not their eggs. It seemed there was nothing that could protect us from the effects of this plague, and the moment we came in from the cold the revolting little beasts had us all over again. The itching had become unbearable, and we set about hunting and squashing them with our thumbnails, which turned black. We named these ghastly creatures after the dreaded Russian tank, 'T 34'. I scratched my chest covered in bite wounds so ferociously that I still have the scars to show today. By Christmas, after repeated delousing we finally seemed to have defeated those pests.

Though each one of us prisoners hailed from a different part of Germany, we managed to build relationships during our time at the camp. We had conversations about our pasts, our backgrounds and families, and found out quite a bit about each other. I made friends like Ludwig Köppel and Xaver Bayer from Unterweickertshofen and Karl Wagner from Weilenbach, near Schrobenhausen. We were all young guys except for Ludwig, who was eight years older than me, had served for many years with the Wehrmacht, and was much more experienced than the rest of us. He truly was a support to us.

Christmas Day 1944 was awful. There we were, sitting next to a cold oven and crying with hot tears running down our cheeks. None of us knew how long this ordeal would last and whether we could pull through. Then, Ludwig Köppel, breaking an atmosphere laden with misery and sadness, came up with an idea. What, he mused, might we do if we survived and returned home? In gratitude for our safe return, he suggested, we should erect a cross back in our country. We agreed, and this solemn promise heartened us. Indeed, a few years after I returned home on 25 November 1948, I fulfilled the vow and the cross still stands today in the corner of our property alongside the road leading to the church of Puchschlagen.

On that bitterly cold Christmas, the Russians had baked a crumble cake for us, using the sugar rations never distributed and which had accumulated in the meantime. Another comrade, Josef Willibald from Odelzhausen (where his family owned the butcher's shop, which after the war was turned into a restaurant), fell ill. He had diarrhoea and was admitted to bunker No. 4, which was full of patients suffering from dysentery. Bunkers Nos 4 and 5 were both earmarked for the sick and surrounded by barbed wire to prevent anyone entering or leaving – an attempt to reduce the danger of the disease spreading. But there was no holding back Ludwig Köppel, who was a friend of Josef's, and he sometimes took me along. It was a dreadful experience, having to watch these emaciated men stretched out in the most miserable conditions and suffering horribly; a miserable heap of what once were men, men who had wasted away in these most squalid surroundings, may their souls rest in peace. Willibald died at the end of January 1945, one of many not to survive that winter. Their corpses would be buried outside the camp, behind the commander's office, but while temperatures hovered in the double-digits degrees below freezing, digging graves was impossible and we simply had to stack the corpses in piles. The initial group that had entered the camp back in October 1944 consisted of 1,800 men and had shrunk by April 1945 to 1,130 – the rest of them lay dead behind the commander's office.

In our camp we only ever had unit officers and sergeants – none of them were exempt from labour. Generals and officers who had been taken prisoner were transported to a camp located behind Moscow. Their work consisted of putting together newspapers, which were then displayed on boards in the rest of the camps. Naturally a paper such as *Freies Deutschland* had the sole purpose of promoting Soviet war propaganda but also conveyed between the lines what was happening in Germany – something that stirred us up. At one point we got to see images of the Dachau concentration camp showing us how cadavers were transported on wheelbarrows out of the camp. Here, in our camp, it wasn't any different, only our corpses were frozen stiff.

Time passed and it was mid-April when my group of 150 men was ordered to board a freight train. We didn't know our destination until we arrived a few days later in the Babayevo camp, a few hundred kilometres outside

Moscow. I will never know why I was part of this group, but fortunately my friends, Ludwig Köppel and Xaver Bayer were also there with me.

The Babayevo Camp

This camp was different. For one, medical care was available because the inmates of this camp mostly consisted of visibly weakened prisoners. We newcomers who were in better physical condition were charged with cutting firewood, mostly for the kitchen. After a short while I had contracted two inflamed fingernails from incessantly chopping and splitting wood while wielding a crude axe, and a female doctor attended to me. Reaching for a pair of forceps, she yanked at the nails until she had totally removed them, all the while asking me repeatedly: '*Balid, balid?*' Does it hurt? Well of course it did, it hurt like hell, the pain was excruciating.

I also once suffered with toothache and was seen by a dentist, again a female, a large and imposing woman who spoke German well and got speaking to me. She had studied in Germany before the war and her comments about my teeth were that they were as strong as those of a horse. That was then. But just two years later, when I was in Cherepovets, they had all become loose due to poor nutrition and there was no way of saving them. By the age of forty I was toothless.

A rare bit of relief came on the morning of Whitsun Tuesday in 1945 when, just before mealtime, Ludwig Köppel and Josef Lankes, who had grown up in the Bavarian woods, taught me the *Schafkopf* card game. They had cut up some paper and made playing cards from them, pencilling on them the proper illustrations and names. The game had barely started when the woman doctor popped in and, despite us guys sitting far back in a corner, she came up to us with a translator charged with asking us what we were up to. 'They're playing a card game.' She ordered him to gather the cards and went on to report us. We were punished by having our lunch and dinner withheld, never mind the fact that the little food we received in any event wasn't sufficient.

Here in Babayevo we were also detailed to the forest. Every day, our silent column, often trudging through brutal weather, dragged itself along a path bordering the forest and past a cemetery where we witnessed the most bizarre local funeral customs, with people visiting relatives' graves and leaving food and drink for them. They'd arrive at the graveside, settle down and eat what they had brought along but also leave the leftovers for the deceased. The idea was that they would consume this food in the world beyond.

One day a small group of us, some six to eight men, were taken to a house in a nearby village where we were supposed to fix a straw roof. It was probably the home of some relative of a guard. A huge pile of rubble was heaped up high in the middle of the village square, the sorry debris of what was once the church. The Bolsheviks had been fighting the Church ever since their October Revolution and most of the clergy had been murdered in the course of the Stalin purges of the 1930s.

After we had finished our work, we were handed large portions of soup along with the customary kasha and a slice of bread; it was delicious, and I was truly glad that I had been allocated to this labour detail. Permission was even granted for us to eat in the lounge of the house where glinting gold-panelled icons depicting religious illustrations hung on the walls. We assumed that the villagers must have rescued them before the church was demolished.

When the war ended on 8 May 1945 nobody was permitted to leave the camp as the Russians celebrated their victory with gallons of alcohol, leaving nobody sober in charge. That lasted for quite a while.

Time passed, week by week, month by month. In June a group of labourers was dispatched to a so-called children's camp and I along with my two comrades had been selected to join. This wasn't a typical prison camp, but was called a 'commando' where we were assigned to one specific building and where we remained for fourteen days. Until today I don't know what to make of the term 'children's camp', but what I remember is learning songs such as the *Internationale*, the combat song of the socialist workers' movement.

> Peoples, hear the signals!
> On to the last stand!
> The international
> Fights for human rights.

Cherepovets

Not long after this stint at the so-called children's camp we were transported to Cherepovets, a good 400 km north of Moscow. It is situated on the train line leading from Moscow to Arkhangelsk, south of the Kola peninsula on the White Sea, bordering a wide canal which was used for ship construction. Cherepovets is connected to St Petersburg on the Baltic Sea via several lakes, and also by the Lake Ladoga. Products from all over were ferried along this canal. It was also the area where the infamous Schaika camp was located, where German prisoners had to fell trees, tie up the cut-up trunks, string them together to form rafts and lug them onto ships that ferried them to their destination. These rafts laid flat on the ground measured some 10 to 14 metres, but there were also some cut trunks measuring 2 metres in length which were stood up in the water and tied together. During the infernal winter of 1945/6 you could count hundreds of such rafts lying in the canal, covered in thick layers of ice.

One of our friends, Max Römisch, had been enlisted to this camp and was part of the group charged with annealing wire, which meant heating wire wound around a large coil at an open fire in order to make the metal more flexible and ductile. In the process and before the metal had become softer, the end of the wire snapped and flipped into his left eye, leaving him permanently half-blind.

I and my close friends ended up in a different camp on the other side of town – in one of the original forced labour camps which, judging from the large number of old barracks, had served to incarcerate innumerable so-called enemies of the people in the time of Stalin's 'Great Terror'.

Our days consisted of daily marches to the nearby workshop where groups of 200 to 300 men were assigned to various types of heavy labour, such as cutting stone or hauling in ships. This was the first time that guards enquired whether prisoners had any professions and, because I hoped that I'd be receiving better rations, I reported as a carpenter. I was soon to regret that move as my first assignment was to construct some shuttering. No sooner had I been found out to be utterly incompetent at this than I was back with the unskilled labourers. Work was brutal. Two of us, for example, had to operate a crude winch to pull a ship in need of repair ashore by rigging it to tracks. Another job they'd allocate to us was hammering at pieces of stone to shape them into cobblestones. By hand, with little food, from morning to night, we sat tightly side by side slaving away, getting injured but forced to fill our quota. It was dreadful.

Somehow I got wind that prisoners who delivered a steel plate would receive from the kitchen a daily supply of 750 grams of soup for a week. These plates were used by the so-called power plant generating electricity for the camp. Keen to take advantage of this offer, I made enquiries and actually came across some of these plates in my workshop.

Swiftly I grabbed one, well out of everyone's sight, strapped it to my body, then covered it with my coat and set off down the 2-km route to the camp.

Back at camp, we lined up in threes, as we did every day, and I made sure to stand in the middle of a row, halfway down the column. The guard shot a quick glance down my row, pulled me out and thrust me to the side – he must have smelled it. Petrified, I shuffled to the station, where the guard tore at my coat, revealing the plate still tied to my shivering body. Carefully placing it behind an oven, he looked over his shoulder. '*Davai baschlie!*' he growled, which meant that I should scram, run through the narrow gate and back to the camp. I obeyed, my heart beating like crazy.

Only once I was back in the camp and among my comrades did I calm down, and that was certainly my last attempt at getting any extra rations. Thank God! I had got off lightly.

Once I was part of a group escorted to an iron foundry. The work here was so exhausting and gruelling that the supervisors had to rotate the groups on a weekly basis. The men chosen for this detail were all strong and in relatively good physical condition and received an additional daily ration of bread and soup, which is why I volunteered. We departed from the camp at 1000 hours to return at 2200 hours. The late start time was due to Russian workers preparing the casting moulds in which we had to pour the liquid iron. Depending on the size of the mould, either two or four men were assigned to this process. The tall furnace would be stoked with an equally long bar and the liquid flowed through a hollow channel all the way from the top and down into a bucket. Once the bucket was full, we sealed off the opening using a pole and a plug. The pole bearer was a heavy-set Russian. One bucket after another was emptied until the evening when the liquid had cooled down and the casting could be extracted, ready for the next morning.

After that particular assignment I was transferred to yet another group, deployed near the Zersai lumber camp where the rafts docked. Horses then dragged the long and very thick tree trunks to trucks where they were loaded onto the open cargo space. Before that, however, we had to somehow remove the wires joining the trunks, with these wires being nearly as thick as my finger. Needless to say, this was hugely tricky, with two men having to lie astride the trunks and, when ordered, simultaneously remove the wires by cutting them with a bolt cutter.

When, at the beginning of November, temperatures dropped dangerously low and the canal and dock were covered by thick sheets of ice, we'd only deal with the shorter rafts, those consisting of the sliced tree trunks that were some 2 metres long and which we were forced to haul up to the camp by ourselves. But not before we had to carve away the layers of ice covering the raft. Iron bars called 'lom' were thrust into our hands and we – there were usually four men at a time – had to balance atop the iced-up raft to pound this massive rock of ice. We hammered desperately away the entire day, trying to loosen the raft until it floated in the water so that we could then retrieve the trunks. But what with the freezing cold and the dense ice blanket, we often failed. At the point when we had nearly succeeded in penetrating the ice, we needed to be especially careful, as any extra force would have destabilised and instantly sunk the lom, which was exceedingly heavy, and that would be followed up by Russian supervisors screaming and swearing at us. We then heaved the wood uphill to the heating plant which generated the electricity for the whole town.

If the weather conditions weren't too rough, Russians joined us on the ice, carving holes measuring about 1 metre in diameter into the ice, through which they lowered fishing nets. They knew that fish would surface through that hole for a gulp of oxygen and if lucky, they'd catch one.

Another job involved transporting flour and barley via a horse-drawn cart from the depot to the town. When the coast was clear, we'd pierce a hole into a sack and gobble up the flakes spilling out while also filling our trouser pockets in order to have a bit left over for the evening. We would often get to meet Russian civilians on the way and we'd beg them for a spare clove of garlic. We prisoners craved some garlic as we used it to spice up our soup. We'd grind the garlic to a fine paste and add it to our brew.

In this particular posting we also worked on Sundays, though we weren't saddled with quite as heavy a workload. We lugged wood from the river to the camp, for example, or were ordered to cut willows which the Russian women used for basket weaving. Though this might seem a light job in comparison, I do remember returning to the barracks half frozen on the snowier days with icy temperatures.

There was one particular assignment which was by far my favourite. During the winter of 1945/6 I was placed with a group working in a bakery outside the camp. Posted there together with my friend Ludwig Köppel and another comrade, we were tasked with preparing the wood to heat the ovens, which came, of course, with freshly baked bread for lunch and yet a further piece which we smuggled back to the camp. All went well, until one day we were searched at the gate, and they took that bread away. If that wasn't bad enough, we were also incarcerated overnight in the penal block where the cells were so cramped you could only stand or sit. Only one man fitted inside and there was no way you could lie down.

That didn't hold us back from trying our luck again the following day and smuggling bread into the camp. Agonising, gnawing hunger was our steady companion, and the possibility of sinking our teeth into some fresh bread was too irresistible. We had learnt our lesson, however, and instead of hiding the bread in our pockets we tied it to the inside of our legs, out of the guard's reach. A fabulous feast for us had been secured.

The bread that was consumed in the camp was usually first sliced in the kitchen, then weighed and placed on trays that were carried into the barracks. None of the bread pieces were identical in weight, as the dough was baked in loaves and yielded two crusty end bits which were considered by us inmates as much more desirable. It wasn't any different when – to even out the weight – an additional portion was added to the lighter slices. Eyes peeled, each one of us was out for himself alone: let me grab the best bit!

At Christmas they doled out so-called *Doppelkarten* [double-sided postcards to allow for censorship] which we were permitted to send home. Such cards had the Red Cross emblem printed across the top, alongside the Turkish crescent moon and were distributed to prisoners in alphabetical order – but by the time it came to S, for my surname, they'd long ago run out of cards and I went empty-handed. Quite honestly, it didn't much bother me as I felt that my family was perhaps better off not knowing my whereabouts, or whether I was still alive. Whether I'd survive this torturous imprisonment was anybody's guess.

While the temperatures dropped to a glacial minus thirty degrees Celsius on Christmas Day, a massive thaw the following day saw water dripping down the roofs, reflecting the enormous weather fluctuations in this area. This wouldn't have been so terrible if it didn't have nasty consequences. The sudden rise in temperature was our most vicious enemy, with our felt boots getting utterly soaked and with there being no possibility for us to dry them. The bitter cold set in a few hours later.

A *politruk* [political commissar or political officer, a supervising officer responsible for the political education and organisation of the unit to which they are assigned] worked in our camp as well and was charged with indoctrinating the prisoners with communist ideology. We just called them 'anti-fascists' and while the people initially teaching the courses were communist émigrés, later on prisoners were also recruited for this job. These volunteers enjoyed many advantages such as being posted to positions in small units and then instructed to promote communism actively once they returned home. Not surprising, as the aim of communism was to instigate global revolution.

At one point I was ordered to report to one of those *politruks*, a certain Herr Wirthig from Augsburg. Though I'm not quite sure I remember his name correctly, I'm certain about the fact that he hailed from Augsburg. He requested I see him in his office, enquired about my details and then came straight to the subject of Dachau. Seeing, he said, that I came from Dachau, I would surely have information about the concentration camp. 'Surely,' he continued, 'you know about the gassing that took place there, and the burning ... Hard to escape such knowledge, as you'd, of course, have smelled that!' I had to disabuse him of this conviction. 'No, I never knew, and nobody ever spoke to me about that.' This kind of back and forth continued for a while, with the guy intent on tricking me into some kind of admission, some form of acknowledgement and of having been aware of the horrors that had taken place at that camp. I knew nothing, and that was the truth. There wasn't anything I could reveal to him. Finally, I explained that Dachau was located 2 km away from the actual camp and Puchschlagen, my home, lay a further 8 km west of it. The man finally gave up and I was never contacted by him again [Dachau had working crematoria and an operational gas chamber, but mass gassing did not take place there].

It was only when I was transferred to the Cherepovets main camp that I found out that Dachau had been a most awful and brutal concentration camp, and that it was one of so many. Plastered on the walls of this POW camp were pages listing in large letters all the concentration camps built by the Nazis, and to be honest, we had no idea of their existence. None of us, especially the younger ones amongst us, had the faintest idea. The fact that I had served in the 376th Division didn't become an issue for me.

We prisoners were regularly checked with respect to our physical condition, how strong and healthy we were and what our capacity was regarding our endurance. We were allocated to the various labour units accordingly, with the strongest men posted to unit 1 and the weakest to unit 3, though they were still capable of work. Then there were the sick, referred to as 'Distrofia' [dystrophic]. These medical check-ups usually went something like this: we'd line up undressed in the courtyard for the doctors to file past us. It was usually a female doctor who'd press our upper arms, checking our muscles by pulling at the skin covering them. If the skin pulled away easily, you'd be registered as 'weak', or your name was added to the list of the Distrofia. Turning 180 degrees, the same examination took place with our buttocks – usually the results were the same. Those listed under Distrofia were actually sick and they neither had to nor could be sent back to work. Among ourselves we called them Strohficker (straw fuckers). My skin was taut, but seeing as I wasn't particularly robust, I usually ended up in the third unit with all the healthy and sturdy comrades placed in units 1 and 2.

Labour details were dispatched to the colliery located in Donetsk and to the paper mill in Sokol, with the workload being so barbaric and horrendous that only men from units 1 and 2 were placed there. It was especially the paper mill, notorious for its horrific conditions, which was feared by the prisoners and referred to by them as the *Knochenmühle* (bone mill). If inmates returned after two to three months, they would inevitably be suffering from extreme exhaustion, malnutrition and injuries, and – soon thereafter they'd be downgraded to the *Distrofia* category. This made me quite pleased to have ended up in unit 3, but I certainly felt pity for those emaciated guys who were physically and emotionally ruined, and practically sentenced to death.

Prisoners from other camps would also often be transferred to our main camp once they were near their end. Such a transport of some 200 men joined us in November 1945 directly from Germany where they had been used as forced labour in Berlin during the summer. Their condition was appalling and they were immediately placed in a separate compound surrounded by heavily guarded fences, much like the main camp. Their quarantine lasted for four weeks, during which time no one was allowed in or out. The Russians had a deadly fear that diseases would turn into epidemics and spread, which they didn't want to risk. That was also the reason that every prisoner was totally shaven, even their heads.

Amongst those who arrived in this transport was Max Römisch from Dietfurt near Grafenwöhr, whom I befriended when we were both posted in 1946 to a work unit in Jorkie. He was four years my junior, so was practically a child when he'd been called up to join the army.

The order to join that Jorkie unit came in April after the harsh winter of 1945/6 had finally come to an end. My group of ten men travelled north towards a remote kolkhoz or perhaps it was merely a subcamp where the Russians had already stabled twelve horses and an entire herd of cattle. It was for us to manage the husbandry, with Paul from Pomerania, a fellow prisoner, in charge of the cattle, but it didn't involve any milking. Horses were tended to by Fritz from Romania, who, because he could speak Russian well, had previously been a driver for the camp commander.

As it was spring, we were also ordered to plough the fields, and were provided with nothing more than a few animals and ploughs – no wheels

66

to speak of. That's certainly not what I was used to from home, but despite my trepidations, it actually all went well. An old, white-haired Russian was in charge and referred to himself as an agronomist. He must have been well over seventy years old.

Much like on our own farms back at home, we initially created large wide beds, but our agronomist was adamant that we revert to the Russian tradition and have small narrow beds with deep furrows in between – understandable as this method allowed the water to drain. Four strong and heavy Belgian horses [Brabant], which the Russians must surely have captured in Germany, pulled the plough up and down the field nonstop from morning to night, and though robust workhorses, they were not up to the task. During those weeks the Russian soil was particularly soggy and muddy, and the horses were so utterly exhausted and weakened that they weren't even able to pull an empty plough. Russian draughthorses seemed much tougher and were probably used to the slog.

The plan was to plant potatoes on a large plot of land, with a truck delivering potato seeds to the far end of a fairly well-paved access road, referred to as the local runway, some 1.5 km away from the kolkhoz. Our group was charged with handling the transport using two horse-drawn vehicles – but it all turned out to be a total fiasco! The path was in much worse condition than we had been told, and our vehicles were constantly sinking into the marshy ground – hundreds of kilograms clean disappeared into the slush.

Much like we were used to in Germany when it comes to normal potatoes for daily consumption, these seed potatoes were large tubers. But while back at home potato growing was just that, in this region the process was quite spectacular. With only a single-furrow plough at our disposal we made furrows into which the Russians then chucked their seed potatoes, leaving us to then cover the pits with soil before digging the next furrow. And this went on all day with the animals working slowly in a steady rhythm and, without pausing, dragging the ploughs through the wet soil until the quota was met.

Some of the fields reached up to the access road, the so-called runway. Once, when Max and I were quite close to that road, we watched a Russian walking towards us. Let's try our luck and approach the chap, we thought. '*Trastishe davarish boshalsta nem shta nye bo pokurit,*' we muttered, which meant something to the effect of 'Good day, comrade, please, something to smoke.' And wouldn't you know it, the Russian reached into his pocket, pulling out a pinch of the coarse but strong tobacco which they called *makhorka*. All we were missing was some cigarette paper, so I boldly asked: '*Bomago nas nyet*', which amounts to 'We also don't have any cigarette paper.'

Tucking the tobacco back into his pocket, he pulled out an expertly folded pack of cigarette paper, tore one apart and handed half to each of us before reaching back into his pocket for the *makhorka*, which he proceeded to spread generously onto the pieces of paper. Arranging it carefully by pressing down, we then rolled it, wetted the ends with our tongues – and hey presto, the cigarette was ready.

The question was how we might light it, and once again I tried out my Russian. '*Spitzkie doshie nyeto.*' We have no fire either, I sheepishly admitted. The Russian drew his fuse cord – all Russians carried one with them at the time – rubbed his flint against it, banged it with a piece of steel until the fuse glowed, and puffed into it. Finally, we could light our cigarettes.

We took leave not without thanking him heartily. '*Spassiva,*' we smiled, and were over the moon to be able to have a smoke. While being prisoners of war, we'd certainly learnt to count our blessings.

It's actually quite easy to manufacture such firelighters. All you need to do is take a handful of dry cotton wool, form finger-thick tubes, wrap them in fabric, light them at one end and then extinguish it by covering the tube with something like a thimble. If you want, you can rekindle the fire with a flint and a piece of steel, but you need to be careful not to sever the glowing end as otherwise it won't work. Indeed, that's how Russians lit a fire, and I followed suit. There were plenty of stones around, and all you needed to do was give it a go. There was also cotton wool to be had, if necessary you just plucked it out of your quilted jacket. As for a piece of steel, well... you just had to keep your eyes open and be swift. Once we had organised for ourselves some tobacco and cigarette paper, we could roll our own cigarettes.

There we were, Max and I, just about to start ploughing the field, but not before we'd enjoy a ciggy. But the tobacco we had managed to scrounge was fresh, with the lower leaves of the stalk having been removed first, before the plant had even matured. What we of course didn't know was that this tobacco was particularly strong, which meant that we only managed to plough half the field before we needed to pull down our trousers and relieve ourselves. But at least we had enjoyed the cigarette.

There was a lot to learn about cigarette paper in general. Russians mostly used printed newspaper. Here again it wasn't as straightforward as one might think, as you couldn't just grab any old newspaper, but had to find a *Izvestia* or a *Pravda*. Both were the official papers of the Communist Party, but it has to be said that they really only printed on good-quality paper, which worked just as well as normal cigarette paper. The paper from all other newspapers turned black and with each puff one would have a flame potentially igniting into a fire.

Towards mid-June temperatures rose rapidly, the heat was sweltering even though we were quite far north. It barely got fully dark at night. Because of the heat we only had to be out on the fields between 0600 and 1000 hours and 1600 and 2000 hours. One day, the sun had been beating down on me from start to finish and I got so sunburnt on my upper body that I had to see a medic, who then bandaged me up.

The summer saw us ploughing at early hours in the morning and whenever possible we sought out the potato fields, where we'd pull out some sprouting potatoes. We chucked them into a fire I had lit with my self-made lighter, which I always carried around with me, and enjoyed the roasted feast.

The only reason why this ran relatively smoothly was because of our guard, an Austrian whom we called by the two letters written on his armband, BK. He had probably emigrated to Russia because of his anti-fascism. He was a decent bloke who didn't blow the whistle on us, but if he had, we'd have been done for.

One day, out of the blue, he admonished me. 'Strasser, why don't you for once write a letter home?' 'How would you suggest I do that,' I asked him back, 'seeing that all *Doppelkarten* have been distributed to others.' He pulled one of those cards out of his pocket, carefully separated it into two and gave me half. I wrote home, and it was the first sign of life I had given my family in the two years that I'd been taken prisoner of war. And wouldn't you know it, after four weeks had gone by, I received a response from back home!

When it was time to harvest the potatoes a convoy of some fifty men on lorries arrived from the camp, each equipped with a small wooden spade to dig out the potatoes and collect them into baskets. It turned out to be a miserable heap of potatoes they collected and much less than what we had harvested in the spring. That certainly was a lot of work for very little.

This was followed by the grain harvest. Two annexes on each side of a large gabled barn close to our barracks had built-in ovens; their construction once again reminded me of our farm, with the only exception being that the arched top of the oven consisted of large stones, each measuring some 10 to 30 cm in diameter. The men would heap the grain onto a grate installed at a height of 2 metres above each oven.

The bulky sheaves had to be transported on foot for several kilometres by the prisoners and, once piled onto the grates, they'd dry out with the rising temperature. That was necessary, of course, because it rained a lot in that area and the sheaves were soaking wet. The guys pulled in from the camp were, naturally, also wet to the bone, but nobody could care less about them. They too gave this little attention as they were overjoyed to be picking grains out of the husk with which they could feed themselves – something they certainly couldn't do back in the camp they had come from.

Every morning my group was ordered to fetch wood from the forest, cut up the trunks into logs, load them onto our horse-drawn carts and drive them back to the barn where they would be used to heat the ovens in the early afternoon. The stones had to be white-hot, and the ovens worked until 0200 hours, leaving the sheaves completely dry the next morning. Then it was time for the threshing, which took place in the barn. This went on for about fourteen days, with our group alternating between ovens. I clearly remember a group of older women who were walking towards us on one of those trips back from the forest and shouting into our faces: '*Gospodie, gospodie, moloddie tcholave!*' 'Goodness me, those are but young lads!' At the time I was twenty-one and my friend Max eighteen.

70

Towards the end of autumn, we were sent to the woods to prune trees, uproot trees, load them and transport them back to the camp. There were loads of them, the forest was overgrown and there was masses of undergrowth. Back at the camp we had to dig flat ditches, again reminding me of shovelling trenches for our carrots. We dumped the shrubs and stuff and covered them with soil. Once again we worked under the eagle-eyed agronomist, who'd use the shrubs in the winter to feed his goats.

Meanwhile my friend Max Römisch was posted with Otto Ersche to a night detail, charged with keeping watch over the horses which were kept out in the fields when they were needed far away from the camp. They'd wear bells crafted out of tin boxes around their necks, the sound of their clanky rings breaking the quiet. They had also tethered the horses' legs, forcing them to cover only short distances and preventing them from escaping. But the comrades' most important task was to stoke a fire throughout the night to keep the wolves at bay. There were many of them around there.

At the beginning of November Max and I were placed with a special unit located at a kolkhoz a few kilometres further away. Along with two horse-drawn vehicles and the Russian commander of our group, Captain Timosche, we were sent to fetch provisions. Kolkhozes were a form of agricultural production cooperative managed collectively by the peasants working there. To that end, farmers had to relinquish their properties and each kolkhoz was obligated to sell its crops or other products to the state for very low prices, or deliver a set amount for nothing at all. If that set amount wasn't achieved by the kolkhoz, whether that was down to bad weather or some other reason, they'd be forced to make up for the loss by ordering their farmers to deliver produce from their own gardens. Each member of such a kolkhoz was permitted to work the soil of his own small garden, where flowers and vegetables thrived, compared to the communal fields.

As it happened, our kolkhoz had fallen behind with its deliveries to the state and this is how, dragged along by Timosche, we ended up knocking on the doors of the farmers to request their products: onions, or other vegetables such as carrots, swedes and parsnips – it didn't matter whether they were prepared to hand them over or not.

Of course they all resisted parting with what they had so carefully stored for the winter, but Timosche could certainly be relied on when it came to every single one of them handing over their baskets. His brutal dealings with his own people surprised us.

Just before we reached our camp on our return trip, a potato field not yet harvested caught my eye. From then on not a night passed when Max and I didn't steal away in the pitch black to fetch for ourselves a few potatoes. On one of those occasions it went wrong, of course, and we were intercepted by the guards, who immediately confiscated them and added the punishment of having to scoop out faeces from the latrines and carry 100 buckets *each* out to the field. As an extra harassment they only opened a tiny hole in the fencing for us to slip through – it was revolting.

Winter came early and the horses needed to be taken back to their stables. Temperatures sank so quickly that when we arrived in the early morning their dung was frozen. Hay for the animals was transported from 20 km away by sleighs from the fields where the mown grass had been bundled up during the summer and had remained there as bad weather had prevented us from transporting it at the time. The sleighs, some 1 metre wide, were constructed with birchwood runners curving up at the end, and attached to the wooden poles was a shaft bow that straddled the horse. That allowed the horse, as was traditional for one-horse carts, to be positioned in the middle, and with the help of its horse collar, to pull at the strap attached to the sleigh and running underneath the animal. The ropes that our farmers used back home didn't exist around here. Another strap slung over the small saddle atop the horse and fixed both to the bars and to the collar ring would allow for adjustments and manoeuvrability. On sleighs like this you wouldn't find a single nail or piece of iron. The whole lot consisted only of wood and willow branches and the sleighs would carry as much hay as we could shove onto them.

We then covered the heap with a sort of timber framing, measuring some 2 x 3 metres, strapped it together like a parcel so that nothing could fall when the sleigh veered around bends or across uneven tracks. At every stop we immediately made a fire to scare off the wolves.

72

That was pretty much how the winter of 1946/7 passed, and when we returned to the main camp in the spring, I was once again posted to the workshop. It became quite warm towards the end of May and the air was stifling, particularly in our barracks.

One morning I woke up and looked left and right but couldn't see anyone lying on their bunkbed. What was going on? Nearly all comrades had chosen to sleep outside, mainly due to the heat that was ideal for the bedbugs, which had become a plague. They didn't seem to bother me, perhaps because of my blood type, and I therefore enjoyed a sound sleep while the others suffered. It was quite different when it came to lice. If there was even a single one in the room, it would most certainly find a home with me.

At the beginning of 1947 new work groups were formed and Max, who had been posted in unit 2, was dispatched to the Schaika forest camp, whereas I, belonging to unit 3, was ordered to work in Armakovo with the harvesting of hay. Armakovo was a 'sovkhoz' and in contrast to the 'kolkhoz' was a state-owned agricultural enterprise with hired workers. Our lodgings this time round was a barn built on stilts some 1 metre high, while the grain was stored in two similarly constructed barns right next to us. First, we were ordered to mow the grass using scythes. But we weren't dealing with a meadow and instead were confronted with marshland teeming with frogs. There were in fact more frogs than there was grass. This turned out to be a blessing for us, as we caught as many frogs as we could and tucked them into our little pouch – something every prisoner carried around with him in case he chanced on something he could put his fingers on. We cooked these frogs that very night and enjoyed a tasty and fatty soup. Hermann Werneke, a comrade of ours, was particularly lucky one day and caught 268 of those creatures, and if one happened to chance upon a handful of grain or indeed a potato, boy – that turned out to be a proper festive meal.

My turn with the horses came after eight days of being there, with mowing grass being the first task on the list. That sovkhoz owned four mowers, two of them old Russians models, but the other two happened to be top German brands, one of them manufactured by Deering and the other by Oelbad-Fahr and I, of course, was familiar with both. Allocated to one of them, I was ogling the Oelbad-Fahr one, seeing as we owned one at home in Puchschlagen. Unfortunately for me, I was landed with the old Russian crate, which I dreaded having to work with. And yet it turned out to be a reasonable sort of mower and did the job. The following day three Russian workers and I harnessed the horses and drove out to the fields. The grass reached up to the horses' bellies and we had our work cut out. All day long we drove the horses around the field, all while shouting the Russian '*Nuuu*', with one length of the field measuring at least 1.5 to 2 km. There was a break after two hours, carriages were arranged in a circle with us lot sitting in the middle. '*Davai bo guried*', meaning 'Let's have a quick smoke', was the kind invitation of the Russians, who handed me a cigarette – not something I could refuse. We let the horses graze in the meantime and then once again were off to our mowers until it was time for the next break. That sort of went on, I can't exactly recall, for some fourteen days. Other prisoners along with Russian labourers gathered the hay and piled it up high – reaching the height of the barn – something the Russians were particularly skilled at.

After we had completed the mowing without any incidents, I was assigned to the stables, which I had to clean and then rub down the horses. A Russian stable master, Simoveum, aged somewhere between fifty and sixty years old, spoke some broken German which he had picked up when he was a prisoner of war in Germany after World War I. He obviously hadn't fared too badly at the time, and he returned this by being quite kind towards me.

After a few days, Simoveum and I as well as some others were dispatched to Berchanov, a subsidiary to Armakovo and located literally in the boondocks. Mowing the fields was on the agenda yet again, I was supposed to use the horse-drawn mower while Simoveum had to use a different mower. This unit was under the leadership of a Russian *natchalnik*, somebody acting like a commander. Rumour had it that he was an animal vet – you really wouldn't have been able to tell, but it was obvious that he was an unfriendly man.

That place only held cows. It was raining incessantly when we arrived, and seeing as we hadn't yet started to work and lived far away from the fields, we were completely isolated. In order to protect us from the downpour, we first had to construct a hut, and to make the roof all we had was foliage – you can imagine how waterproof this turned out to be. Then on to the mowing, but compared to the large and beautiful fields we had mowed before, this was awful. Grass grew in the relatively small and very bumpy clearings. I couldn't help whacking my mower into one or two humps, which naturally held me up. Where the mower was unable to reach, labourers worked with their scythes.

I worked both on the field and in the stables as diligently as I had done back on my farm at home and in Armakovo, but I seemed to be failing this time round. I simply couldn't do anything right in the eyes of that beastly man, who just kept laying into me, claiming I did everything wrong. It was obvious that he couldn't stand me.

This went on for several days and it really got to me, especially as I did everything he ordered me to do, he was continuously piling more work on me and then criticising it afterwards. To be honest, I saw no way out. I was so exasperated one day and was feeling so dreadfully bullied that I knelt down at his feet and folded my hands. '*Dawai, Natchalnik, boschalsta bo bum*!' 'Please, Natchalnik, quickly, please just shoot me dead!' At that moment, I didn't care to be alive any longer, I felt that I simply couldn't go on.

He shrugged his shoulders and replied: '*Ja nie je moschno.*' 'Well, I'm not allowed to.' And with these words he turned around and left. I was devastated and close to the end. Collapsing onto the ground, exhausted and desperate, I wept. After a while I fell asleep.

After I had woken up and dragged myself to the horse-drawn mower, which had moved a bit further on, probably because they'd found better grass, I noticed that the connecting rod which functions as a lever arm was broken. I suspected that the horses must have forced the machine across a tree trunk, but that was it for me. I took the horses and the mower to where the other labourers were working to show them the damage and, surprisingly, the *natchalnik* who had so bullied me didn't say a word. In fact, he left me to it from that day on.

I was then ordered to gather the hay with the help of a horse, which other comrades then helped rake up and gather into bales. We then tied them together and transported them to the nearby barn. From there the hay was picked up by sleighs, just like in Jorkie.

After we had finished that job, part of the group along with Simoveum and the horses returned to Armakovo. I remained outside to chop wood for the winter, but this time round we were lodged in an old house which proved exceptionally pleasant. During lunch hours we'd disappear to the nearby forest to pick the many mushrooms growing there. It only took one or two knee-bends and, before you knew it, our pouches were filled to the brim with a whole variety of mushrooms. We didn't bother inspecting them closely for worms, but if there were any, they'd simply go into the broth. It didn't do us any harm and the priority was to fill our bellies. Nobody could leave the house during the night because of the howling wolves that roamed around in our immediate vicinity.

After a few weeks we returned to Armakovo, where I could once again join Simoveum in the stables. My chores were to muck out as well as then to chop the wood for the kitchen. It was the five of us, just as it had been during the winter: Simoveum, three other Russians and myself. At the house, we had a small room with a table where we could all sit, have a smoke and drink our tea. It was nice for me to be part of this group, who'd welcomed me as one of their own, and every morning, after finishing my work in the part of the stables where I was in charge of grooming fourteen horses, I'd join them and they'd offer me a cigarette and some bread. It felt good.

After the break I needed to tackle the other part of the stable, where there were only six horses, with a few riding horses among them. They were being trained for Antonovich, the director, to ride, which suited him well as the stables were close to the sovkhoz administration building and he lived nearby. He also kept some chickens on his property which often ventured into 'my' stable and made a mess of the horse manure I had carefully divided into heaps. This one day infuriated me to the point that I lifted my fork and bashed that poor animal from behind, and though I had only wanted to shoo her away, she died instantly. A tragic accident, so to speak, but seeing that it was the director's hen, I had to be creative. I quickly shoved the dead animal underneath the dung; when the coast was clear I dug her out, hid her under my jacket and carried her to the house, where we then plucked and cooked her. When the others

76

returned, they could smell the aroma of cooked chicken soup and there was plenty of meat to go around. Another festive meal, as it turned out.

This sovkhoz not only had a cow shed but also a pig sty, both very close to where I worked, and they too had a prisoner of war allocated to them. He'd often bring us a special sort of turnip which over in Russia was fed to the pigs. This type of root vegetable was much tastier than the vegetables we usually received and was very much coveted by us lot. Other prisoners brought us potatoes. Gradually we got more resourceful at procuring everything and anything that could assuage our hunger and indeed we'd often have so much that we couldn't even use it all. That led us to keep some extra in stock.

We decided to store all of this underneath the raised floor of the various houses, seeing as these buildings stood some 1 metre above ground, so finding hiding places wasn't that difficult. There was, however, the odd crackdown, with the Russians raiding our homes, but they never could get their hands on the whole lot, and cook always had what he needed.

And once again winter arrived. From where I worked in the stables, I had a good view of when the turnips were being delivered at the pig sty. On cold days, when the courtyard was frozen, I slid across to the sty, swiftly tucked four or five turnips under my arms and slid back to the stable. The *natchalnik*, the supervisor of the sty, must have seen me, as he ran after me without me knowing and when he had caught up with me, tripped me up. I fell and let go of the turnips, which tumbled to the ground. Without giving my lost booty another look, I scrambled up and ran for my life. That was the end of my forays to the pig sty.

In late autumn we returned to Armakovo and my task, much like the year before, was to procure wood for the kitchen. On our way back from Berchanov I had spotted in a village just short of Armakovo several tree trunks, and I intended to get those loaded up for the kitchen. Just picking them up, getting them onto my horse and cart and fastening them tightly would be a whole lot easier than having to fell the trees first. Without further ado I set off to the village named Iskra and carried out my plan. All done, and I was back on my way to Armakovo. But once again I'd made a miscalculation, and the Russians were soon onto me. The minute my cart arrived at the first house on the outskirts of the village, two Russians leapt onto the path from behind, grabbed the lead-rope of my horse and led it behind the house. With a few sharp cuts they tore through the strings and flung the logs down on either side. '*Davai bashli!*' they hissed menacingly, which meant 'Get lost!' With no wood, I quickly dashed off.

Another time, when I happened to find myself on the other side of Iskra, I chanced on several birch trees standing far apart from each other in a forest. Somehow, I must have lost my sense of direction and I couldn't for the life of me figure out which way led to Armakovo. I tried to retrace my route, but reached a village I hadn't ever come across before. What should I do? I was panicking but then plucked up the courage to approach some Russian folks. '*Trastishe davaris, od guda sovkhoz Armakovo?*' 'Good day, comrade, what's the route to the sovkhoz Armakovo?'

I was lucky in that these guys were a friendly lot who showed me which direction to drive in. But the further I travelled, the more sparse the snow on the ground, which meant that I had to unload my birchwood as my horse could no longer pull the sleigh. I arrived in Armakovo after a strenuous and extremely lengthy trip, it was already 2200 hours and by then pitch dark. It turned out that my absence had not gone unnoticed and cook sarcastically added that it wasn't such a good idea to travel so far. As for me, I could only sigh with relief that I wasn't being punished.

Simoveum, who held the position of foreman of the stable, once took me back to his home, situated two villages away from us. He wanted my help with making ropes, and I immediately figured out that the yarn came from Germany, as I was familiar with the sisal provided by the Baumhüter company [the company still exists to this day] as we had used the exact same stuff for our straw baler and our binding machine. It just showed how the Russians had taken everything they could lay their hands on in Germany and brought it back to their farms. Using a simple rope-maker's top with one hook at one end and three on the other, we twisted the sisal fibre into three strands before tightening the single hook, which in turn twisted the three strands into one rope. After we finished work, we were treated to a plentiful meal at Simoveum's, along with a hefty piece of bread. Life felt good.

What my excursion to Simoveum's confirmed for me was that a prisoner of war fared best with those who had lived under Tsarist rule, anyone over the age of forty really. The younger lot consisted mostly of fanatic communists hostile to us Germans.

In Iskra, the nearby village where I had been ambushed because of the wood I had carried, there was an additional camp holding Russian prisoners – a so-called penal camp – who were treated even worse than us prisoners of war. Punishments meted out under Stalin's rule were draconian and the theft of say 50 kg of grain carried with it four years in one of these infamous penal camps.

It was winter when it was time to say goodbye to Armakovo where, thanks to my *natchalnik* Simoveum, I had generally fared well. Such was our success in having organised and stored our own provisions during that year that we had a lot to leave behind. We felt especially upset not to be able to take along all the turnips and potatoes we had hidden away in various places.

The Panovka Camp

At the beginning of January 1948 we were carted off again. Loaded onto a train that went from Armakovo to Vologda in the north, another group of prisoners who had worked in Vologda joined us, including Max Römisch, my friend from back in the days when we were prisoners in Jorkie, in 1946. Russians yelling 'Get off' told us that we had arrived in Panovka, a forest camp where labourers were charged with chopping wood – nothing I wasn't already used to doing. The camp structure consisted of log cabins lining one side of the train tracks and disconnected wagons spreading along the other side that also served as barracks. My group was lodged in one of the larger log cabins, which was barely lit and infested with bugs. There were so many that one had to be careful not to crunch down on them accidentally as invariably they'd fall from the ceiling into our tin container. That would have stunk to high heaven! But at least we were no longer plagued by lice.

The following day we were marched to the wood, located down a 1 km road following a narrow-gauge track towards a large shed containing our

79

We marched towards the train station dressed in *valenkis* (felt boots) and fur gloves.

Prisoners were forced to work in the woods despite the freezing cold.

equipment such as saws and axes. Once we had shouldered our tools, we had to trudge down the path for a further 500 metres into the middle of a forest that consisted mainly of spruce but also some poplar and birch trees. Teams consisting of three men each had to clear a chosen section of the trees, with the spruce to be turned into telegraph poles of between 10 and 14 metres in length. The rest was turned into firewood. With the snow more than 1 metre deep we first had to shovel it away in order even to reach the trunks before sawing them into pieces. Fortunately, we had received hooded fur coats and felt boots called *valenki* to protect us against the icy winds and bitter cold – any ill-clad prisoner would not have been able to survive.

We were plenty busy trying to meet the prescribed socialist quotas, but once we understood how these were being calculated, the job became easier. Some of the comrades who had joined us from the Vologda camp and had worked that past winter in the Shaika forest camp knew precisely what to do in order to 'simplify' or speed up meeting the quota, or in other words, cheat. A first step would be for each group to claim for themselves a densely covered section of forest. It wasn't uncommon for brutal fights to break out over one thick tree or another. The spruce trees which would be turned into the telegraph poles would be felled and then chopped by us into lengths measuring 1 metre longer than stipulated. We would heap them up, ready to be counted on that given day, and on the following day we'd cut off the extra metre and present the shorter trunk to be included in the new quota. It wasn't difficult to pull off, as when they registered our output at the end of, say, day one, they'd draw a line where the trunk had been cut using a piece of coal. That was that – once the trunk was marked and included in the quota, the *natchalnik*'s job was done for the day. Our trick was to shorten the trunk exactly where the line had been drawn and then present the shortened trunk to the *natchalnik*, who'd mark it again for the quota on day two. Only the marked trunks were eventually transported away and anything left over was used to make a fire, so we had one going the whole time.

Cheating the so-called system was even more common when it came to producing firewood. When heaping up the sticks and logs, for example, we'd make sure to pack them up only loosely, often leaving such a large cavity in the middle that a person could easily have taken a seat inside. All that mattered was that it looked tightly stacked.

Cheating with tree trunks piled into smaller heaps was easier if there was snow around. We'd then often cover the trunks already marked with a black coal line and accounted for in a given day's quote with snow, allowing only the unmarked end of the trunk to be visible to the *natchalnik*, who'd mark it again. These and other tricks would bring us an entire day above the set and expected quota and gain us advantages such as, in my case, being allowed to return to my lodgings on the last day of the week immediately after others had set out to work early in the morning.

The long poles as well as the firewood were stored alongside the train tracks from where another crew would load them onto the trains for transport. This was a murderous task, with the trunks ordered to be stood up vertically into the wagons with one of the wagons often slipping off the rails, which forced us lot to then heave it back on. It was harsh and exhausting labour, often carried out in brutal and dangerous weather conditions.

A small locomotive driven by diesel power and meant to draw the train was often broken and constant repair was required as a result.

A small diesel-powered locomotive transported the wood.

With the start of spring and the snow melting, the train tracks emerged from under the cover of snow and ice and we realised that the tracks, in order to compensate for the uneven bits in the landscape, had been propped up by wooden beams laid crossways. This improvised and sub-optimal way of running the tracks certainly explained the many breakdowns even during the winter when ice and snow concealed the bumpy terrain. Before us now lay a muddy and squelchy stretch of land which made it totally impossible to cross with the felt boots to reach our workplace – and yet, it had to be done. No dry patches or firmly compacted paths existed – it was all a wet mud bath. The only way to manage was with two men marching along the track, side by side and holding a stick between them, while each one carefully balanced himself along the rail line and – in step – moved towards their destination. Same routine on the way back. It went quite smoothly and also gave me the opportunity to observe how the Russians went about the repair of their train line. Wherever they'd come across a beam that was loose they'd just reinforce it from below with planks of hardwood laid criss-cross.

Chopping wood close to the train tracks in the forest surrounding Panovka.

During that time, it was announced that a 'visitor' from the Krassovitz camp would arrive. That camp housed high-ranking German officers and though they too were prisoners of war, they weren't forced to do any labour. If an officer expressed the wish to work, he was permitted to be transferred to our forest camp and, in such cases, one of us was given permission to take a week off. It so happened that one day, along with Colonel Freiherr von Hallberg, an officer came to visit us in Panovka and regaled us with his life story. This provided us with some, albeit brief, relief and I didn't feel quite as despondent, especially with this officer speaking in the familiar Munich dialect.

In fact, Panovka was nothing more than a train station serving the timber transport industry, with no regular trains ever stopping there. We'd write messages with bits of information and wrap some small items into a small packet and string that to a 2-metre-long willow rod with a loop at the end. We'd attach this to the track and when the driver passed the spot, he could grab and haul it into the driver cabin.

However, when provisions needed to be supplemented, the train was forced to come to a halt and several men would hop on and travel to the next town. I don't recall the men's names nor their destination, but the train certainly didn't stop on their return trip. The comrades simply had to chuck the goods out of the train and then leap off. Fortunately, the track was quite windy around that area, with the train forced to slow down, and the guys didn't have any safety issues.

The Krassovitz Camp

It was towards the end of April or beginning of May when we were once again ordered to move. The train, we were told, would take us 'somewhere else', but seeing that we generally weren't ever properly informed, nobody knew where the hell we had landed once we'd disembarked. Nor did we have a clue what our work would consist of. Let's please not be posted to the 'Sokol group', we fervently hoped. Dubbed the infamous 'bone mill', the name alone filled us with dread. Again, I was lucky and ended up in the Krassovitz camp (written 'Grjasovez' in Russian).

The camp was located a few kilometres outside the town of the same name and must once have been a monastery, of which nothing more than a small stone building remained standing. Here, high-ranking German officers were interned, including General Schwarz, our previous division commander of the 376th Infantry Division, and since none of them were obliged to do any work, it was down to the lower-ranking comrades – some junior officers and a very few senior lieutenants – to carry out the chores. There must have been around 100 labourers in total. The higher-ranking officers also received better food, all very similar to how it was in the Russian military.

The wood structure of the two large buildings at the entrance of the camp grounds also resembled monastic architecture, with the camp itself built up an incline overlooking a narrow river, some 150 metres away from the entrance. Two large barracks to the left of the entrance and a bit up a road, and three to its right housed our groups, and then a further three very comfortable wooden lodges were located even further up, one of them home to the German camp administration! Yes, that type of thing also existed!

One of the large buildings at the entrance to the camp.

Prisoners produced creative art and craft items during their time off.

The other lodge nearer the river also served as a sort of community hall including a café. The officers were not only exempt from working but also received pay of 14 rubles, while we were categorised as simple labourers and therefore couldn't afford to go to the local café. Having said that, out of all the camps we'd been placed in, this one was by far the best.

I'm not quite sure what was housed in the third lodge near the path, on the other side of which was a sports field, but it seemed to be something special. A laundry could be found on the other side of the river and after a short uphill walk from there, some 100 metres to the right was yet another barracks and to its left the dining room. From the laundry and looking towards the entrance stood the two buildings mentioned before which housed the higher-ranking officers and generals. In the times of the monastery these buildings were probably used for agricultural purposes.

Behind the dining room was a large house constructed of stone, which, judging from its size, might once have been the monastery's church because, as we know, Russian churches don't have steeples.

Prisoners were accommodated here as well, amongst whom was Colonel von Hallberg who had paid us a visit back in Panovka.

A large flowerbed greeted us right at the entrance with colourful flowers outlining the Soviet star and surrounded by noticeboards on which were fixed the daily papers, primarily *Izvestia* and *Pravda* informing us of the latest news, albeit of course from the Soviet perspective. But there was a German paper as well, *Freies Deutschland*, that was published, mostly voluntarily, by allegedly anti-fascist German officers who geared their contributions to the higher officers but not to us simple labourers.

At this camp too our main task was felling trees and chopping wood in the nearby forest. In the mornings we set off down a path running alongside the camp, crossed the river to then march uphill, passing through a small village called Talitza, a name I will always recall as the German translation for it is the 'village of sin'.

The entire day was spent outside in the forest, but we'd often steal away and go foraging in the nearby village, something we had become

Conditions in the officers' camp at Krassovitz were more pleasant than in other camps.

used to. We knocked on farmers' doors and begged for potatoes, milk and bread. If we couldn't use them ourselves, we took them back to the camp and bartered with them, exchanging them for other goods. Seeing as we had at our disposal a mare, we often drove by horse and carriage to the woods, and on top of that, as the mare had given birth to a foal, we also benefited from her milk. Deviously, we locked the foal away and milked the mare, using the milk for our potato mash – delicious! Horse milk is so sweet that it cannot be turned into sour milk.

Seeing as the summer weather was mild we were able to wash in the river and one time we even had a water party. We had relay races and used the 3-metre-high diving board, but I only watched on as I wasn't a confident swimmer. I particularly remember Jupp Bös from that event. He had thought of putting on a bit of a show by jumping from the diving board in full prisoner's gear, along with everything such a *wojna plenni* would carry on him: a bread board, a bread scale, a few tins and even some cooking utensils! His plan was to dive, then rid himself under

Jupp Bös from Cologne jumps from a 3-metre-high diving board.

88

water of all his accessories and re-emerge dressed only in a bathing suit and surface as a 'new man', so to speak. But his scheme failed miserably once he went under, as all the stuff got entangled with his clothing and prevented him from coming up. Luckily we had enough life guards on hand who dived in and rescued the poor fellow. He'd surely have died a 'hero's' death otherwise.

We even staged a boxing tournament one time. And yet, for all the cheerful intervals brightening up our imprisonment, the overall experience for most of those interned in this officers' camp wasn't what you might call pleasant. The reason for keeping them at the camp wasn't to give them a break and allow them to recover from the stresses of the war. Far from it. The purpose was to interrogate them repeatedly and intensely about everything they had experienced and done during the war. Every single detail was analysed and scrutinised, both with reference to Germany's advances during the war as well as to its withdrawals. The Russians were masters at finding out the tiniest fact about us, which unit we belonged to, where it was deployed, for what purpose, and who had led it. Officers were interrogated by the Soviet Secret Police, the NKVD, whose offices were in the large lodge. They took place day and night, often for weeks, sometimes even for months until the officials had received the answers they were after or had extorted a confession. Rumour had it that some officers had been locked away for over a year. During those interrogations the officers, who were kept in solitary confinement, would receive nothing but bread and water. Us lot would only get wind of such things from people whispering in hushed voices and casting anxious looks around their shoulders, but secretly we were quite relieved not to have been granted any of the officer privileges.

The NKVD was the notorious Secret Police Agency feared even by the Russians themselves. The organisation had been created after the October Revolution by Felix Dzerzhinsky, a Bolshevik who named it Cheka, which turned into NKVD in the early 1920s and was the forerunner of the KGB. While names changed, the brutality wielded by the members remained constant. We know that Felix Dzerzhinsky signed thousands of death warrants, and his successors were no less criminal. Genrikh

Yagoda and Nikolai Yezhov were perpetrators of Stalin's 'Great Terror', which claimed over 1 million victims.

For us, therefore, working outside in the woods and not being aware of the machinations of the Secret Police sat with us, in comparison, quite well. At most, we might have been summoned to go fetch a document or something of this sort from the administrative building, and I still remember the first time I was requested to run such an errand. Max Römisch and I were charged to do something or other at that building and immediately upon passing the threshold we got a fright as we heard a heavy thud on the floor. It turned out to be a rather simple device that closed the door: a rope fastened to it and strung across a track had a weight attached to its other end, and when we opened the door the weight crashed to the ground with such a loud bang that the two of us leapt up in complete panic. We thought we had broken something and scurried around to see what might need fixing, but we were interrupted by the warden, who addressed us in a pleasant, and for us calming German dialect: 'Boys, what are you up to now?' and with that, the matter was closed. I'll always remember this man, a Herr Eisenmann, whom I'd recognise later in photographs as the 'fisherman with a cigarette'.

Many readers may well ask themselves where I got all these photographs taken in Panovka and Krassovitz, what with prisoners only thinking about how to survive and not how to take good pictures. Moreover, Russians certainly wouldn't have had any of that. There was one man, however, who had permission to take photographs, a professional photographer by the name of Steinberg who had served in the Wehrmacht as a senior lieutenant.

In that same camp, a Russian officer, holding the position of a captain, which was equivalent to a sergeant in the German army, was also a photographer. Originally German, he had fought in the German army in World War I and was captured by the Russians and imprisoned. He remained in Russia, became a Russian citizen and fought against us Germans in World War II. His mission at the camp was to enable prisoners to send home a picture of themselves. To this end he enquired of the camp administration whether there was a professional photographer amongst the inmates, and this is how Senior Lieutenant Steinberg came into the picture, so to speak. He was immediately handed a Zorki Rangefinder camera, a Russian replica of the Leica, and charged to take portrait pictures of prisoners, if they agreed to it. Inmates were allowed to sew these onto a postcard to send home, comforted by the knowledge that relatives would finally be assured that they were still alive. Only one border of the photo was sewn onto the postcard so that it passed censorship, when the back of the picture would often be checked for any hidden messages. I didn't manage to connect with Senior Lieutenant Steinberg in Krassovitz and I imagine that it was primarily officers who got their pictures taken.

As you can see, Steinberg also used his camera to document what life was like in the Krassovitz camp as well as giving a glimpse into our activities in the Panovka forest camp. When he was liberated, he managed to smuggle out the negatives, but I only got to hear the story of how he managed to do so when I met him back home on 23 November 1994. His version of events was that he'd snip away the edges in order to reduce the filmstrips in width so that they were narrower than the leather straps of his rucksack. He then carefully stitched the filmstrips into the straps and succeeded in getting them past control. In the early fifties some of these pictures were published in a magazine which I happened to look at and I immediately recognised that these were pictures taken in Krassovitz and Panovka.

Naturally, I desperately wanted to get hold of these photos but didn't know how to go about that. It just so happened that a doctor, named Dr Schreier, who had been a comrade working alongside me in the Krassovitz forest, got in touch with me one day via a patient he looked after. That patient from Puchschlagen had come to see him at the Dachau hospital where Dr Schreier had recently got a job. Because inmates knew each other well, knew each other's names, life stories and where they came from, Dr Schreier remembered that I too hailed from Puchschlagen and enquired of the patient whether he perhaps knew if I had returned from Russia. Relieved to hear that I had indeed returned, he got in touch, and we met up. We embraced, and the two of us couldn't have been happier to have found each other alive and well. We got talking about Steinberg, the photographer, who had apparently opened up a shop in Munich. That

The orchestra playing in front of the building housing the theatre group.

same autumn, a customer of ours in Munich had booked a delivery of potatoes, and after I offloaded my horse and cart, I made it my business to pass by the photography shop. That's how I got hold of all the photos – I just purchased the lot of them. Yet another coincidence followed shortly thereafter when Dr Schreier opened up a private practice in Pfaffenhofen an der Ilm and married one of the daughters of Herr Eisenmann, the warden at the Krassovitz administration whom I mentioned earlier.

When in Krassovitz, Steinbach took many pictures of performances by the camp's orchestra. Indeed, we had a dedicated orchestra of well over fifty musicians playing a wide range of instruments. Not that I ever attended such a performance, as I was always working outside, felling trees. But I always knew of this orchestra and could actually hear them from afar, practising above the dining room in the large brick building. Someone told me that a musician from Munich was part of the group, so I went upstairs during one of their rehearsals and asked to see him. All I really wanted was to chat to someone from back home, but he was rather stand-offish. Well, at the end of the day, he was an artist who probably thought he was a cut above us simple folks. What on earth could he do with someone like me – a lowly farmer's boy? A very few cold words were exchanged before I walked away, disappointed.

During one of the concerts, it must have been summertime, Steinberg took a picture of the audience sitting outside on a grandstand, purposely constructed so that everyone had a good view of the musicians. Though not in the audience at the time, I certainly knew just by looking at the pictures who the so-called prominent guests were. In the first row, in the middle, sat a Russian officer holding a small child clad in a white cap and surrounded by four women. He was the camp commander. The woman in uniform and sitting to the left of the camp commander was the medical officer; we prisoners had given her the pet-name *Vitaminchen* (small vitamin pill) as she was charged with distributing the medication. Right at the front and leaning his head on his left arm, a typical pose for a thinker, sat Keller. The group was flanked on both sides by Russian guards with hats and uniforms. We named one of them 'thin towel' because of his slight stature, and he'd usually wear his hat pushed right to the back of his head. He was definitely not a nice guy when it came to us prisoners of war. So there they were, sitting with a few hundred German prisoners at the back, listening intently to music. Even at the time I couldn't quite understand why the Russians supported this orchestra and mounted such an extravagant classical concert. Was their intention to make German officers more favourably disposed to communism and then, once they returned, portray Soviet Russia in a positive light? At the time, the goal of communism was to revolutionise the world and even back in 1948 we could see the signs of the future power struggle between the political systems that would later develop into full-blown confrontation – the Cold War.

Various work assignments kept us busy during the summer of 1948, when we were detailed both to the forest as well as to a project in the town where, at times, we were fortunate to get our hands on some additional food. Max Römisch was often part of my crew, which was a lucky break as far as I was concerned. He had a knack for being able to get hold of all kinds of things, mainly food, and he never once got caught. Quite unlike me, who'd be spotted a mile away. I was, however, good at connecting

Looking towards the grandstand.

with the locals in Russian, speaking to them or begging from them. And I knew whom to approach – I always picked older Russians who felt sorry for us. Compared to the Mozhaysk death camp or the hellish winters in Cherepovets and the forest camp in Panovka, our experience in Krassovitz was fabulous. Not one of us suffered or succumbed to cold or hunger! How very fortunate indeed. Some were even so heartened by how well we were treated that they concluded they would soon be discharged and regain their liberty.

The Poprotzkie Camp

At the beginning of September 1948 any hope that this would happen soon was quashed. All of a sudden, we were told that every prisoner who had arrived in Panovka in the springtime would be transferred. Once again we were marched to the train station and loaded onto cargo wagons. Our journey took us via Vologda towards Cherepovets, or to be more specific, to the nearby Poprotzkie camp. I knew the town from three years ago when I was there in the autumn of 1945. But this particular camp was located on the other side of town and their barracks were larger and of a more recent construction, unlike the main camp.

The barracks were so spacious that they were more like halls; furnished with normal bunkbeds, we had a decent place to sleep. With it being autumn and time for harvesting, we were assigned to help farmers with the potato gathering; they too were probably camp employees. At times we were asked to work for private townsfolk, which turned out to be a treat as it usually meant us being provided with ample and wholesome meals and even being offered some bread to take back. The lucky ones to get such jobs could also ask local civilians for a bit of extra provisions. 'Poshalsta, nem noshko chleb!' 'Could you please give us some bread.' Bread meant everything to us.

Sometimes it was bread we asked for and sometimes we hustled for something to smoke. As mentioned, the older Russian townspeople usually felt more generous towards us and were understanding of our circumstances.

A football pitch which was also attached to that camp often allowed for matches between prisoners. Watching one of these games, I witnessed a horrible incident when a Spanish player nearly bit off the ear of his German opponent. Without exception, all the Spanish inmates of this camp had belonged to the Blue Division that had fought on the side of the Germans when they were just outside St Petersburg.

We also had some Catholic priests amongst the inmates, something I had never before encountered in the Soviet Union. I remember one of them in particular as he was a noted theologian by the name of Johannes Stelzenberger. At least the clergy were entitled to much better food, and they made sure there were some leftovers for us lot.

Much like in other labour camps, some work crews here were saddled with having to carry out the most gruelling tasks. One of them, the 'SMU', was ordered to dig out, layer by layer, concrete foundations, which I suspected may have been laid down as far back as before the war, without any further construction carried out. It's quite common practice in Russia. Most unfortunately, I ended up there. The excavation work, the hacking away at rock-solid layers and using mostly primitive tools to reach deep below ground, was brutal and exhausting. After dragging our worn-out bodies back to the barracks in the evening we collapsed on the bunkbeds.

At Long Last: Release from Imprisonment

November arrived and, as in the past years, I dreaded the upcoming Russian winter. But it was different this time round. On 2 or perhaps 3 November, a list detailing all those prisoners due for release followed by a return to Germany arrived in Poprotzkie. That evening our barracks elder read out all the names, one by one. With each name, we hoped that we would be the next one called out, and yet neither I nor many of my comrades seemed to be on the list, leading to a sleepless night. Elation for some, disappointment for others. Many felt utter despair.

For those left behind, reporting to work the next day was torture. Shuffling to the SMU, we felt completely despondent, shuddering at the thought of yet again having to dig out the grey mass of concrete. Grabbing our axes and shovels, we hollowed a pit right next to the foundations and made it so large and deep that we could huddle in it all together with nobody able to see us. We sat there in silence, pain written on our faces. The world seemed to have forgotten us and we had lost all hope.

On our way back to the camp we heard someone mention that yet another list had been published. 'New names are on the list of men who're permitted to return home.'

Böhm, our barracks elder, stood ready to greet us at the entrance. Previously, when with the Wehrmacht, Böhm had served as a sergeant major and was often referred to as the 'company's mother', and here too he looked after all the admin stuff.

Officiously he read out the new names, and Strasser and my name, Michael Kaspar Strasser, was on the list. I could hardly believe my ears. 'Have I heard it right?' I couldn't help but approach Böhm privately in his 'office' afterwards. 'Yes, you're on the list!'

While this was, of course, a huge relief for me, I was sad for Max Römisch, my comrade and friend, who wasn't on the list. Not many

96

words were exchanged that night – emotions were high. There was joy, as well as bitter disillusionment.

The next day, the fortunate ones were requested to report to a different barracks where they received new clothes. Next, we took leave from our comrades who remained behind. We shook hands, last wishes were exchanged and bittersweet goodbyes. Everyone knew that those leaving that day wouldn't come back and nobody could quite imagine that a day would come when we'd be able to reconnect. And yet, it didn't prevent us from memorising the names and addresses of our comrades. Jotting these down was pointless as everything was taken away from us.

My friend Max stayed behind, but he too committed to memory names and addresses of those returning home. Many years later, towards the end of the fifties, there he was … standing in front of our door.

So, everyone went to the barracks to get changed into the new clothes we were provided with. I received linen underpants and not just one, but two shirts. We had never seen such luxury during captivity, or was it just propaganda, trying to demonstrate how well we had been treated while prisoners of war? The shirts, also made of linen and barely reaching our navels were uncomfortable to the touch and felt like tin. A new pair of cotton quilted trousers, a new quilted anorak and an old fur cap, a blue uniform jacket still from the German Luftwaffe – that was our luggage.

But the worst was yet to come. The inspection of whether one had belonged to the SS would be the downfall for many. Anyone who had been attached to the SS was immediately sent back and not allowed to travel home. Each prisoner had to lift his arms so that the guards could check for any tattoos, as all soldiers enlisted with the Waffen-SS had their blood group tattooed underneath their arm. My heart sank, because when I was posted to Holland back in 1943, I suffered from an abscess on my glands that was removed and then left a scar, and apparently many SS men had their tattoos surgically removed, leaving a tell-tale scar behind. But the Russian guards just waved me through. Only later did I find out that the tattoo of the blood group had been engraved on the inside of the arm and not into the armpit – I needn't have worried. But three or four men had indeed been found out.

The process, however, was still not over. Sent to a different barn, we were inspected yet again, this time to ensure that no one carried any forbidden goods. Finally ... we passed through the entrance of the camp where we were gathered to then be lined up and marched off to the train station which was more than 1.5 km away. It was pouring with rain, and we arrived on the platform totally soaked to the bone. But luckily the wagons had already pulled in and we boarded immediately. Wooden planks divided the carriages into an upper and lower deck, allowing sufficient room for men to sleep on both levels. It was an amazing experience to move around in so much space compared to being cramped in miserable conditions when transported as prisoners of war. And we even had an oven – something I had never seen before in a freight train – though no wood was available to make a fire. But nobody grumbled. After five years spent in Russian labour camps this was a minor inconvenience, and we simply wanted to get ourselves organised. At long last we were free to do so. In a jiffy we had gathered enough wood, and before too long a crackling fire warmed up the carriage. We hung up our clothes to dry and, even before the train set off, we received some soup with kasha. The train finally left the station, it was 4 or 5 November – I don't recall the exact date, but it was certainly just before the official Remembrance Day of the 1917 October Revolution, the so-called birthday of the Soviet Union that was celebrated widely through the land.

After several days travelling, our transport of 400 to 500 men reached the outskirts of Moscow, with the Moscow public transport – gorgeous gleaming red carriages – driving past us. We actually got a glimpse of the Kremlin with its golden cupolas sparkling in the sunshine. It was dreamlike.

The journey continued with several interruptions along the way, tedious and long waits at various train stations, but it gave us time to collect wood and we managed rather well, using every inch of the wagons for storage. It would have lasted us up to the Urals and we would never have been cold for even a minute.

Was it 1946 or 1947 that Stalin gave a speech on Labour Day, 1 May? He was quoted as having said all prisoners of war are coming home in '48.

Well, it certainly was true for me. Just.

Back in Germany at last

After about three weeks we arrived at the Frankfurt an der Oder train station on 21 or 22 November. The war had ended three years earlier and I had been imprisoned an additional four years. I had survived it all, which seemed miraculous as so many comrades had succumbed to hunger or disease.

Many people had gathered at the train station, but it wasn't to welcome us home. No, all they wanted was to search the empty wagons for firewood. All of Germany lay in ruins, buildings and streets had been destroyed by the bombing, and even after 1948 the survivors searched for anything they could use to make their lives more bearable. Though there were stacks of wood left in the wagons, they were gone before we even turned round. We couldn't care less, as we returnees were well looked after.

First off, we were taken to a camp, likely once used as an army barracks, where we could wash and have a meal. We also received some money, 40 Ostmark, but that immediately went towards two pints of beer and some bread. So that was that, but we were also allowed to spend the night there. That first evening with us comrades sitting together for the first time free and happy was also tinged with sadness. We spoke till so late into the night that we nearly missed the onward journey the following morning.

The journey took us to Oelsnitz, where we were put up for the night in the town's castle. We went onwards the following day by passenger train to the border town of Hof-Moschendorf. Here, the Americans welcomed us and, while offering us generous meals, they didn't miss the opportunity to enquire about our experiences in what they called the 'Socialist Paradise'. After literally stuffing ourselves all day, it was time to get ourselves to the train station and board the train to Munich. We finally arrived there at 0700 or 0730 hours. At long last I had arrived home, after six years spent on a hard, gruelling path and enduring so much.

My first thought was to look up my aunt in Sendling. Leaving the main train station via its southern exit, I was shocked at what lay before me. All I could see were the remains of the war, heaps of rubble, ruins and debris. So many buildings had collapsed that I had a clear view to the Goetheplatz and the Lindenwurmstrasse. Turning my back in dismay, I boarded the number 6 tram and travelled to Sendling, to my aunt. Well, more precisely I walked to the house of Onkel Josef, a brother of my father, and his wife. This 'aunt from the city' was dearly loved by all her family – she always brought something special for the children when she came on a visit and was a clear favourite of mine.

Indeed, I found her at home. At first, she got a fright – my arrival was so completely unexpected – but then she spontaneously threw her arms around me in a joyful embrace. Of course, she immediately set about preparing a festive dinner and heated up the boiler so that I could take a bath. She mentioned my mother, who needed to be alerted and mentally prepared, I was gently informed, as she had turned completely blind over the past years. My aunt immediately called the restaurant owner in Puchschlagen, the only one who owned a telephone at the time, and this Anton Holzmüller, a cousin of mine, was charged with informing my family of their son's homecoming. The day was 25 November, celebrated as the *Kathreinstag*, an old peasant holiday when farmers traditionally took half a day off from work.

He went to my father, who was busy threshing wheat and informed him of the news: his son had come home from Russia and was staying with the aunt in Munich. Father immediately cut the engine and shut the doors of the barn. That was it – he'd take the rest of the day off seeing as it was a holiday in any event.

My sister took a taxi that very afternoon to Munich to fetch me – much to my aunt's disappointment, seeing she was all set to spoil me rotten for just a bit longer. But back at home the excitement at seeing me at last was tremendous, with there being so much to catch up on.

As is common practice on a farm, work and the call of the animals, along with having to tend the fields, soon caught up with me. The next day, once the stables had been cleaned out, Father approached me and asked whether I wouldn't mind helping them with the threshing. Without a moment's hesitation I set off to the barn just barely one day after my return. Quite honestly, this seemed quite normal in my eyes. That's the relationship Father and I always had and what mattered most was that we were together once again: my father, my blind mother, my sister and my older brother. We had survived the war!

That summer, my mother passed away. Come April 1950, my plan had been to embark on an apprenticeship as a mechanic with the Reiter firm in Dachau, manufacturers of forestry equipment, but it wasn't to be. In the springtime of that year, my brother died in an accident. Back in Russia he had suffered severe head injuries. Released from the Wehrmacht in 1943 and slated to take over our family farm, he kept delaying that move for some reason, saying he'd rather leave this to his younger brother once he'd returned from the war. When I did, we discussed this between ourselves and I insisted that he was foolish and that he, not I, should take over. Then, one day, he was dead, killed by a tractor that had toppled over after colliding with a steam engine. That was the end of my plans to train as a mechanic and instead I became a farmer in Puchschlagen.

I met up with my friend Max Römisch who had memorised my details and the name of my hometown. At the end of the fifties, Max, who had been released only in 1949, was the proud owner of a gravel plant and regularly attended the Bauma trade fair for construction machinery held in Munich. During one of his visits, he spontaneously drove himself to nearby Puchschlagen and looked me up. What a happy surprise that was and a wonderful reunion. We happily remained in contact from that day on.

I think back to those miserable years in Russia, fighting in the war and in Russian captivity. Yes, I suffered immeasurable pain and distress, but I honestly feel no hate towards the Russian people. I thank God that I am still alive, quite miraculous actually. I emerged with a much better understanding both for Russia and the Russians and came away feeling that they love peace, just like the Ukrainians do, like the Germans do, and like all other nations on this globe. War is the last thing man wants. This is the only reason I have decided to write my experiences down on paper. May it be a call for peace and for understanding between all people.

I Was Protected

EYEWITNESS ACCOUNT BY JOSEF HAMBERGER

I was born at the end of December 1925 in a small village located at the foot of the Bavarian mountains, on a farm in Pfannstiel, some 2 km from Frasdorf. My family managed a medium-sized farmstead with twenty-two cows, some chickens, pigs, rabbits and pigeons; we had fields where we grew grain and a forest where we'd fell trees and cut firewood for the winter months. It was a pleasant and normal life imbued by the Christian traditions pervading those parts of the country as well as the religious education offered in the schools. With all family members doing their bit, I grew up as a typical and content farmer's boy. We got up at 0400 hours to cut the fields or work in the stables and once a year we'd slaughter a pig. The meat, once smoked and stored in the attic, had to last us the entire year. Rationing was to the letter and strictly controlled, as we couldn't

103

afford for someone to help themselves to whatever they wanted. So, if the portions weren't distributed as planned, another pig would still only be slaughtered the following year.

When I turned fourteen, World War II broke out and directly impacted our household, with the day's political events featuring heavily during our dinner conversations. My parents were deeply opposed to the fascist regime, which caused us no end of trouble in the village, where most inhabitants supported it. Informers were prevalent and we had to be on our guard. Much like all youngsters, I too was encouraged to join the Hitler Youth, but I refused, and this too caused a lot of problems in my school – but I had to obey my parents, who forbade me to participate in any activity that was even faintly related to the Nazis. In this respect, it was my mother who had the last word in our family, but none of us cared about whether any of the village boys were for or against the Nazis.

When the war broke out, the womenfolk attached to the five farmsteads of our village broke down crying. 'It's our turn now,' they sighed and burst into tears.

I was personally feeling quite split, seeing as my primary school teacher was an ardent Nazi who joyously applauded the start of the war and screamed enthusiastic 'hurrahs' on the day Germany invaded Poland. In the end, however, we youngsters cared more about the rabbits and the pigeons hidden underneath our desks than the war. We cherished these pets of ours who calmly sat between our legs waiting for the end of the lessons with no one, not even the teacher, taking any notice of them since they caused no trouble whatsoever.

After finishing primary school, I immediately took up farming jobs on our homestead, but Mother was of the opinion that our farm couldn't afford to feed a family of six children and decided that I should ask another farmer to hire me as his farmhand. I lucked out as he was a kind man, but he knew no shortcuts when it came to getting the jobs done, which meant I worked hard for seven days straight every week. It was no different for my brother, five years older than me, who remained at the family farm.

I returned home a year later as so much work had piled up back at home that they couldn't cope without me. Of course, it wasn't easy with my four sisters outnumbering me, which meant that they continually ordered me around, probably because they'd much rather have been boys themselves.

At some point a letter from the ministry arrived and it felt like a bomb had been dropped. I was drafted to the Reichsarbeitsdienst [RAD] and was to report on 7 January 1943, with my brother called up one year later as he was still, at the time, needed on the farm. Eventually this would leave only my father to work the land. Mother would often break down in tears, she so dreaded the family being split up and losing her boys. The mood at home became depressing, everyone had their problems and worries. I, however, had no choice, and was off to Donauwörth.

At the very start of my training with the Reichsarbeitsdienst I realised that lining up in the first row was always a mistake. I instinctively knew that the last row offered the best chance to survive the longest. We always had to line up in three rows, and without fail you'd find me in the last one. Once we'd graduated from Donauwörth we filed through the exit of the barracks where SS men stood at the threshold, busily recruiting. Patriotic slogans such as 'Do you want to serve your homeland?' sounded convincing.

Many were drawn in and eagerly signed up for the Waffen-SS, but I certainly wasn't one of them. Determined not to be swayed by whatever they enticed us with, I made quite sure to be among the last to leave the barracks. Questioned about my plans, I pretended to be dumb, and they soon lost interest in me, probably thinking that they could do well without such an idiot. My answers to their questions were too daft for the SS men to engage with me.

The comrades selected by the SS were dispatched immediately to the SS-Totenkopf Division based in Warsaw and deployed to crush the ghetto uprising. I was most fortunate not to have been part of that group as the operation proved brutal, cruel and criminal.

After a short three weeks, we were off to France, to the St Nazaire submarine base on the Atlantic coast. Our main job was to clear the area of any undergrowth, making sure that it didn't provide any hiding places. Equipped with our spades, the usual RAD tools, but also provided with forks and saws, we flattened the area. The food handed out to us guys was very sparse compared to the outstanding meals our superiors enjoyed, and we regarded them as a pack of bastards only concerned with their own well-being and not giving a toss about us. Once, permitted to inspect a submarine inside a pen, I was horrified at how narrow it was and relieved not to be part of that division. I wouldn't have wanted to travel in what seemed like a floating coffin.

In July 1943 I was deployed to the anti-aircraft artillery in Kaliningrad, which was a long journey by train. My training on the heavy guns lasted for several months but was otherwise calm, with the surrounding raging war having little impact on us. Other than our routine drills, not much seemed to happen, and I would rather have been posted to the Luftwaffe. But my request wasn't answered, and I soon forgot about it.

Then, six months later in January 1944 my superior approached me and mentioned my application. 'Didn't you want to go become an aerial gunner?'

And, indeed, shortly after that meeting my transfer came through. The training school was located in Rumia near Gdańsk, which meant that I had to relocate to the north-east, where I had already been posted before. Still, it was better than the Eastern Front.

These weeks were also pleasant enough, even though not much was going on and all we did was wait around. I was given responsibility for the airfield control, but no enemy plane was sighted, not even once – which, in retrospect, proved lucky.

One day the commander enquired whether any of the trainees had a background in agriculture and I immediately came forward. From then on, I was charged with delivering the mail by horse and carriage, which was quite marvellous, and even though I was often dealing with a stubborn animal, the job was rather cushy and certainly not dangerous. It was actually a somewhat grotesque situation, us lot positioned here and leisurely driving our horses through the landscape, with the rumbling noises of gunfire not far away. The Russians were close to Warsaw.

While I was occupied in this way just east of Rumia, the English launched an aerial attack from the west, targeting the Rumia airfield, which lay just outside the town. The airfield was completely destroyed and many of my comrades were killed, having had no time to escape into their bunkers. After that our airfield was practically useless, strewn with wrecked aircrafts. Buildings had been turned to rubble and hangars were shredded to pieces.

That's the first time I felt that a 'guardian angel' must be watching over me, and seeing as I was of a religious nature, I instinctively knew that nothing untoward would befall me. Though I often questioned why it was me who was spared while so many of my comrades around me lay dead, I couldn't come up with an answer other than concluding how important it was not to stand in the front row.

In the summer of 1944, the fortunes of war had unquestionably turned against Nazi Germany. The Soviets launched a large-scale offensive against the Heeresgruppe Mitte [Army Group Centre] and the Allies landed on the sloping beaches of Normandy. Suddenly, chaos erupted. After these operations, my aerial gunner course ended and we were ordered to assemble at the West Prussian SS training area located in the Chojnice district, from where we were subsequently dispatched in different directions. These events took me by surprise; I felt unconnected and it dawned on me only gradually that Russia would be my next destination. Travelling by freight train to the east, towards St Petersburg, we were facing an unknown future and could only hope we would survive it. Amidst total confusion the transports were organised in alphabetical order.

I was expected to join a group headed for Toruń in western Poland and located north-east of Warsaw. When we lined up on the military field, none of us knew anyone else. My erstwhile comrades had been sent elsewhere and I was filled with a profound sense of loneliness. I was utterly lost and yet around me frantic activity was taking place with sharp orders barked out and wild rumours making the rounds. Somebody thrust a rucksack containing laundry and a gun into my hands. Would we receive any instruction? 'You'll receive it when you are behind the front line,' was the blunt reply. It seemed it was every man for himself.

We departed on 20 July, travelling through East Prussia towards Klaipeda in Lithuania. It was a balmy summer's day. But then we could advance no further as the Russians had meanwhile created the Courland Pocket, surrounded us and thereby isolated the German army from the rest of the German forces. Us lot were loaded onto boats and, circumnavigating the pocket, we landed in Riga. Heavy fighting inside the pocket continued on both sides and ours suffered horrendous losses.

At the quay in Riga, a group of the so-called *Goldfasane* (golden pheasants) waited for us – we called them by that name because of their golden-brown uniform. They watched us get off the boats and then went home. Before the war and for many years, they had led quite a comfortable life, paradisiacal, but with the Russians pushing forward it came to an end. Meanwhile we were left to march through Riga's streets, singing patriotic songs to drum up some propaganda for the Nazi regime – a totally bizarre situation seeing that at the same time our comrades were fighting for their very existence back in Courland, only a few kilometres away.

Following this hypocritical display of a regime which was sinking into an abyss, we were transported on a narrow-gauge railway to the hinterland, a wide, barely inhabited and sparsely wooded expanse, with our group of some twenty-five to thirty men ending up on some farm or other. While on the upside this took us further away from the Courland Pocket, the downside was that we were inevitably coming closer to the Eastern Front. This brought us down emotionally and our fighting morale was low as anxious questions were asked: would we ever survive the

Wehrmacht units making their way towards Moscow – the beginning of the end.

inferno that would surely befall us? Would we manage to return home? None of us were in any doubt about the Germany army's fading power. We knew full well that despite all assurances about the so-called *Endsieg* (final victory), the war had been irrevocably lost a long time ago.

After three or four restless days during which tensions rose, a lorry suddenly chugged down the track leading to the farm. We clambered up and travelled through the vast landscape, always eastbound towards the front line, without the faintest clue as to what lay ahead of us, but aware that it would be disastrous. We slept in the flatbed of the truck, not the most comfortable night's quarters, but we were so exhausted that we could have slept anywhere. One guy pressed against the other and in between us were our guns.

We reached our destination just short of the front line at dawn. They had eagerly expected us as we were to replace a battalion which had been deployed to secure the runway of a nearby airfield, but we weren't even able to take up our positions. With the Russians so close, the field had already become an identifiable target and we had no choice but to wait. That afternoon some sergeant made an appearance. 'Everyone is under my command. The Russians have penetrated the line. We take position!'

He marched east, towards a deserted field, with nothing in sight.

'Line up in twos, everyone, and dig holes thirty steps away from each other. Those pits will be your night quarters and for you to hold guard against the Russians.'

Really? Our sorry handful of men, inexperienced and untrained, should act as Germany's stronghold against the Russian army? The Russians were firing incessantly and indiscriminately; bullets hit the ground, sparks flew and yet we had still not quite cottoned on. We were out of our depth. And because we had never been properly instructed, our confidence was low. I could handle a gun, at least, but that was about it. Anything past this most basic activity was beyond our capability.

We dug the pits, as we had been ordered, two by two, equipped with our shovels. As usual, I was the last and was left to do the shovelling by myself at the end of the row. With the soil being rock hard it was a gruelling task and, all on my own, I sank to the ground utterly exhausted. There was stillness all around me. It was the first of three days I will never forget.

Alone, crouched in the crater, I was left to listen to the unsettling noise of the screeching *Stalinorgel*, hoping that their rockets would not plough into my protective hole. Despite the howling of the explosives and the shots raining down, I fell asleep, such was my exhaustion from the past few days.

I must have been lying down for hours in this mud hole when I suddenly woke up with the sun shining into my face. I had lost my bearings, but quickly came to. Goodness! Here I am in a foxhole and I'm meant to fight against the Russians. But it was completely still around me, with only some dull rumbling noises not far away. Outside my hole, it was peaceful.

I was fully awake by now and asked myself what I should do next. I carefully turned onto my stomach and crawled up as far as I could to peer over the edge. I wore my steel helmet, of course, and cocked my gun. Nothing. No man, no animal, no sound, nothing – just the wide open field. At that particular moment the war seemed to be far away and I felt no fear. I dragged myself out into the open, slung my gun around my shoulder and went about searching for my comrades in the foxhole further along. It was empty – all the pits were empty. My comrades must have left during the night and must have forgotten me. There I was, stranded alone in the plains of Lithuania with no idea what to do. I did, however, know how to reach the command post of my battalion. I set off westwards, towards a small village we had passed the day before. That's where the command post had been set up.

Walking along the railway embankment, I was the very picture of a lonely soldier savouring the solitude of the Baltic, right in the middle of the war. A walk through nature. I arrived at a small hut, but it too was empty, with only two scraggy horses calmly standing there and not paying any attention to their visitor. Following the path through the deserted village, I turned the corner and expected to see the command post just beyond the last farmstead, but not a soul could be seen. The battalion had disappeared – it was completely gone.

Sounds of shooting came from woodland a bit further away. Russians! Where there were Russians, there must, I concluded, be my comrades. I decided to walk in that direction, but en route started to worry that if I was spotted by a German, I'd be in for harsh punishment. In the worst-case scenario they'd even consider me a deserter. Such offences resulted in execution. You were sentenced to death and shot. That was the end. It would never have occurred to me that I might actually bump into Russians. Just to be on the safe side I walked through the grassland bordering the roads and reached a wood, where I had to fight my way through dense patches of undergrowth.

Leaving the wood behind me, I realised that the Russians were nearby and that I was behind their line. Scram, I said to myself. Instantly! I turned on my heels and ran all the way back. I was confused and couldn't make out where west was. I reached the house I had come across before, sped down the village road and past the command post.

By that point, I was naturally extremely hungry, but I had no food on me. Finally, from afar, I saw a house. Perhaps I could put my hands on some food, I thought, and having nothing to lose, I approached. I turned the western corner and got the fright of my life: a group of Russian soldiers deep in conversation stood around smoking their horrible Russian cigarettes. To this day, I am proud of myself for having grasped the situation and reacting correctly. I slowed my pace and calmly walked past the soldiers, adjusted my gun strap and smiled at the Russians. Yes, that's what I did. I just smiled at them and kept walking, reaching a narrow path that led into the wood. You should have seen their faces! They were dumbfounded. Staring both at me and then at each other, they couldn't believe their eyes. 'Who's that? Wasn't that a German guy? Impossible!' they said.

It took a while for these guys to figure out that I indeed was an enemy and by the time they did, I had already covered a good 100 metres, with the wood within my reach. Ducking against a blast of whistling bullets whipping around my ears, I ran the last bit and then flung myself into the dense undergrowth at the edge of the wood. That was a close shave, admittedly, and, once again, a guardian angel had watched over me.

But then they set after me, yelling at the top of their voices. Luckily, they had lost sight of me and I kept running westwards until I reached a row of hedges bordered by spruce trees. Beyond, Russians again. With Russians at my back and my front, I panicked. But somehow I had to make it through. Desperate, fearing that my luck had run out and not knowing what I should do next, I simply crawled into the hedge. Somebody will find me and pull me out, I thought desperately.

The group of men who had stood by the house had now caught up and were conversing across the hedge where I lay hidden with the other Russians. They walked past where I was at least twice and should have discovered me. Why didn't they capture me? Even in retrospect I can't make sense of it. I was unbelievably lucky once again. It was such an indescribable situation – divine intervention. I felt protected.

I spent the whole day in this hiding spot within the hedge, near the railway line. No food, nothing to drink, but I was alive. This unbelievable day neared its end and darkness fell, but I could feel the proximity of Russian soldiers on patrol. After all, I was behind their front line. I decided to walk along the tracks as, for some reason, I thought that they constituted the border and something told me that if I kept going west, I'd finally reach a larger village, perhaps some 3 or 4 km further along.

I was right. But when I did reach the village, most houses were burnt-out and in ruins. The whole village was deathly quiet, no movement. No bark of a dog or miaow of a cat. All I could hear were scratchy sounds from a loudspeaker in the wood to the left of the village. These were calls attempting to convince us to desert to the Russian side. 'Come across to us, you won't come to any harm!'

This was a ruse, the type of propaganda with which we were familiar, and I didn't fall for it. Moreover, it told me I should move in the opposite direction and bear right. At first, I hesitated, then mustered my energy and entered the village, glancing every so often over my shoulder in fear that someone might jump out from the ruins and attack me. There was nobody around, and I reached the other end undiscovered.

Once again, I found myself out in the open, with farmland stretching ahead, blotted by demolished farms, blazing roofs and beams. I could hear the crackle of fire and had the smell of gunpowder and burnt soil in my nostrils. It was dreadful, smoke still lingering above this apocalyptic scene. The Germans had set fire to everything they could on their retreat.

I ran on, continuing across the field like a chased animal, keenly pricking my ears – I was running for my life. Onwards! Keeping my eyes on the gruesome spectacle above me where concentrated fire was at work,

I knew the front line was moving. Tracer rounds illuminated the sky as they hit their targets and exploded on both sides, indicating that I was in between the two front lines. But I didn't know what time of night it was, I was utterly disoriented. Ending up in yet another forest, I was completely lost, totally exhausted and desperate. I crawled underneath some undergrowth and fell asleep. The sun woke me up and allowed me to get my bearings. Leaving the undergrowth behind, I set off, keeping west. I must have roamed around for a good two hours before finding my way out of the forest – hours of feeling abandoned and panicked.

From an incline I made out what appeared to be a larger farmstead, which I approached, crossing some cornfields while ducking my head as best I could. Seeing that I was in a slightly elevated position, I noticed some freshly dug pits, but wondered who had dug them, Russians or Germans? Cautiously I edged forwards, careful to remain invisible. It didn't actually matter whether it was Russians or Germans who detected me, as either would surely shoot without warning.

Luck was on my side again. I happened to run into the arms of a friendly lieutenant who instantly understood the situation and listened to my story.

'Get yourself down this hill and you'll find a unit who's just having a meal. You must be terribly hungry.'

I followed his instruction, and who do I meet up with but my company, my own unit who were busily tucking into their food! But from my replacement unit of thirty men who had joined this company, only two remained. The others were gone. Were they still lying out in the field somewhere, perhaps? Most likely they were killed. Those guys sitting around their mess kit seemed in shock. They certainly didn't show the slightest interest in me. They knew there was no way out for them, the Russians would arrive shortly in tanks and all that we had left were our guns. And if comrades had jumped into ditches for cover, the tanks would simply rumble across, then reverse and crush their bodies into pulp. These experiences during my first three days at the front are indelibly imprinted on my brain to this very day. I keep reliving the memories. I realised that on some level I resembled the 'good soldier Schwejk', seeing as I had as much idea about the war as the man in the moon [the figure of Schwejk was created by the Czech author Jaroslav Hašek: he was a simple-minded, loyal soldier who collided with military bureaucracy]. It also became clear to me that all along we had been deceived and lied to.

We were now a depleted and disillusioned lot of demoralised men, and our retreat had left us in total confusion. What were we meant to do? Surrounded by the Russians, we knew full well that we wouldn't stand a chance.

At some point the moment arrived which we had strangely and secretly hoped for, as this damned war had utterly worn us out. We were depleted – no fighting spirit left in any of us. The Russians pushed forward and, coming face to face with them, we cast away our guns and put our arms up. Finished! It's over. Despite not knowing what the future would hold, I felt relieved.

The Russians collected our weapons along with everything else we carried on us. Sluggishly stumbling forwards, we were ordered to move towards St Petersburg. I no longer gave a damn about anything. I didn't even have enough energy to think, not even about my family. Our destination was some kolkhoz located near St Petersburg and we were immediately put to work upon our arrival – labouring in the fields, from morning to night! The circumstances were horrendous and made even worse considering the physical condition I was in. The food was ghastly. A watery soup with barely anything nutritious in it, a piece of bread stuffed with sawdust – we never felt full. Plagued by hunger, extreme hunger, we often saw dead bodies chucked on a heap, death by exhaustion or dysentery. Not surprising, what with the filthy water we were given. Would I be able to survive?

And then it was my turn. I weighed barely 43 kg and I suffered not only from dysentery but also from pleurisy, and at that point I was transported to the prison infirmary. But with the lack of medication, ongoing bad and insufficient food, I didn't recover. After the female chief medical director checked me, she wanted me returned to the kolkhoz, which would have entailed certain death. I wouldn't have survived the following winter had it not been for a Jewish doctor who examined me and immediately ordered my dismissal. 'Domoj,' she decided, home, back to my home country. With this single word she

And that's what it looked like: a Russian hamlet where German prisoners of war carried out forced labour.

opened the gateway and gave me the rest of my life. A guardian angel, once again, had protected me.

In September 1945 I travelled by train to Munich, via Berlin, Leipzig and Kronach. The first leg on Russian freight trains took us two weeks to reach the German border, with the 'menu' featuring one thing only, a soup made of crushed corn [grown primarily for industrial processing and stockfeed] – many comrades didn't survive and were buried beside the tracks.

I finally reached German soil, albeit still in the occupied Soviet zone, a sorry figure clothed in a black military coat that flapped around my emaciated body that was still severely weakened by the inflammation. I still had the crossing of the border between the occupied zones ahead of me. With the help of someone familiar with the area I managed, and with that behind me, I no longer feared the danger of being sent back to the east.

Trudging past Munich's Ungererstrasse and Leopoldstrasse leading up to Munich's Siegestor (Victory Gate) past the Feldherrenhalle and up to the gutted train station, I saw a city in ruins with heaps of rubble, debris, rubbish and broken glass wherever I looked. I took the train to Rosenheim and then on to Frasdorf, the village I grew up in. It was evening when I arrived; I was overjoyed to be held in my mother's arms as she embraced me in my broken state. I was home, at long last.

The next morning, Mother took me to the village doctor. He spoke little during the examination, only expressing the hope that I'd pull through. Dysentery struck again and, because of the lingering inflammation that meant that water kept pressing on my lungs, I was bedbound for several weeks. Being in my childhood room was comforting, though. Recovery was slow and made me think long and hard about my life. Why had I been spared? Why wasn't I lying in some wet pit in the icy fields of Russia? What had allowed me to survive? I was a religious man, a God-fearing person, and concluded that a divine power, a guardian angel so to speak, had protected me. Yes, someone had watched over me.

My Dramatic Voyage with U-234

EYEWITNESS ACCOUNT BY ERICH MENZEL

I was born in the summerhouse belonging to the Jagemann family in Radebeul on 27 January 1921, a bitterly cold day but one filled with joy, so I was told. At the time Father was employed as a bank clerk with the ADCA (Allgemeine Deutsche Credit Anstalt) and he was mightily proud of his son and heir.

He himself had been brought up in a household ruled by strict discipline, firmly believing that this was the right sort of upbringing, and his rules concerning my siblings' and my behaviour were similarly rigid. My mother, Lisbeth, came from Crimmitschau in Saxony and, perhaps by way of compensation, she was a more benign figure in my life, as is often the case with mothers. Once my little sister Margit was born, our family was complete, and my parents didn't wish to have any more children.

The house I was born in was attached to a garden complex with a hothouse, nurseries and vast plant and flowerbeds reaching down to the banks of the Elbe river. I used to run wild there together with my schoolfriend Horst von Jagemann and my sister, which often earned me a good thrashing from my father, especially the time when I decided to shove Horst into a barrel filled with rainwater from which he was just about able to escape. At the same time, I got to learn about plants and animals and the journey down to my grandparents who lived in Raditz, a village close to our town and situated along the Elbe river, was short. My grandfather was a well-respected locksmith who also worked as a farmer, postmaster and even as a dance teacher in the local restaurant. I, his oldest grandson, was a welcome visitor and he'd often allow me to ride on the backseat of his special bicycle, where he'd usually place his parcels. I was allowed to potter around in his shop while grandmother spoiled me with a cup of sugar mixed with cocoa powder, called *Schokoladenteig*, as chocolate bars at the time were way too expensive.

We loved playing cards in our family, with my father particularly favouring the game of Skat, for which he'd often invite his brothers and in-laws. We kids complained about these gatherings mainly because the lounge would then reek of cigarette and cigar smoke despite Father being a sworn non-smoker. I've been passionate about card games ever since, and I clearly remember odd customs, such as passing on the hat to determine who would shuffle the pack. These were relaxed and happy times and those who had to step out used the latrine on the next floor up.

Radebeul Primary School

In 1927 I was enrolled in Radebeul's Pestalozzi primary school. At intake, a medical examination stated that I was undernourished, which meant that I was entitled to receive school meals, but academically I was among the average achievers. The years 1927 and 1928 were memorable in terms of summer vacations spent at Kölpinsee near the Baltic Sea, a sought-after holiday destination for Saxons and where we would be joined by my aunt, Father's sister. Carefree and happy, we enjoyed roaming around the area, appreciating the landscape. My father was quite talented when it came to building sandcastles, which he decorated with shells and fir cones and which he then made us water and maintain, while he took all the credit.

At the time, pupils had to pass a relatively difficult exam to be accepted into secondary school. Though I was a nervous sort of lad and physically not particularly strong, my father nevertheless insisted that one day I must make something of myself. He requested that my mother take me to see a student of Coué, the French founder of 'conscious autosuggestion', which had patients use a method of suggestion and imagination for themselves. By using the mantra 'every day, in every way, I am getting better and better', I was supposed to rid myself of my weaknesses.

In any event, I did well in my exams, and at Easter 1931 I, along with thirty other students, was admitted to the Sexta A. Father was happy to see me wear the green and silver school cap and immediately added cocoa milk to my meals to combat my malnutrition. We lived quite frugally, with meat a rare delicacy at our suppers.

I was barely settled into high school when a friend of my father's suggested that I, then ten and a half years old, join the boy scouts. I was the youngest in that group. I received a neck scarf, something that resembled a safari hat and the field shirt, and learnt all the usual scout skills such as reading maps, identifying stars, building makeshift bridges, and finding one's way through the forest in the dark and without a compass. But above all I enjoyed the solid camaraderie, though seeing I was the youngest, it was often quite tricky to keep up.

In 1930 the number of unemployed people in Germany rose to some 6 million out of a total population of 85 million. Though all parties promised to lower that rate, all they did was fight each other and nothing happened except politicians trading vicious verbal attacks. This paved an easy way for the NSDAP [National Socialist Workers' Party] to establish itself and they won 230 seats as early as 1932, with the SPD [Social Democratic Party] gaining 140 seats, the KPD [German Communist Party] 80 seats and the Zentrum [German Centre Party] holding 75 seats, while all the remaining splinter groups and factions lost out.

The mood in school was conservative-liberal. Nearly all teachers had served as officers during World War I, belonged to the Stahlhelm-Bund [the Steel Helmet, the League of Front Soldiers; their steel helmets were a symbol of soldiers who had undergone hardship and were willing to sacrifice themselves], and they resolutely refused to vote for the NSDAP. Generally, they didn't take the rise of the Nazis seriously, and their attitude rubbed off on us pupils.

As an employee of the ADCA my father feared for his continued employment, as jobs were being terminated up and down the country. He trusted the NSDAP and proudly wore the party badge and, with him being the only Nazi in our own home, it caused a fair bit of trouble. Increasingly worried about his employment, alongside his job, he founded a 'margarine distribution business', which worked along the following lines: once a week we'd receive a special delivery of fresh margarine from Schleswig-Holstein which was then stored in our flat or cellar, but first had to be made airtight and specially wrapped, all taken care of by my mother and my sister. I would then deliver orders to immediate and extended family, relatives and other households in the area – each one of them a party member. We made a decent profit, the margarine was fresh, but for us youngsters it was a bit of a slog to carry the stuff around and up and down many staircases. For each delivered block of margarine I received a Reichspfennig, the first money I earned, and it filled me with pride.

After the NSDAP came to power in 1933, all the other political parties were disbanded. Father no longer had to worry about keeping his job and was able to dissolve his margarine distribution business. It also meant that many other groups, such as the Freemasons, the Rotary Club and the German Scouting Association were branded as 'ideological enemies' by the NSDAP, leading the head of our scout group to request that we be integrated into the *Jungvolk* [the youth wing of the NSDAP]. The request was refused, which landed me, a squirt of twelve years, into one of the *Jungvolk* groups already operating in our district, sporting the black beret, neckerchief and tan shirt. Later, at the age of fifteen, we automatically moved to the Hitler Youth.

Angry at the dissolution of our scout group, but perhaps also emboldened because of where my school stood ideologically and how that influenced my thinking, I refused to accept any leadership position in the Hitler Youth, but instead reported to its marching band and played the drum. Because my parents had to pay the costs stipulated by the Hitler Youth, especially for the band uniform, I decided to perform (but not wear my cap) a wake-up drumming spectacle every Sunday morning to get people out of bed, something my father-in-law still holds against me today, seeing as he couldn't bear the deafening disruption on a Sunday.

As I grew older I improved academically, especially in the sciences and sports, where a lot of importance was placed on swimming, including obtaining the lifesaving certificate. I excelled in athletics and boxing. After my first year, the school had a certain tradition of allocating classroom seats to the pupils based on their grades, and youngsters were allocated seats corresponding to their performance, and this would change every six months. As I went up in years, I was always among the top ten, for which I can primarily thank our excellent teachers, who cut lonely figures within the community as they didn't belong to the Nazi party. I particularly remember our Latin tutor, a Dr Tuisko Reibstein. When the traditional morning address was banned and replaced with the Hitler salute, he'd start the lesson with: '*Heil Hitler*, may God help us, open the windows, it stinks!'

As for the young student teachers, things were different. Unlike their older mentors, they kept with the times and proudly wore their party badge, being overall quite pleased with how matters were developing. They made a point of sharing with us, their students, the political advances achieved by the Nazis, which we only knew as they were portrayed by the Nazi propaganda: breaking the 1919 Treaty of Versailles, withdrawing from the League of Nations, the Wehrmacht crossing the Rhine bridges and occupying the demilitarised Rhineland while establishing full authority over the Saarland. The 1936 Olympic Games in Berlin, where all nations marched into the Olympic arena raising their arms in the Hitler salute, the annexation of Austria, the creation of Grossdeutschland and the reintegration of the Memel district ... it all made an enormous impression on us. There was more: the Sudetenland was incorporated from Czechoslovakia – every single success was achieved without a gunshot and celebrated throughout the land.

The Allies could have put a stop to that on several occasions, but in the mindset of 'appeasement' they were prepared to accept the new developments. Had they intervened at the right time, World War II could have been prevented. Instead, they didn't put any obstacles in Hitler's way, and he proceeded to invade Poland.

Indeed, the economic situation within Germany improved by the day. There was rapid implementation of job creation, with, for example, unemployed people being put to work on highway construction (*Autobahnen*) and rearmament, or another example, increasing production in manufacturing and heavy industry, which contributed to an economic upswing. Over and over again, everywhere, these accomplishments were attributed to the efforts of the Nazis. Why would we have questioned it, what did we have to compare it with? Permitted to listen only to German radio broadcasts, we had no access to foreign news, and travelling abroad, at least for the general masses, was unimaginable – there was only one way of going on a journey and that was via the organisation *Kraft durch Freude* [Strength through Joy – the KdF was a leisure operation set up by the NSDAP to compensate for poor wages and loss of trade union rights].

We had no idea, and were never informed, about the negative aspects of the regime, such as the concentration camps, the arrests of citizens that disagreed with it, and even their murders. We knew nothing.

When it came to the *Judenfrage* [Jewish question] we got our information from the *Stürmer*, the virulent anti-Semitic paper published by Julius Streicher, which focused on describing Jews as sex offenders who violated innocent Aryan maidens. When a Jew had – allegedly – raped a German girl, it would be announced in large headlines. Even during the war, we never heard of any crimes committed against Jews, nor of their annihilation. Never.

On 14 April 1935, I and my cousin Elsbeth were confirmed in Rade-beul's Martin Luther Church. This celebration was an opportunity for all godparents and families from Kaditz and Crimmitschau to get together, but it was unfortunately just when a split within the Protestant Church occurred and two groups formed, with some believing in the Church and others who called themselves German Christians and were particularly committed to the National Socialist Party. Nearly all party members were German Christians, my father included. The Catholic Church stepped away, but equally didn't take any action and made no objections.

After not having had a holiday for some years, we were finally able to take summer vacations in both 1936 and 1937. A family friend owned a summer lodge at Yamno Lake close to the Baltic Sea, located alongside the beach. We all shared a room, and unfortunately there was no bath or toilet, but it didn't bother us. It was here that I met Elisabeth Goldmund from Bad Polzin, my first love, and I kept up a warm correspondence with her well into the war years.

When we returned home a noteworthy event took place. In autumn 1937 all the boys of our class were invited to attend dance classes under the leadership of the ballet master Schade and his wife. It took place in Radebeul's *Grundschänke*. A whole slew of issues had to be dealt with, such as what to wear, since proper etiquette was essential and dictated that we wear patent leather shoes and a suit. Because Father at the time only earned 300 Reichsmark per month, we couldn't afford many extras and I had to make do with my confirmation suit.

The lesson usually ended at 22.15 and I had to arrive home at 2300 hours at the latest, as my father was very strict about this. Since in our first 'good manners lesson' we were told that one must escort one's lady dance partner back to her home, the choice of who'd be one's respective partner depended on where she lived. My choice fell on a tall, blonde and relatively scrawny girl by the name of Lilo who didn't find much favour in my father's eyes. 'How can a man marry such a bag of bones!' he dismissively commented, though I was barely seventeen and marriage was far from my mind.

With our dance classes being short of girls of the same age as us (because they had already mastered the art of ballroom dancing much earlier), the ballet master sought out daughters of respectable families in our area who'd be willing to join. A girl called Ruth Meister from Radebeul came along and she impressed us boys with her fine physique and a rather curvy behind. Though we were still young, we had a thrill just looking at her, and she was a lovely and high-spirited girl, to boot, whom I got closer to during the final ball with our parents watching on from the spectators' gallery. According to our card, we had to perform a waltz, which suited us fine, and Ruth's behind was definitely an advantage when it came to twirling her around. From then on, we remained dance partners and would walk home together, much to the annoyance of the others.

It was the beginning of a long friendship. Ruth's brother needed extra help in maths and his maths teacher had recommended that Ruth's father use me as a private tutor. It brought me into Ruth's large family home, which offered two advantages: I received five Reichsmark per lesson which was a handsome amount for a poor chap like me and, on top of that, I could play with Ruth in the garden both before and after the private lesson. Both of us were very good at gymnastics, showing off our skills on the high bars as the family had lots of equipment at their disposal. Ruth's mother often pulled a long face when she noticed that Ruth was happily exercising on the bars without the proper clothing, but it was fun. I was quite a shy and reserved sort of lad and none of us had any clue at the time about what was what, except that babies aren't delivered by a stork. That much we knew.

A definite highlight of our friendship was Ruth's father inviting us to the ball given by the Association of German Engineers in 1938, and Meister senior asked me to accompany his daughter. That was my first time inside a Mercedes, with dear Ruth by my side, holding my perspiring hand. The dinner was excellent, albeit entirely unfamiliar to me, and with it we received going-home presents, a packet of Salem, produced by the Yenitze firm in Dresden and which, seeing as I was a non-smoker, I immediately handed to my heavy smoker of a host.

That summer my father and I went on a KdF trip to Gössweinstein in the Fränkische Schweiz. Our hotel was located directly opposite the convent, right in the middle of the village. As was the custom at the time, all the famous sights in the area had been renamed to honour important Nazi personalities, so for example there was the Göring Rock or the Adolf Hitler Panorama. During our walks we got to know the Klein family and I got along well with their daughter Margot. A lovely picture of Margot which I later stuck inside my locker raised suspicions from my comrades, but the two of us were little more than pen-pals and nothing ever developed. Perhaps Margot would have liked the friendship to go further, but it remained at that, seeing as I got married to someone else.

Life Gets Serious

It was about the middle of 1938 when questions regarding what I would choose as my profession began to take on a more serious tone as I was about to graduate. My grades were good and Father and I decided that I should have an officer's career in mind and have a position in a technological troop, something like the Luftwaffennachrichtenschule [the LN is usually referred to as the Luftwaffe Signals School] but Mother wasn't thrilled with that idea as she sensed that there would be a war.

I myself was quite excited and applied to the academy based in Halle along with submitting proof of my Aryan ancestry. My parents added their letter confirming that they were able to support me with a monthly amount of 25 Reichsmark, but I still required three references. My father wanted to impress and approached D. Burghagen, a retired lieutenant commander who had been the commander of a U-boat during World War I, and Senior Lieutenant D. Krantz, both of whom he knew from his honorary positions in the local council. As a third reference, I put down my class teacher, Dr Reibstein, and added for good measure Dr Zimmermann, the headteacher.

My application was successful, the references had positive things to say about me and my family, above all because my father was a party member and a 1914–18 decorated war veteran. I went for my first interview, where the school's officers put several questions to me, and this was followed by lunch. They probably wanted to assure themselves that I had the proper table manners as befits an officer. I went away believing that I had made the right choice. But prior to the final confirmation, I still had to pass a two-day psychological exam, which was known to be untraditional in terms of the methods and testing they used. The goal was to test the individual's level of endurance, how much pain they could take, a process where the candidate would be given electric shocks while playing with magnetic balls. Additionally, we had to answer 300 multiple-choice questions with hardly any thinking time allowed. The final part entailed several specialists interviewing us.

Before day one had even ended, I had had enough; I turned belligerent and stubborn and was convinced I had failed the exam. After the war I was permitted access to the school's files and it turned out that I hadn't totally misjudged the situation. I had indeed been considered 'lazy, sleepy, lacking any initiative and without the potential to offer any significant contribution to the officers' corps'. But still they invited me for the last part of the application process, a final event along with a further exam organised by the Luftwaffe Signals School, which was much more pleasant. I did well with the science questions and excelled in the initial sport exams, which meant that the rest of the exams were optional for me. Instead, I had to act as referee. On 27 February 1939, much to my father's delight, I received a letter confirming that I had been accepted as probationary officer cadet to the Luftwaffe with a start date of 1 October 1939. Many of my classmates were also accepted to this officer-training course.

Reichsarbeitsdienst in the Middle of Nowhere

At nearly the same time I also received the order to report for the six-month service with the Reichsarbeitsdienst (RAD), which was obligatory for all eighteen-year-olds. That's how they availed themselves of cheap labour, as both boys and girls received only pocket money for this. Another of their goals was for the various social classes to mix and all who had until then not worked in any physical capacity would now learn to do 'hard physical work', as it was called. The section I joined had just been formed and was located in the village of Kotten, somewhere in the sticks. I was called up to report on the 1 April, and it was certainly not a trick.

But ahead lay the all-important preparations for our *Abitur*. Everyone took their studies seriously and worked diligently towards the written and oral exams set by the Reich Ministry of Education that existed from May 1934 until the end of the war in 1945.

A random question from the German exam paper might have read: 'What will the world look like in 300 years when coal is no longer available?' It was a question that interested even me at the time.

Luckily, none of my year failed the *Abitur*, which meant that the graduation ceremony from the renamed Hans Schlemm School was thoroughly enjoyed by parents, teachers and the younger classes.

It was then time to face harsh reality. I only had three weeks to say my goodbyes to friends who all knew about my career hopes with respect to the Luftwaffe Signals School. And taking leave from my family as an eighteen-year-old was especially difficult, with none of us knowing what the future might bring. With the call-up letter folded in my pocket and my few belongings packed in a cardboard box, I travelled to Kotten on 1 April, my head filled with doubts. We were handed our uniforms, both for work and for when on leave, and a spade – our trusted companion for some time to come.

We were about 120 men aged between eighteen and twenty, with us high-school graduates being in the minority. We were housed in a barrack with 112 bunkbeds covered with straw mattresses, checked bedding and a square pillow, and had to come to grips with how to make beds properly, the rules demanding that the sheets be folded around the corners at exact right-angles and that the duvet covers were not allowed to have any creases. Regulations with respect to how we arranged our lockers were equally strict.

That first day we lost a good part of our individuality when all of us had our heads shorn to barely a fringe and once we were dressed in our uniforms, we all looked basically the same. Needless to say, the task of 'cleaning the area' fell to us new graduates. We were ordered to scour the latrines, some twelve of them situated in the centre of the wash zone, and the equipment we were given was inadequate. A filthy and disgusting job! The urinals were arranged along a line running down the middle. I was fortunate in that when our superior enquired whether anyone knew how to play the piano, I dropped out of the cleaning rota and instead played marches and songs to entertain the troop leaders during mealtimes.

After roll-call, raising the flag and room inspection, we marched to our work, each group assigned a different job. Ours was to 'flatten' the Schwarze Elster [the Black Elster is a 179-km river in East Germany], heaving wet mud from the riverbed and loading it onto dumper trucks, with hardly any time allowed for this. After only a few hours, our lot – mostly 'non-labourers' and high-school graduates – were exhausted, and because we hadn't met the quota, we were duly punished.

We were fortunate enough to have a truck driver among our group, one hell of a strong guy who could easily manage the quota and often saved the rest of us from punishments. These varied in severity: one was to crawl a certain distance while holding the spade between your arms. I was once ordered to request from the troop leader a *'Böschung* plane'. Not having a clue what I was asking for, I naively approached the leader, relaying the request. 'D'you think you can take the piss out of me?' he bellowed. 'Get out of my sight – ten push-ups, with full gear!'

After a few weeks they managed to break our will and deaden our brain – that indeed was the goal of their educational methods. When my parents came to visit for the first time on a Sunday, I was standing in the square – where I was being punished for the making-beds-routine – out in full view of the public. It really spoiled the visit as they weren't even permitted to speak to me.

A special exercise was the *Spatengriff,* how to handle and carry the spade, another one was to march in the Nazi-style goose-step. Thanks to me shining in sports, I was soon counted among the best 'marchers'.

After three months had gone by, our camp commander received the order to dispatch the best parade men, officer candidates if possible, to the Nuremberg department in Hoyerswerda. About twelve men were selected, all delighted to now turn their backs on that particular camp. In Hoyerswerda they put together a RAD unit to prepare for the *'Reichsparteitag* of freedom' scheduled for the beginning of September [from 1933 onwards, they were used as propaganda events for Adolf Hitler by the state leadership in Nuremberg, called the 'city of Nazi party rallies' from 1936 to 1945].

The leaders of this unit were soldiers who had benefited from training that was superior to what was on offer in Kotten. And though their drills proved equally grinding, we felt much better treated and properly instructed. We polished our spades with 'Sidol' to the point that they could be used as mirrors, and greased our hobnailed *'Knobelbecher'* boots so that they shone. The various commands as to how to carry the spade – 'spade – over the shoulder', 'spade – in grip position' – soon worked to perfection.

Furthermore, working outdoors was not as hard as in Kotten. We had to fell trees, prune hedges, clear forests, strip bark from trees and take measurements. After a while, taking measurements was the only assignment I was tasked with, which allowed me to sneak off and catch a few naps hidden away in the woods. Thanks to my athletics skills, I was also chosen to join the camp's handball league.

When August came, the Gau [the term used by the Third Reich to describe a district] leader in charge of our work informed us of the details of the *Reichparteitag* ahead. But it all turned out differently. Suddenly, in mid-August, our unit received a delivery of thirty rifles and our leader, previously a sergeant, began to instruct us in the use of arms. Each one of us practised at a shooting stand and it wasn't long after that that we were loaded onto a freight train. The journey, however, did not take us to Nuremberg but instead to Upper Silesia, or more precisely to Bobrek-Karb near Gliwice. We were taken to our lodgings, previously a school building located close to the border with Poland, and slept on straw mats and also had a blanket. But otherwise we spent a leisurely few days enjoying the nearby outdoor pool and befriending some of the locals.

Piercing noises from aeroplane engines and gunfire ripped through the air during the night of 1 September, rudely awakening us with bullets shattering the school building's windows. Alarm!

At dawn we received the order to leave and march to Poland. Arm bands with '*Deutsche Wehrmacht*' printed on them turned us into soldiers overnight. The first division carried the thirty guns, with the rest of us shouldering the spades. Marching along the roads, we headed towards Częstochowa.

World War II had begun with Great Britain declaring war on Germany. A treaty of non-aggression between Germany and the Soviet Union was agreed [the Molotov–Ribbentrop Pact], in other words a pact was made with Hitler's arch-enemy Russia, which in turn invaded Poland and later Finland. But we only heard the news after the fact; meanwhile us lot were steadily marching on throughout the day. We didn't clap eyes on any German soldiers; in fact, the area we crossed seemed totally deserted except for a destroyed Polish light aircraft, where I sliced away the white and red cockade.

We took up night lodgings in yet another school, where we were woken up by a gunshot cracking through the air. It turned out that our guard had shot at our unit leader on patrol, who had responded too late with the codeword. Our first casualty! The second one was our cook, shot dead by partisans while standing right next to his *Gulaschkanone* [mobile kitchen unit].

Our invasion of Poland took a mere ten days, without our group ever being involved in any operation. At that point our command post received a telegram with the order to send all officer candidates back home. And with that the six of us traipsed unarmed through the fields towards the nearest German train station, where crowds greeted us as if we were returning war heroes, though not one of us had ever come face to face with an enemy or been involved in any battle.

Signal Intelligence School in Halle

After a brief vacation spent with my family I travelled to Halle on 1 October and reported to the Luftwaffe Signals School. Allocated decent lodgings in newly constructed buildings, we were four men in one room fitted with bunkbeds and parquet flooring which we had to sand three times a week using wood shavings before waxing it. On the first day we were already provided with our kit, uniform, tracksuits, sport outfits, underwear and the famous *Knobelbecher* with which we were familiar from our time with the RAD – those boots with hobnailed soles. We were then lined up according to our height. Our company of the 7th Officer Supplementary Cohort, which consisted of 192 candidates, was split into four platoons, each consisting of three groups. Due to my height of 1.8 metres I was deployed to the second platoon in its third group, which was a unit of sixteen men. Its leader was a corporal, but the platoon was headed up by a sergeant. Two platoons answered to a lieutenant, and the company reported to a captain. We, of course, also had a sergeant major, who was the sergeant's right-hand man but was not necessarily the highest-ranking soldier in the company and was commonly referred to as the Company Mother, looking after administrative tasks.

Our training was harsh, but unlike the RAD, it was fair. We were trained on guns (Karabiner 98 K), pistols (08/15) and bayonets, and above all instructed how to look after these weapons, termed the 'soldier's bride'. During daily roll-calls we were drilled in discipline, neatness, obedience and cleanliness, while in the classroom we were taught technical know-how. After two months we were sworn in, when we dutifully lined up at the air base in front of two Ju 87 dive bombers and swore allegiance to the Führer. We swore to serve the country and dedicate our lives to this mission.

Who could have predicted how soon we'd be called on to make this sacrifice. Of the 192 soldiers, most had been killed by the end of the war or were declared missing. But in 1939 we all believed that the war would end soon. My father was also completely taken in by the idea of the *Endsieg* (final victory) and, come Christmas, when we were all sent home on leave for a few days, he fixed a large swastika wrapped in silver paper to the top of our Christmas tree. The Christian cross was replaced by the swastika – what a travesty, in hindsight.

On 1 February we were promoted to the position of probationary officer cadets and had a silver triangle sewn onto the left sleeve of our uniform, the rank of an airman. At the same time our company was transferred to Potsdam-Eiche, near Berlin, to 'fine-tune' our education.

Erich Menzel with his mother, Lisa.

We studied Morse code, radio traffic, how to lay telephone cables and operate switchboards. Furthermore, we were instructed in tactical warfare, night manoeuvres and practised combat readiness. For us, much like for the Roman legions, the principle of 'if you want to command, you must first learn to obey' was the underlying doctrine.

On 1 April 1940 the promotion to officer cadet followed, and we were granted time off to explore Potsdam, Berlin and its sights. Our training came to an end with what they called a 'celebratory ball', consisting of a power march of 25 km around Potsdam in full gear. While some of us were not up to this mammoth challenge, I didn't mind what was considered torture, seeing as I was extremely fit. At the end of the trek we were received by a military band who accompanied us, notwithstanding our aching feet, through the town centre and all the way to Potsdam-Eiche. 'Left Shoulder Arms'.

The news that Denmark had been invaded by our forces on 8 April, with Norway attacked very soon thereafter, took us by complete surprise. It was reported that the English too were on the warpath and had wanted to occupy Norway, with Polish, French and British units landing in the north. Heavy battles and substantial losses were sustained and Norway capitulated on 20 April 1940, with King Haakon and his government fleeing to England. The campaign ended with the Allied troops, just short of victory, withdrawing suddenly due to the critical situation in France.

The Western Campaign in France

After a brief leave of absence, we were deployed to the Western Front and allocated to different regiments. The Wehrmacht prepared to invade the Netherlands and Belgium and laid the groundwork for the French campaign. As of 10 May the plans that had been conceived by General von Manstein were carried out, and here is an excerpt from the *Kriegsstammrolle* [war logs] of Luftwaffe Signal Intelligence, Department 34, with reference to me: 'Participated in battles fought from 10 May to 4 June 1940, [participated in the] advance to the English Channel, deployed in the battle in West Flanders and around Artois.'

132

Erich Menzel with his father, Willy, 26 April 1940.

The Netherlands capitulated on 15 May, followed shortly by Belgium on 28 May. On 13 May Italy declared war on France and England. On 17 June Maréchal Pétain became the new head of state in France, formed a new government and requested an armistice. General de Gaulle, who had meanwhile fled to London, created the French National Committee and called for the French to resist Nazi occupation.

Finally, on 22 June an armistice between Germany and France was signed in Compiègne, ironically in the same railway carriage in which the Germans had requested a ceasefire in 1918. In their dizzy flush of victory, Hitler and his followers believed that from then on, they would be able to conquer all of Europe.

At the same time the Soviet Union invaded and occupied Lithuania, Latvia, Estonia and parts of Poland. Meanwhile I was sitting in a radio car in the occupied airfields, charged with communications between the ground and the air crews. The streets were crowded with refugees, destroyed tanks, burnt-out vehicles and corpses.

Somewhere in the south of Belgium, I am not sure what the place was called, we took over a conservatoire whose director, an enthusiastic pianist, permitted me to play on their Blüthner grand piano. Curiosity got the better of some of the female students and they were keen to come face to face with one of the despised Germans. Eventually we gave the conservatoire permission to open their classes again, bade them a polite farewell and left them with what I believe was a good impression of us, which at the time was not to be taken for granted.

Posted to the Orléans-Bricy airfield, I operated out of the radio truck and was charged with communications between ground and air crews during the Luftwaffe operations against England, while by night I took up lodgings in barracks previously used by the French.

Back to Halle

On 1 July I was promoted to the rank of ensign and returned to Halle for further training in the 16th Luftwaffe Signal Intelligence Company. Sadly, we were already mourning our first losses, but these first three months in Halle were actually most pleasant and I thoroughly enjoyed the

Erich Menzel (with cap) surrounded by a few of his comrades.

training. Highly decorated officers from World War I (bearers of the Pour le Mérite) instructed us in strategy, tactics and methods in leadership, but still allowed us lads enough free time to spend in the town's bars. Sundays we'd often drop into Grüns Wine Bar, where we might meet Luckner, a German nobleman, naval officer, author and sailor who lived in Halle. He had great physical strength and was noted for his ability to bend coins between the thumb, index, and middle finger of his right hand and to tear up telephone directories. Or we chose to have a drink at Café Zorn or Café Danneberg. On 1 December we were finally promoted to the rank of senior ensign and wore many of the officers' special items such as the silver braiding attached to the cap, an officer's dagger and leather coat. All we felt was pride, not realising for a moment that this terrible war snuffed out the lives of countless human beings and plunged many families into deep mourning and despair.

At the end of officer training, we had to decide to which special unit we wished to be deployed: to the flight crew or ground operations. Those training as radio operators and for reconnaissance were deployed to the flight crew, whereas those attached to ground operations were instructed in sending and receiving radio signals from operators in aircraft or tank units.

Luftwaffe Intelligence School 1 in Nordhausen

I signed up for the flight crew and from 1 December 1940 to 31 March 1941 was transferred to the Signal Intelligence School in Nordhausen [later the location of the Mittelbau-Dora concentration camp]. Along with me came Klaus Müller, Hans Meurer and Martin Stambrau, all friends of mine. We were lodged in barracks with the company commander subjecting us to a Prussian-style drill that was quite over the top, in our opinion. Practical lessons included radio communication on the ground, but also from inside a bomber, such as a Ju 52 or an older Ju 86 with diesel-powered engines. A rather unpleasant way of learning the art of radio communication was us being placed in steel tubs and lowered down from the aircraft on a rope to get better reception. It was ghastly!

At the same time, we had so-called etiquette lessons, an induction course of how to behave in noble company. By the end we knew how to kiss the hand of a lady properly, dance in step and cut the right figure at the occasional ball. I was introduced to a young lady who had previously experienced an unpleasant encounter with an officer and I was 'on my toes', so to speak. She was very pretty and intelligent, and enjoyed the evening. A delightful friendship developed and much later she visited me and my family in Radebeul, where she was attending an 'Institute for English Misses' in Dresden.

The end of the training was marked with an award ceremony where we were handed the certificate for Luftwaffe Aircraft Radio Communication. It was a period in which I saw no war, no terror, nor any injured or dead soldiers.

The Tutow Fighter Pilot School

After a brief vacation, we were transferred to the 'Great' Tutow fighter pilot school, south of Stralsund in Mecklenburg-Vorpommern, where we stayed until 15 May 1942. My friend Klaus Müller was also part of the group as we were both among the highest-achieving graduates of Nordhausen and stood to be further promoted, meaning we were the first to be selected for reconnaissance and navigation instruction. There were only two others from the crew who were also accepted to this course, which involved instruction in the process of dead reckoning, blind-flying manoeuvres, using fire-control radar, night navigation (especially celestial navigation) and landing techniques. In order to gain experience, we were trained extensively in all kinds of conditions and practised on old plane models such as Focke-Wulf Weihe, a fabric-and-metal-clad twin-engine multipurpose aircraft, or the Junkers W34, a single all-metal transport and passenger aircraft.

Because the Tutow airfield was located in the midst of the Vorpommern countryside, there was very little to take one's mind off things, other than a visit to an officers' mess, doing some sport or going to the one cinema in the area. But by mid-May we were prepared for deployment. The motto

Erich Menzel in uniform.

rammed into us was to never show any fear, demonstrate impeccable behaviour and die a hero's death for the homeland!

After the defeat of France, the Tripartite Pact between Germany, Italy and Japan followed, with Hungary, Romania and the Slovak Republic joining afterwards. The possibility that the Soviet Union might also join was held 'open'. On the other side, Churchill formed a new British government and was preparing his country to enter the war with his famous phrase 'I have nothing to offer but blood, sweat and tears.' Spain refused to enter the war, despite Hitler holding two meetings with Franco.

Operation *Sea Lion* [the codename used by the Wehrmacht for their planned invasion of the United Kingdom] was soon abandoned as the German Luftwaffe was unable to achieve air superiority during the Battle of Britain, and indeed suffered heavy losses. The German Africa Corps, led by General Erwin Rommel, on the other hand, scored a great many victories over Britain, causing them to suffer heavy casualties. German troops who occupied Bulgaria, Hungary and Greece and landed there with parachutes suffered considerable losses.

On 10 May Rudolf Hess, the deputy to the Führer, boarded a Me 110 and flew himself to Scotland, made a parachute landing, and intended to initiate peace talks with the British. This prompted the government of the German Reich to declare him mentally ill, with the British taking him prisoner. At the end of the war, he was sentenced to life imprisonment in Spandau, but he committed suicide in 1987. The British only released records and files in respect of this event in 2015.

Deployed to Combat Unit 100 (KG 100)

Straight after finishing at the 'Great Fighter Pilot School', Klaus Müller and I were transferred to Kampfgruppe 100 [henceforth: Combat Unit 100], a special unit formed from parts of the Luftwaffe Signals School in Kotten and everyone flying the Heinkel 111 while using the latest equipment and systems of radio navigation (*X*- and *Y-Gerät*) that allowed pilots to find targets within a range of 500 metres. Bomber units would follow up at night and drop their lethal cargo on the targets marked by flares.

The process was relatively simple: by applying a particular frequency the radio beam from a single transmitter in the northern part of France would identify the target, for example Sheffield or Coventry, and a second transmitter was set up so its beam crossed the first guidance beam at the point where the bombs should be dropped. Beams from these pathfinders, the aircrafts of Combat Unit 100, would be carefully aimed to define a precise bomb-release trajectory.

It didn't take long for the British to identify our radar techniques and come up with counter-measures, such as setting up false beams and sending our machines wildly off course. Later, they deployed nightfighters equipped with rotating aerials and many more elements and shot down the pathfinders. As a result, the Luftwaffe's losses increased despite further developing our tactics, such as changing frequency, sending additional bad beams and installing automatic defence weapons in the tail unit.

Combat Unit 100 was stationed in Vannes-Meucon (in Brittany) and led by Captain (later Major) Aschenbrenner. We duly reported to the unit, hoping to be deployed for operation imminently, despite knowing full well that many machines often didn't return from their combat mission. The commander, however, refused our application, believing that we were too young and inexperienced, and instead dispatched Klaus Müller to Hanover-Langenhagen to join the reserve squad, while I was ordered to embark on leading an NCO training course on radio intelligence for Combat Group 100. Both of us were disappointed, but, in hindsight, this might have saved our lives.

Vannes was an interesting small town located on the Gulf of Morbihan. At first, we were booked into a large room in a hotel in the centre and were introduced to the secrets of radio navigation. The port was marked by a large crucifix standing on an elevated platform from which one had a splendid view over the Atlantic. One evening, we were in for a surprise: the famous Barnabas band provided musical entertainment lasting till the early hours of the morning, providing us with some light relief in such dark times. [Initially a personal favourite of Adolf Hitler, this band quickly became popular across the German Reich, with Barnabás von Géczy leading his versatile and talented orchestra and dance-band. By 1941, over 50 million listeners were tuning in to the regular and popular broadcasts by Géczy and his pianist Erich Kaschubec.]

When I had completed the training course in Vannes, they transferred my group on 19 July 1941 to Chartres, an impressive city with its massive cathedral looming over it, but our mood was low in the face of losing some of our crew to the war. At the time I was 'chief' of the ground unit and at one point travelled in an open-top BMW along the highway leading from Vannes to Chartres, when three low-flying squads attached to Combat Unit 100 zoomed past – what a sight to behold!

On 22 June 1941 German forces invaded the Soviet Union from the Baltic Sea to the Carpathian Mountains, taking us all completely by surprise. We couldn't comprehend why this was happening and why this decision had been taken. In his book *Mein Kampf,* Hitler himself wrote that the reason for Germany's failure in World War I was rooted in its two-front offensive. We were horrified! German soldiers were recalled from Italy, Romania, the Slovak Republic, Hungary and Finland and began marching into the expanses of Russia. At the end of October 1941, the front line ran from Lake Ladoga via Smolensk and Poltava to the Sea of Azov, and with that the siege of St Petersburg began. In October 1941 German tank units had arrived on the outskirts of Moscow, encircled and conquered Odessa and overran the Crimean peninsula, with only Sevastopol failing to fall into their hands.

Winter arrived early and unexpectedly. It was a winter that brought misery, chaos, immense suffering and proved the army's woeful shortcomings. We were completely unprepared. Meanwhile newly formed and rested Russian Siberian regiments embarked on a counter-offensive, and though Hitler had made some comments about the war in the east ending at Christmas-time, his target date was nothing but an illusion. He promptly dismissed Commander-in-Chief Brauchitsch and took over himself, alongside Himmler and his Waffen-SS, Göring's Luftwaffe and Raeder's navy.

Deployed to Operations in Russia

A very large part of the German flying units were transferred from France to the east and took off for operations from conquered airfields. These involved Messerschmitt and Focke-Wulf fighters, and fighting and reconnaissance units flying He 111, Ju 88 and Ju 87 planes. Our special unit was also ordered to leave France for Bobruisk on 1 August.

I was deployed to the 2nd Squadron of Combat Unit 100, but Klaus Müller was dispatched to the front line. The lodgings we were provided with were very basic, with neither a bathtub on site nor a toilet, leaving us to wash in a kitchenette using bowls of water. Food was served in a nearby canteen which belonged to Tes, an erstwhile Russian airbase. Senior Lieutenant Langer was my chief and also kept an eye on my first enemy operation. He had decided to leave behind his main observer and instead chose me as his co-pilot and observer. Sitting right next to him in the He 111, I had to my right the all-important radio equipment for direction finding, in front of me, covered by a sort of blind you could pull up, the Zeiss Lotfe-bombsight, and all the way at the front, two machine guns. After the evening briefing it became obvious that our mission was to attack Moscow, and in particular to destroy as many factories and train stations as we could target.

Senior Lieutenant Langer was an experienced pilot, having flown successful operations over Norway and England and was decorated with the Iron Cross First Class as well as the Narvik Shield [awarded to all German forces that took part in the battles of Narvik between 9 April and 8 June 1940]. In our crew we had radio operators, a flight engineer and one gunner. When we took off, the engineer sat behind us, squeezed into the tight corridor leading to the bomb shafts, but later on moved to the fuselage, where he operated the machine guns together with the gunner and observed what was happening on the ground. In the rack underneath the fuselage were stored some 2 tonnes of explosives.

The moon was shining, the engines revved up and then slowed down, and the airbase control flashed his 'green light'. Both engines rumbled into an instant roar which saw us speeding down the runway, lifting off just short of the end. Our course was set to 70 degrees, north-east. Gradually we climbed to an altitude of 4,000 metres and donned our oxygen masks. It was freezing cold. Coming closer to the front line, we could see a long stretch lit up by explosions and fires as far as the eye could see. The distance between Bobruisk and Moscow measured some 800 miles. Down below, radio beacons had been installed in Roslavl, Yukhnov and later on in Kaluga, making it easy for me to determine our position accurately.

We didn't have to press down on the plane's Morse code key. Approaching Moscow from the south, we were immediately greeted by accurate flak and fire, which luckily did not hit us. Large searchlights had been put up in the west of the city, their pale, corpse-like fingers reaching out for our German bombers. If an aircraft crossed one or two beams, they were immediately shot down by nightfighter planes. When the weather was calm, so-called barrage balloons floated in the sky which could easily tear off the wing of an aircraft and bring it down.

We executed a sharp turn and had Moscow below us, with the S-curve of the Moscow river and behind it the Kremlin clearly visible, despite us having reached an altitude of 6,000 metres by then. Drawing closer, we throttled back, sank lower, opened the Lotfe, and I took over control. Through the bombsight I could pinpoint the target with utmost precision, focusing on the crosshairs. The bomb-bay opened and our precisely calculated bombs dropped, carpeting the area below. With the aircraft significantly lighter, I closed the doors to the bomb-bay; breaking away, we looked at the fantastic scene caused by the explosions, with smoke rising from the burning factories and loading stations. Leaning into a wide sweeping curve, we left the danger zone behind us and headed west, our course set to approximately 240 degrees. It was a cloudless sky and the bright stars illuminated our way as we returned to base.

We contacted the ground crew and I was commended on the calm execution of my approach and how I had handled the instruments to position the aircraft, though at that point I was feeling hot and uncomfortable in my thickly lined flight suit. It was miraculous, really, that we hadn't had any enemy contact, hadn't been hit by flak, even though a hurricane of fire and explosions had filled the air.

All five of us sighed with relief as we crossed over the front line, for if we then had to make an emergency landing or bail out, the ground troops would have been able to assist. Landing was not a problem, as firing ceased whenever home aircraft were on their approach. Reaching for the flare gun mounted on the outside, right next to my seat, I fired a warning signal.

Several more operations earned me praise and commendations by my commander and Staffel captain, and after having been deployed to daytime ground attacks as well, I was given my own crew. Otto Siebert became my senior sergeant, an experienced pilot but not a daredevil, and radio operator Claes and flight engineer Ehmke made up our little group. I was the commander and had overall responsibility for anything relating to the operations. What followed was a string of relentless battles that saw us dispatched on one operation after another, interspersed by night outings to Moscow and frequent contact with artillery bombardment. I witnessed my friend Götz, who had trained with me back in Tutow, being shot down while flying close alongside us, caught by the claws of the searchlights. It was horrific to watch. Every single one of us was close to death at all times, but to reflect upon this reality was pointless; our nerves were at breaking point.

A little later I witnessed a nightfighter plane ramming the aircraft of my friend Klaus Müller, forcing him to make an emergency landing behind the front line. He turned up three days later with his pilot, but the rest of his crew had been killed, with Klaus and the other guy taken prisoner by Russians somewhere in no-man's-land. At first, Klaus and his comrade were threatened with execution, but for some reason were let go in the end. Lucky.

I didn't altogether escape danger either. With my engine hit by a flak salvo near Gomel, we were forced to toss out all the weapons and armour plates and managed to return using only one engine, but thankfully we did return. These are moments when the test of our nerves happens, with fear only coming later. During another flight my left wing was badly hit but the aileron was missed by just a few centimetres, and we soldiered on. Several more operations were launched every day, embroiling us in battles over Chernihiv, Konotop, Bryansk and Kursk, all intended to weaken the Soviet offensive. Spraying their infantry columns with splinter bombs and intense flak, we attempted to destroy them but failed. Our operations cost us heavy losses as practically skimming the ground at extremely low altitudes of 100 to 300 metres had us exposed to every single bullet. And yet, we had to persist and continue and annihilate all the cargo transports of the Russian railway, all of them heavily armed.

On 8 October we were moved further east to the Seschtchinskaya airfield, where we were lodged on its base. All officers except for the commander shared one large room, which was extremely basic and yet grand compared to what the poor chaps of the infantry had to live in during those days. They always waved to us from the ground and my only hope for them was that they'd survive this inferno.

At that time we had a change in command and Major Aschenbrenner, who disliked and hence avoided joining the actual sorties, was replaced by Major Küster, best known for being the 'last Prussian' and who had also been part of our training course back in Tutow. He was always correctly dressed, during operations as well, and chose to alternate the He 111 planes he boarded. Once it was this one, then another one, and he was intending to get to know the respective crews 'before the enemy did'. He'd sit in between the pilot and his observer in a sort of emergency seat and, donning a helmet with the intercom attached, he would listen in on the radio messages. It soon made the rounds that something was sure to happen in the particular plane where 'the old man' could be found. Before take-off, he had the crew report for duty, which was followed by the commander announcing that they were ready. 'Crew GN-GK complete with five men reported and ready for enemy attack, emergency equipment complete, machine tank full, bay loaded with so-and-so many bombs.' Nothing was left to chance. During daytime operations he even went as far as to check on the cleanliness of hands and fingernails.

When, one evening, he boarded our plane prepared for a night-time operation, we knew it boded ill. And indeed, I had to attempt the approach to Gomel three times, at an altitude of only 3,000 metres, with another He 111 zooming past our cockpit and nearly causing a collision, followed up by a bull's eye shot into our engine. Luckily, this only happened after we'd already got rid of our bombs. He proceeded to coach us as to what our strategy should have been, but I simply switched off his intercom and that was that.

Going down a bit lower, but still flying above enemy territory, I had the machine on a steady course and switched the intercom back on. 'Bull's eye,' I radioed, 'right engine cut off, flaps down, airscrew in feathered position, machine lowering 1 m/sec, briefly full throttle, climbing up to discard anything detachable and heavy, position X, landing in one hour.'

He then thumped my back. 'Excellent,' he smiled. 'Outstanding achievement, Lieutenant Menzel!' And after that, I never had any issues with the guy. After our emergency landing, we reported to the command headquarters and, thanking us all, he shook our hands – it was a lucky break.

After our landing and a quick stop to go to the toilets (there was none on board except for an enlarged 'condom' [sic] with a cork stopper) we filed our report with the operation officer, providing him above all with the details of the target area, the hits and the crashes observed, of enemy fighter planes, flak and the searchlights. This report was then compared with others, thus offering a fair overview of the situation, as alongside us, there were other squads carrying out attacks as well. Studying these, one also could uncover the odd 'cowardly fighter' who had decided to discard his bombs somewhere over an open field instead of attempting to hit the target.

After all that was taken care of, we received some 'post-midnight' dinner in the canteen, which was in fact an early breakfast, and we then hit the sack, protected by a mosquito net.

Another operation in which I was involved deserves a mention. The plan was a raid on a tank plant near Gorky, the main city in the Volga region [the bombing of Gorky by the Luftwaffe was the most destructive attack on Soviet war production on the Eastern Front in World War II]. The reason this raid was particularly noteworthy is because our gunner, 'Captain Thönssen' – he was given this title as he came from the navy – managed to destroy the flak's searchlights by accurate fire when flying low. Ingenious!

Once the German advance came to a halt in the middle section of the Eastern Front and we were hit by the brutal, severe winter, General Guderian redeployed nearly the whole of Combat Unit 100 to support the infantry, which in turn caused us to suffer such a high number of losses that in mid-November the unit, now consisting of only a few remaining aircraft, was transferred to Hanover-Langenhagen to be refitted and replenished. In the meantime my friend Klaus Müller and I had been awarded the Iron Cross Second Class, the Iron Cross First Class and the *Frontflugspange* (Luftwaffe Bomber Clasp) in bronze and silver and had turned into experienced fighter pilots at the age of barely twenty-one, with each of us having over 100 operations under his belt. However, being confronted on a daily basis with the reality of death caused us enormous emotional stress. The thought of how our operations brought us close to death, relentlessly and viciously, plagued us at night and robbed us of sleep.

Returning Home to Hanover

The period of time my friend Klaus and I spent at home was like paradise. We lodged in officers' quarters as if it were peacetime and recuperated. During Christmas 1941, however, we were on duty, charged with administrative tasks or with communication issues. While in the office, we got to see a photograph sent to us from London, showing a shot-down aircraft attached to my Staffel and its crew lined up in front of it. I had indeed witnessed that particular hit and had attempted to prevent it, so we were mightily relieved to hear that the comrades had survived. Sadly, they all died in Russia after being taken prisoners of war. It was a tragic ending that profoundly affected me.

Only married soldiers were allowed home at Christmas 1941, leaving Klaus and me, the youngest guys, to hold the fort. On the first day of the break, we decided to leave Langenhagen and take ourselves to Hanover, to the Karsten, the best hotel in town at the time. Seeing as we were highly decorated soldiers, the staff naturally gave us an excellent table, and the atmosphere was jolly as everyone was hoping that the war would end in 1942. Nonetheless, the two of us felt sad, as we hadn't been able to visit our families.

Then, suddenly, an older gentleman approached our table and introduced himself. 'May I say, good evening! Since my sons are about the same age as you both and are deployed in Russia, my wife and I are sitting alone and we would be delighted if you would agree to join us at our table. Would that be to your liking?'

This allowed us to spend a truly wonderful evening reflecting and discussing the situation. Time went so quickly that we missed the last bus and ended up legging it all the way back to Langenhagen at around midnight.

Something similar happened the following day, when my parents came for a visit and a lady from East Prussia (she was staying over in town) joined our table when we were having a meal in a restaurant. While chatting, my mother touched upon the dire situation we were facing with respect to the scarce food supply. Some days later my parents received a parcel with ham and sausages, rare delicacies at the time. We kept in touch with the lady until 1944.

Come New Year's Eve, Klaus and I got permission to travel home. During that visit I met up with Margret, my pen-pal from Nordhausen, when she also took the opportunity to inform me that, at the request of her parents, she would marry an older army doctor. That, of course, put an end to our wonderful and harmonious correspondence, though there had never been any mention of love. And yet I felt disappointed as, who knows, maybe something could have come of it.

Off to Romania

There was no point and no time to ponder the matter. An order I received over the telephone called me back to Hanover-Langenhagen on 2 January 1942. My group had already left for Focşani in Romania flying brand-new He 111 planes and I was to follow with a small section of three Ju 52. Weather conditions were fair which meant that I took off for Kraków on 5 January, but once close to the city it turned out that landing was impossible due to heavy clouds, forcing us to divert to the Dresden-Klotzsche airfield, which was clear. I took that as a sign, as on that very day my father celebrated his fiftieth birthday, with me now being his big surprise, walking through the door of our home and congratulating him.

Fortunately, Kraków was overcast for another two days, and then we were finally given permission to fly there. Upon arrival, we filled up our tanks to then continue onto Focşani without delay. Once in the air, bad visibility caused by a heavy snowstorm was reportedly making landing impossible and, to top it off, we were also running low on fuel.

An emergency landing was inevitable and we came down on the oil fields of Ploeşti, covered in deep snow. It all went well and two days later we finally touched down in Romanian Focşani, where they had been desperately waiting for us. By then our crews had already put behind them several operations on Sevastopol, which was being bravely defended by the Russians. During one of those missions my friend Piotter suffered a direct hit and was forced to perform an emergency landing in the sea. He was the only one to survive. He was floating in the sea with his life jacket on for over twelve hours, nearly unconscious, until a fishing boat picked him up. Back on firm ground, he told us that this way of 'dying' had brought him great comfort, as he didn't actually feel anything, no pain, no fear – he had curiously lost the will to live and was at peace.

After having completed a large number of operations, we were awarded the Romanian Medal for bravery and the *Krimschild* [the Crimea Shield, awarded for service between 21 September 1941 and 4 July 1942 for the capture of the Crimea].

Even now, when I reflect on the eery sensation I felt when pursued by an enemy aircraft who intended to shoot me down, I still get goosebumps.

Focşani was still relatively peaceful. You could go shopping, purchase food and even fur coats, so I decided to treat myself. I bought a musk fur collar for my leather coat, and two leather jackets, one for me and one for my sister. Of course I bargained and got the prices down as is customary in Romania. With my purchases under my arm, I suddenly bumped into Major Küster: 'How much did you pay for this?' he asked. 'Some 600 Lei.' He immediately sent off his aide to purchase him a similar collar and upon the guy's return he was called in to report to the major. How much had he paid, was Major Küster's question. The aide dutifully reported that he had paid the requested price of 1,200 Lei. 'Well,' I interjected, 'I bargained, of course, that's what got me the lower price!'

'A German officer does not bargain, Menzel, and keep that in mind!' he retorted, clearly annoyed. What could I say … the man had never visited the Balkans before.

After my twenty-first birthday, which we celebrated quite extensively in Focşani in the company of the Romanian officers, Klaus Müller and I were selected by General Martini. [Martini conceived and set up the Luftwaffe Luftnachrichten Abteilung 350 (Air Signals) in 1936. In 1938, he was promoted to major general and named Chief of Signal Affairs of the Luftwaffe. He was then elevated to General of Luftwaffe Signals Troops in 1941, and remained in this position until the end of war in May 1945.]

He withdrew us from the operations at the front line in order to attend general staff training. Though fully appreciative of the honour bestowed on us [only the best officers of each year were selected for general staff training], we were also sad to leave behind our comrades who continued to fight in the increasingly fierce operations, as nearly all officers were ordered to fly basically until their machines were shot down and crashed. This essentially spelled their death or led to them becoming prisoners of war. We had, in the meantime, become accustomed to a strange tradition of slicing off the egg-white of our breakfast fried eggs and then trying to fork the yolk 'without an accident' into our mouth. If we succeeded, we 'knew' that we'd return from our mission unscathed on that day. It was a habit that didn't leave me even after the war.

Klaus was transferred to the Radio Intelligence School in Pocking, Bavaria, whereas my school (Luftwaffe Signal Intelligence School 5) was located in Erfurt. Our group was deployed in Kropyvnytskyi [in central Ukraine]. We packed our bags, but also took along bomb crates that were no longer used and filled these with food, liquor, eggs and butter. Major Küster added two extra crates that I was to deliver to his family in Erfurt as we were all aware of the food shortages in Germany.

The train from Bucharest, reserved for those on furlough, pulled into Focşani on time and we boarded the first-class wagon with all our luggage. When the Romanian station master waved his signal for the train to leave, half of our luggage was still on the platform, so I bounded up to pull the emergency handle and Klaus drew his pistol and his shot barely missed the engine. The train stopped and we loaded the rest.

The German official overseeing the train, an elderly army captain, started to make enquiries about who had fired the shot. When he entered

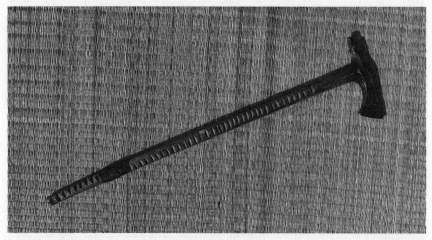

Every groove in Erich Menzel's axe represented a successful operation with his He III.

149

our compartment, we had already taken off our coats, which allowed him to verify that we were highly decorated '*Frontschweine*', and that was that. We had a few drinks with him later, celebrating that we were still alive after having flown a large number of missions.

At Erfurt Airbase

I arrived in Erfurt with all my luggage, made the delivery to Frau Küster and reported to the Signal Intelligence School, where I was signed up for the academy's training section. It just so turned out that here again I was the youngest lieutenant 'bedecked with tin' and was asked to give lectures to the officer corps on what we had accomplished in the east, the experience I had gained, and what life was like there. Once again, I was asked to head up a six-week training course for sergeants and I came away realising that young soldiers were still enthusiastic about the war. They all subsequently passed the exams and after completing a series of flights testing their skills on radio and radar equipment, they were awarded their certificates.

In Erfurt I also bumped into Jochen Stein, who had studied in my cohort back in Halle, and I also became friends with Ottheinrich Hertrich from Inzell, a resort town in Upper Bavaria where we were invited to spend our vacation after having been deployed in Romania. What a lovely time we had, and relatively peaceful! An invitation to a wedding in Radebeul was a further highlight in the summer of 1942 – Ruth Meister, who had in the meantime turned nineteen, was getting married to Artillery Sergeant Siegismund Meinhold, who was nine years older than her, and I was chosen to be the best man. Seeing as I had been a friend of the family and was Ruth's dance partner as well as her brother's tutor, I arrived in my dress uniform, complete with white cap and all my decorations. The festivities were stylish, of course, and took place at their home in Meissnerstrasse. Vater Meister was at the door. A major of the Reserves, he turned to me and exclaimed: 'Well, then, what's the Luftwaffe up to, Menzel, young chap?'

Ruth looked exquisite, but much too young to be getting married. Nonetheless, we got on well. Sergeant Meinhold came back home on

Erich as a best man (second from left) has a grim look on his face as,
in truth, he wanted to be the groom.

a visit only once after their wedding. He died in September 1943, shot
in the stomach while fighting in the Caucasus. That meant that the
beautiful Ruth's married bliss was short lived indeed, a mere few weeks,
as shortly after the nuptials her husband had to return to the front line,
and unsurprisingly never returned. Not long after their wedding Ruth's
doorbell rang and, based on army practice, a highly decorated soldier
stood there announcing in carefully-chosen words that her husband had
died for his country and the Führer and that she could take pride in that
fact. Ruth collapsed on the threshold, was lifted to a couch inside the
house and within an instant this youthful girl had turned into a grieving
widow. I so pitied her!

During the winter of 1942 the high command of the Luftwaffe sent me to
recuperate in Gampabing near Schruns in the Tyrol and because Ottheinrich
Hertrich happened also to be there we became even better friends.

Following many operations along the Mediterranean Sea, Jochen
Stein got married in October 1942 to a sweet little woman by the
name of Inge Kloos. To get to the church, we travelled in a festively
decorated tram through Dresden and were then invited to celebrate in

a well-known restaurant located along the River Elbe, the Italienisches Dörfchen [it still exists to this day]. At the table next to me sat Inge's sister, and the evening turned out to be very jolly, with the war seemingly far in the distance. All officers were in dress uniform, complete with the 'aiguillette', a silver bullion cord, a silver-buckled belt and a sword reaching down to the floor.

But the war wasn't quite as far away as we had hoped. The United States had, by then of course, entered the war, and with the Wehrmacht's 6th Army being defeated by the Soviets at the Battle of Stalingrad, people started speaking in hushed tones about the beginning of Germany's downfall. But one had to be cautious in respect of voicing negative comments, as any sort of subversion was punishable by death.

Margot Klein came to visit me in Erfurt and maybe she thought of marriage, but I really didn't feel any desire whatsoever to commit. A few months later I received a notice that she was set to marry Werner Meyer, an SS officer.

At the Luftwaffe Radar Test Centre

In January 1943, totally out of the blue, I was transferred to the newly created Erprobungsstelle der Luftwaffe für Funkmessgeräte (Luftwaffe Test Centre for Radar Devices), which was responsible for testing and developing targeting devices for air and maritime reconnaissance. Only later did I find out that Major August Hentz had been responsible for this transfer and that he had pressed the issue with General Martini from the Signal Intelligence Corps. It was great to meet up with my friend Klaus Müller, who had been promoted to senior lieutenant along with me and who then served as an aide to the commander. Werneuchen, located between Berlin and Frankfurt an der Oder, was indeed a peaceful sort of place at the time; nothing about the war seemed to have filtered through yet.

Our task was to test airborne and ground-based radar devices and study captured equipment. The devices we developed ourselves were to be used by the fighter planes. In order to test equipment effectively, we had to fly planes fitted with devices used by the enemy even during actual operations, which in turn allowed us to come up with the respective defence devices. Serious and critical issues arose that required solutions.

The high command of the Luftwaffe [Oberkommando der Luftwaffe, OKL] consisted mainly of soldiers who had fought in World War I and who consequently weren't up to speed with modern technology. The sore lack of expert engineers who were properly trained and available was hugely troubling. The army even resorted to pulling some physicists out the front line and transferred them directly to our group. The scientific know-how demonstrated by the Allies, above all by the Americans, far exceeded what we were able to do, and as the war dragged on, this became increasingly obvious. The various German firms such as AEG, Siemens, Telefunken, Lorenz or Askania didn't coordinate with each other and their respective research sometimes ran in parallel despite the OKL's technical branch doing everything it could to get this under control.

Several groups were answerable to Major Hentz: the staff of the signals division – and I was one of them – and the technical test centre led by Sergeant Major Hans Gienecke, who'd later become a very close friend of mine, as well as the entire airbase command centre headed up by Lieutenant Colonel Helm who had previously flown for the Lufthansa airline.

This airbase command centre under Helm included all the guards, the entire staff serving in the canteens and the officers' mess, then all the communication centres and the ground staff controlling air traffic. Major Hentz, in turn, was accountable to Petersen, chief of the entire Erprobungsstelle der Luftwaffe in Peenemünde [which tested experimental aircraft and also developed night navigation and radar systems].

My office was housed in the command centre building and I shared it with Senior Lieutenant (later Captain) Gose, a very experienced pilot who came to us from the Flugfunk Forschungsinstitut Oberpfaffenhofen (FFO) [the Air Radio Research Institute, though at that time the research was stopped and instead concentrated on developing processes and devices for the war effort]. Gose wasn't just an outstanding pilot but a hugely talented inventor, with whom I completed most of my test flights.

We at the institute discovered that thin aluminium strips cut to a certain length [codenamed 'Window' by the British] simulating

Erich Menzel in his office.

aircraft echoes and ejected from enemy planes were jamming our radio equipment, with the aim of confusing and distracting us. The cathode-ray tube display was compromised, resulting in us being unable to locate the target. Our respective *Gekados Meldungen* [*Geheime Kommandosachen*, top secret information] was filed with Göring and his staff, and this produced a terse one-line response: 'Put your files behind lock and key so that the enemy is not informed.'

Instead of developing counter-measures, nothing happened. This was until the deadly raid on Hamburg had been carried out, with Mosquito planes ejecting tons of these strips which completely clouded our radar. Nothing worked! We developed devices such as Hohentwiel, Lichtenstein and SN2 to equip nightfighters to locate ships and trains, and airborne radars for air interception, targeting enemy planes at high altitudes.

Several older commanders were opposed to installing the required antennas, since they caused drag and slowed down the aircrafts. And then there was a Professor Hinzpeter, who then successfully invented a device operating at a higher frequency against the 'Window' that was based on the Doppler effect, and he was subsequently awarded the War Merit Cross.

Although life seemed calm, it wasn't entirely without its dangers. When I returned to the Werneuchen airfield, flying one of the FW 200 Condors, I was only able to lower the right wheel of my undercarriage as the left one was jammed. Much good advice, such as hand-cranking the mechanism, was radioed up by the ground crew, but it was to no avail, and we were ordered to divert to Berlin-Tempelhof, where they all stood in readiness: fire engines, an ambulance and a crowd of spectators. But my good friend Senior Lieutenant Wrede, who'd later become a captain flying with Lufthansa, didn't disappoint as he very gently touched down with one wheel only. It turned out that the machine had only suffered minor breakage, which was reason enough for the guys to welcome us back over a glass of sparkling wine.

Then it was my friend Klaus Müller who announced his wedding, which was to take place in Radebeul with me, once again, asked to be the best man. My commander, Major Cerener at the time, released me from duties even though I was about to embark on a critical test flight with the Condor and Sergeant Gose in the pilot seat. So, off I went to the wedding, followed by an evening celebration held in the Bussard wine cellar when I got a telephone call with the shocking news that the FW 200 had been shot down by a Mosquito. Had I not been given permission to attend the wedding … Well, I'd be lying in a grave. Unimaginable!

The next day saw me drive alongside Major Cerener to Brannenburg am Inn to bring Frau Gose the news of her husband's death. I found these kinds of assignment personally very disturbing, as witnessing a young woman's world just crashing right in front of you is a deeply upsetting experience. Here was a young couple who had dreamt of creating a family and dreamt of a peaceful world where nothing was amiss. And then, before me, stood a distraught wife receiving the news that none of this would ever happen, that her husband had been killed.

The moment Frau Gose set eyes on us standing on her threshold, she of course knew. She remained composed, however, and simply covered her eyes with her hands to hide her pain. Asking us to step inside, she then gratefully listened to our memories of experiences we had shared with her husband. Well aware that once we had left she would be filled by emptiness, we, as we so often did, concluded that war has simply no regard for human life.

During a stay with friends in Berlin we were rushed into the air-raid shelters, listening to the relentless bombing, and then decided to stay on and help citizens to extinguish the fires. The suffering these people had to endure was quite unbelievable! Houses had collapsed, turned into heaps of rubble, many still ablaze, and dead bodies lay strewn on the streets and needed to be recovered.

In the partially destroyed Berlin opera building we listened to a concert with the young Karajan, eyes closed, conducting Beethoven's symphonies. Dressed in our winter coats and shivering in the unheated hall, we kept asking ourselves: 'When will it be our turn?'

Thanks to our equipment we could listen to all foreign broadcasts, and we knew: the war was lost. Nonetheless, we had to continue our efforts, and we kept on flying. As of 1944 we collaborated closely with the Kriegsmarine, which led me to fly the He 111 to test the potential impact U-boats could have and also saw me deployed to a U-boat that participated in the naval campaign in the Baltic Sea.

At one point, it was around midnight, I flew with my aircraft above the battleship *Gneisenau*, having alerted them previously that I'd be launching a fully lit test torpedo that would be landing amidships. In response, the naval crew fired wildly at us with all their guns, sending waves of tracers in our direction and trying to shoot us down. The flak battalion had obviously not been informed, and we zoomed off at breakneck speed while the shells exploded nearby, lighting up the sky.

Sometime later I was court-martialled in Szczecin, accused of causing death by negligence. What had happened was that when carrying out a test flight over a specified grid-square just short of Gdańsk on board a U-boat of the type VIIC with a rubber coating to avoid detection, air traffic control suddenly spotted a second boat which hadn't previously contacted them. Tethered to the boat by a cable was a 300-metre high kite. But, hovering some 10 metres above the water, we crossed the wrong boat, our propeller cut the cable, and the lookout (observer pilot) plunged straight down into the water and died. After we had landed, we noticed a 10-cm gash in our propeller. A split second was all that stood between life and death, but we were acquitted.

Transfer to Tokyo as Luftwaffe Attaché

Considering what had happened to me, I was quite surprised when General Martini transferred me as radar specialist to the Luftwaffe attaché staff in Tokyo in the autumn of 1944. This assignment should have been kept under wraps, but soon afterwards, radio broadcasts from London and Moscow mentioned our names, such as General Ulrich Kessler, appointed by Göring as Luftwaffe attaché, Colonel von Sandrart and Senior Lieutenant Stepp.

The Japanese *Tenno* [emperor in Japanese] and his general staff were prepared for a war of aggression but hadn't been trained for defence. The *Tenno*, therefore, directly approached Hitler, Göring and Dönitz and requested specialists to be deployed for the following: the production of fighter-interceptors to defend against attacking enemy aircraft, particularly bombers; the creation of a proper air defence on Japanese territory; the installation of communication devices for early detection of approaching units, which meant ground-based radar and airborne radar devices, including know-how with respect to operating them (as these had been retrieved from a four-engine American bomber which had crashed). Furthermore, we were to share with them our empirical findings on attacking submarines and how to defend against them, as well as checking over their naval activities.

Twelve officers were part of the Luftwaffe attaché's staff, while the naval attaché's office had six, including engineers operating the naval radar. The plan was for an aircraft to take off from Petsamo, an airfield located in the north of Finland, near Murmansk, fly across Russia and then continue straight to Japan. An FW 200, equipped with additional tanks and crates containing a Leica, white tropical uniforms, fabric for suits, elegant underwear and new uniforms, was loaded up. This whole operation was supposedly top secret and yet even the girls working in the insurance offices kept asking me whether I too was headed for Japan.

Senior Lieutenant Schumann was tasked with serving as General Kessler's aide and I accompanied him to Brandenburg to attend a first meeting with the general. We had barely arrived at the airbase when the Liberator bombers opened up on us and we were subjected to a carpet of bombs that whistled past us and exploded. Trying to get clear of it and running for my life, I came away with little more than a superficial wound caused by shrapnel. I had flung myself into a ditch and buried my head into the ground, thus avoiding the marker, while my cameraman who intended to photograph the spectacle was killed. My He 111, meanwhile, was reduced to flaming wreckage.

Discussions with Kessler were frank and fair. Previously deployed to the Fliegerführer Atlantik [the naval air command supporting the Kriegsmarine's operations in the Battle of the Atlantic], he had been opposed to Göring, who then basically shoved him off to Tokyo. To us lot it was totally clear that the war had been lost by then and that the transfer to Japan was pointless.

Petsamo was captured by the Russians in autumn 1944, and in September an armistice was signed between Finland on one side, and the Soviet Union and the United Kingdom on the other. In light of these political events, my flight to Japan seemed too precarious, because Japan had not yet entered into war with Russia and if our plane was forced to make an emergency landing on Russian territory, it would certainly have complicated matters. The decision, therefore, was for us to travel to Japan on submarines. But nobody could quite make their mind up as to who should travel and with which boat. Naturally, this delayed our departure from Kiel which, as luck would have it, allowed me to remain in Werneuchen and pop over to Radebeul, where I helped celebrate my parents' silver wedding anniversary. During my visit I got together with my erstwhile dance partner Ruth – she too dressed in black as her husband had been killed in 1943. Along with her parents she was visiting an anti-aircraft position quite near to our house and where her brother served. He had been called up at the age of seventeen, without ever graduating from high school. Ruth was twenty-one, I was twenty-three, and we fell in love. We made music together and enjoyed each other's company; we became inseparable.

Ruth was working as an assistant doctor – she hadn't quite finished her formal studies – in the Radebeul hospital. Every hour we spent together was precious. Once, when Ruth came for a visit to our home, I'd cycled her back to her house on my bike and got stuck in the snow piled up along the road and in the tram tracks and we toppled over and landed on the pavement, unhurt. We had fun. In November 1944 Ruth visited me in Werneuchen and we decided to get married the minute we knew that we had both survived this ghastly war. My parents, at least, could rest easy in the knowledge that they'd gain a daughter-in-law who was charming, intelligent and studied medicine.

In December 1944 groups each consisting of three attaché staff members were allocated to four submarines, all carrying secret documents. Just shortly before getting underway, however, Dönitz decided that these boats would not leave for Japan, which meant the general was forced to reduce his onboard team to six members, and this again gave rise to a whole slew of discussions. He, however, was very keen to keep me on board, firstly because we really got on well on a personal level and could communicate with each other openly, but secondly because the particular U-boat earmarked for this trip had been equipped with the Hohentwiel maritime patrol radar, which I knew how to operate [this was a surface search radar adapted to shipborne use]. And besides that, we would both happily join Colonel Sandrart in a jolly Skat game.

Once again we experienced delays but it turned out well for me. I was able to spend Christmas at home and New Year's Eve with my friend Hans Türcke in his home in Berlin, though I was completely drunk by midnight and no longer good company after that. Fortunately everyone was well aware of the 'suicide missions' I was involved in and the stressful impact these had on me. In 1945 his home was bombed and Hans Türcke's parents along with his sister were killed.

In mid-January General Kessler and his team, by then shrunk to five officers, were ordered to make arrangements to travel by train from Berlin to Kiel at the beginning of February. At Kiel, we were to take a ship to Oslo and then continue by railway to Bergen, where we'd board a larger U-boat, U-854, navigated by Captain Wolfram. However, the repairs it had to undergo after suffering snorkel damage during a prior attack were not completed. This gave rise to me being granted further leave and I returned home to celebrate my twenty-fourth birthday with my parents, Margit and Ruth. But on 20 January it was time for me to say goodbye, a sad departure as it was well known that 90 per cent of all German U-boats were sunk.

Nobody knew whether I would return or not and, frankly, I didn't really want to think about how it might feel if our boat were spotted, fired at, with no one able to escape as the water rushed in. And yet I couldn't banish such thoughts altogether and I will readily admit that I was scared stiff. It would, I feared, be no different than being in a life-and-death struggle while in an aircraft engaged in action. Being trapped in one of those damned submarines and struck by a torpedo would be slow, dark and terrifying. And though I had taught myself to suppress my feelings and remain highly focused and operate my equipment mechanically, I became increasingly apprehensive. Indeed, even today I feel uneasy about boarding a plane, deep down always fearing that I am climbing into my own grave.

Once, when visiting Ruth on one of my vacations from the Luftwaffe, I annoyed her with my insistence on first and above all establishing the best escape route from her lodgings. Obviously, such fears had deeply embedded themselves into my psyche. In order to find calm in these times of inner turmoil I took to playing my harmonica, both when serving with the Luftwaffe and on board the U-boat. My repertoire was eclectic, with Christmas songs, folk tunes, just anything that popped into my mind. My comrades joined me and sang along as we temporarily managed to scare away the evil ghosts of war.

Departure for Japan

Our journey to Bergen proceeded via Oslo, where we were taken to the local officers' lodgings and received a meal. The fact that we survived this trip was actually due to the lethal aerial bombing attack on Dresden launched by the Allies on 13 February 1945. It appeared that Dresden was their single most important target and they focused on nothing else.

That night, tucked away in Oslo, I was able to reach Ruth in the clinic by telephone and got the reassuring news that she and her family were all safe and that the incendiary bomb that had hit my family home could be extinguished.

After some days had passed and despite receiving nothing but catastrophic Wehrmacht updates reporting on defeat, destruction and devastation we took the train to Bergen which takes you through the most beautiful landscape. Unforgettable! After more than fifteen hours' train ride we arrived at the U-boat pen and were greeted by a group of depressed marine officers. The submarine designated for our journey had been bombed by a Mosquito just short of entering the harbour and sunk with the entire crew and guests on board. All were killed.

What were we supposed to do? Secretly we hoped that this would be the end of our assignment. But then again, what would be our alternative? In the face of total defeat, we could neither escape to Sweden nor find a hiding spot in the Norwegian mountains. Had we chosen the first option, the Swedes would have immediately handed us over to the Russians, and the second option would have been tantamount to desertion, and if German soldiers discovered us we would have been executed. And had we fallen into the hands of the Norwegians, much the same fate would have befallen us.

Discussions in Berlin revolved around whether we should sail to Japan at all, and if so on which boat. Then, suddenly, I was ordered by the OKL to join the flying units in Trondheim and train them in radar technology, in preparation to attack Allied convoys headed for Murmansk.

Surprisingly, all trains were still operating in Norway, though heavily guarded by the military. I took the train from Bergen to Oslo, again enjoying the spectacular views, reported to Luftwaffe commander General Kühne in Oslo and then travelled to Trondheim; it was all quite leisurely. Whatever I offered to the crew, clever as it might have been, didn't appeal. They seemed quite prepared to capitulate and pitied me as they all pointed to the fact that I was heading for Japan. Lodging in private quarters in Trondheim, I mistakenly left my dog-tag behind in my room and, if I was killed somewhere later on and my dead body were found, it wouldn't have been possible to identify me. But, quite honestly, when I realised my error, I didn't much care any more, and General Kühne, to whom I reported the details with respect to my efforts, showed no interest either. He was pretty much finished due to the desperate situation we were all facing.

On the U-234

Back in Bergen I was informed that the large U-234 (a Type XB originally built as a minelaying submarine but completed as a long-range merchant submarine) was to sail from Kiel to Japan. Due to the space constraints, only three Luftwaffe crewmembers were allowed on board, with General Kühne selecting General Kessler, Colonel Sandrart and me. The fact that the other three officers promptly complained didn't help them one bit. They, of course, were rather relieved to stay on in Norway and wait out the end of the war, as nobody really believed that this submarine would ever return from Japan. At the very least, we all knew that the voyage was going to be highly risky seeing as the Allies had full command over the sea at that point.

Worried, we returned to Oslo with all our luggage and expected the boat to arrive at Horten, the main base of the Norwegian navy. My entire radar file with all its documents had been stored on microfilms, which in turn had been welded into metal containers. When the boat finally landed, the general ordered me to board with both my luggage and his fishing gear. Captain Falcke even gave me a hand stowing the many items – private and official material and kit – showing me a few tricks of how to make optimal use of limited space.

After that, I was provided with my 'U-boat pack', which contained a diving suit (a kind of leather frogman suit), the traditional souwester (collapsible oil skin hat), scarves, underwear including thermal items, and socks. It was time to test the boat and, when submerged, we rammed into another boat, resulting in essential repairs in Kristiansand. It was quite embarrassing, to say the least. Unsurprisingly, the question being asked was whether we would even manage the voyage to Japan under this commander. The ballast tank had ripped apart and needed to be welded, and because there was no dock available, the bow was flooded in order to raise the stern out of the water, thus enabling the repair to be carried out.

At the beginning of April we were all set to sail. Apart from our crew under the command of Captain Hein Fehler, we had two high-ranking Japanese officers who had officially bequeathed their swords to the commander back in Kiel, a symbol to say that they were entrusting

Lieutenant Commander Hideo Tomonaga.

their lives to him. Their names were Lieutenant Commander Hideo Tomonaga, a submarine engineer, and Genzo Shoji, an aircraft specialist and former naval attaché.

Furthermore, we had two civil engineers who were dispatched by the Messerschmitt production department and carried with them designs and drawings pertaining to the construction of the Me 262, the most advanced German aircraft – a light bomber, reconnaissance and nightfighter – which was far superior to any of the Allies' fighter planes. Their names were Bringewald and Ruff.

We also had Gerhard Falcke, a naval attaché, Nieschling, a naval fleet judge advocate who was to rid the German diplomatic corps in Japan of the remnants of a spy ring, Dr Schlicker, a scientist and radar specialist, and Senior Lieutenant Hellendorn, an expert in shipboard counter-measures.

Three Luftwaffe officers made up the rest: General Kessler, Colonel von Sandrart and me, who was an aeronautical communications and radar expert. We all had diplomatic passports and visas, which the Japanese embassy in Berlin had issued just for this trip. Among the 300-tonne cargo (including three Messerschmitts, other aircrafts, an airborne radar, bombsight computer and a lot of other equipment) it also contained ten canisters with 560 kg of uranium oxide to be used by the Japanese for the production of synthetic methanol towards the development of future atomic energy and weapons.

Captain Hein Fehler was thirty-four years old and, to my mind, a calm, reflective and thoroughly decent officer who had been on the legendary auxiliary cruiser *Atlantis*. After it sank twenty-two neutral merchant vessels in the Indian Ocean and the South Atlantic, it was sunk by the British cruiser HMS *Devonshire*. Part of the crew survived, was picked up by a submarine operating in the area and after an adventurous passage reached a French port. In 1942 Fehler became an instructor at the naval war academy in Mürwick, after which he completed several courses in Pillau, Flensburg and Travemünde that trained him up to the rank of submarine commander. In March 1944, instead of being assigned to attack enemy vessels, he was ordered to command U-234, designed to lay mines, but now converted to a merchant ship for its voyage to Japan. The ship was also fitted with a snorkel which enabled it to motor beneath the surface while powered by diesel engines.

It was easy for me to have meaningful chats with Fehler as we got along extremely well and trusted each other. He was an utterly responsible captain who was of course well aware that our chances of survival weren't great at all. With the war in its final stages, we not only carried important cargo on board but we also had to traverse dangerous waters absolutely teeming with the enemy. Hein Fehler never lost his nerve and only had one aim: to get us all out of there alive.

Dönitz himself wanted to decide on the date we were to set sail. Delayed three times, we were led to believe that perhaps some high-up Reich officials wanted to leave the country and that we needed to wait for their arrival. We finally departed on 15 April 1945 but remained puzzled, as the war had practically ended. Japan, however, was still at war and had paid for the valuable material on board with foreign currency, some 5 million dollars' worth of mercury stored away at the bottom of the U-boat. Then there were all the blueprints and construction drawings as well as the Japanese crates with U-235 written on them and filled with uranium oxide ore (for use as fuel in nuclear reactors). The labelling referred to a uranium isotope, but was meant to be a red herring as our boat was the U-234 whereas the U-235 had accidentally been sunk by a German torpedo on 10 April 1945.

Considering the food reserves on board and the fuel in our tanks we could have remained at sea for several weeks and not required any further supplies. We could have easily navigated around Cape Horn and the Cape of Good Hope near Cape Town. We were bound for Penang [George Town], a base for submarines under Japanese occupation in Malaysia and from there we would have continued to Kobe in Japan.

The mood on board was at a low, except for the Japanese officers. Seeing as most submarines had been sunk thanks to the Allies' finely tuned tactics, we were conscious that this was a suicide mission, and yet the commander kept promising us: 'My aim is to return all of you back home, alive and well.' And with that his order was clear: 'Set sail!'

The British and Americans were, of course, well aware of our departure date. After the auxiliary vessel had left us on the evening of 15 April, U-234 ran at snorkel depth and remained submerged for several hours, which confused search aircraft and ships as they weren't able to determine its location.

As I was familiar with navigating a submarine, I wasn't at all surprised at the alarms being sounded. The cabin that I shared with Senior Lieutenant Hellendorn was located at the bottom, but much like all the others, we too had to be on guard duty, because the two of us on board were the reason other crewmembers had been rejected. A typical watch rotation was four hours. While on the starboard side of the conning tower, my job was that of a lookout; inside I worked as the communications officer liaising with headquarters.

My Voyage with the Oceangoing Minelayer U-234

At 2130 hours we glided out of Kristiansand, then remained stationary till dawn broke. A few hours later, still submerged, we travelled at a speed of 2 nautical mph. The snorkel mast complicated our routine. The boat dived to a depth of some 14 metres. The snorkel, which takes in air from above the surface allows the diesel engines to continue running, powering the boat and recharging the batteries. It consisted of two tubes, one for intake, the other for exhaust. But when the sea was rough or if the boat was steered incorrectly, the ballcock valve (that prevents seawater from being sucked into the diesel engines) would slam shut and the engines would then draw the air from inside the boat itself. In turn, the engine exhaust fumes fill the hull, breathing becomes difficult, the drop in air pressure causes painful earaches and eyes to start hurting. To offset this, one could bring the boat closer to the surface. It happened to us three times that the boat accidentally surfaced. With that, the order 'All hands forward!' was given and all the men dashed to the bow in order to use their weight to bring the boat below sea level again.

And if the planesmen at the control station used the wheels incorrectly, the snorkel would submerge and the game would start all over again.

On 21 April, now surfaced as the sea was too rough for the snorkel and radar to function properly, we were positioned about 90 nautical miles north-north-east of Shetland.

On 22 April, our first Sunday on board, we were submerged, listening to the first depth charges launched at us.

On 24 April by periscope we spotted four aircraft on patrol. That means an immediate crash dive, but fortunately we remained undetected and weren't attacked. Later on, with the help of our sound-detection gear, we heard some propeller noise and continued at a snail's pace to remain undetected.

Then on 27 April we surfaced in a sea scale of 8 (very rough seas) and gale force 10 storm. I was on the second watch, which meant I had to spend another four hours on the conning tower dressed in my diving suit and souwester, with two towels wrapped around my neck and my belt with an iron chain attached hooked up to the tower. From the bridge we had a fascinating view, despite the darkness: waves with long white breaking crests threatened to topple the boat and bury us in the ice-cold sea. Breathing became impossible. The next moment the boat was lifted by an immense force as if it was a toy, to then be swallowed up in the crest.

The storm was fierce and the visibility practically nil, but it meant that we didn't have to fear an aerial attack, not even by radar. But then, suddenly, there were audible 'pings' coming from the ASDIC system and we immediately dived deep. Totally drenched, I scrambled down the tower ladder, fell to the ground and was immediately pulled away to make room. I was a bit the worse for wear, but intact. Then the boat submerged to a depth of some 100 metres, and it would all have been fine had it not been for the depth charges. This is what we were confronted with: beneath the keel was 4,000 metres to the sea bed, and above us was, at best, 200 metres of water, and the nearest land was some 1,000 nautical miles away – all in all we were not filled with any confidence. In comparison, when in an aircraft one eventually, one way or another, gets down to earth. But under water? Well, that's a different story.

On 28 April we were positioned 120 nautical miles north of the Faroe Islands and 135 nautical miles south-east of Iceland. The waters were exceptionally heavy and we surfaced. During my watch I was hooked up again, of course with hail and rain whipping against my face, and I simply thought to myself that it couldn't get much worse.

We spent 29 April listening to a concerto of depth charges exploding and feeling the shockwaves, but luckily they were hitting other targets. We had not been discovered.

On 30 April our sonar system picked up two combat fighters and we spotted smoke traces on the horizon. Nothing to do but go back below the surface! Our speed was greatly reduced and all crew off duty were back in their cabins, no word was uttered and we focused instead on breathing calmly. Would we survive this? Would we ever get back home and see our families again? Or would we be hit by an explosion and drown?

On 1 May we heard the news of Hitler's 'hero's death'. While the Japanese expressed their deepest condolences, they still insisted that our destination remain Japan. Personally, I had some issues with that, seeing as the war would surely be over quite soon. Wouldn't that raise the question of whether continuing our voyage to Japan made sense? Where would this lead us? Our heads were buzzing with all the possibilities.

On 2 May, at midnight, we were positioned 60.55 north, 15.45 west. More bombs detonated, straining our nerves. Meanwhile I discovered that my large suitcase stored away in the forward mine compartment was covered by a layer of mould. The general had emptied his, filled it with potatoes and left it right next to mine. I covered it as best as I could with a thick oil cloth. In my time off I played chess with Tomonaga and harmonica with Hellendorn and Bringewald. Playing chess, we didn't speak and instead focused on our moves; we felt anxious and were both aware how laden with tension the atmosphere was. Tomanaga was a highly intelligent comrade, a friend whom one could really rely on.

In the days between 3 and 8 May, when we had surfaced to get stronger signals, we heard about the end of the war. Our position on 8 May was 55.25 north, 23.24 west.

Capitulation

On 9 May the commander picked up a shortwave transmission announcing Germany's unconditional surrender. Dönitz, who had taken over as head of state from Hitler, issued an order to all U-boats to surface and return to the Allied ports. This 'would save millions of Germans in the east', was the message. Then we received a radio message from Captain Rösing in Bergen that we either continue sailing to Japan or return to Norway. Allied broadcasts also called on all U-boats to surrender, otherwise they would be treated like 'pirates' – that was the warning.

Huge discussions took place on board during the following days, from 10 to 13 May, among all ranks and in all rooms. Firstly, we established that considering the situation we were in, we no longer were bound to our oath to Adolf Hitler. A unanimous decision followed, confirming that Captain Lieutenant Fehler should remain in his position as commander and be ultimately responsible for our boat.

A Reuters report informed us that Japan had broken off diplomatic relations with Germany and that finally clarified once and for all that our voyage to Japan was not going ahead. The Japanese officers were briefed on the recent events and at the same time guards were put in place to ensure they didn't sink the boat. An open and frank talk between them and our commander convinced them not to entertain any such thoughts.

Seeing as they were submarine specialists, they could have quite easily gone ahead and sunk the boat. In return, Captain Lieutenant Fehler assured them that nobody would stand in their way, should they choose to commit suicide.

At the same time we motored southwards through the water at full speed. We had radio contact with Halifax in Canada, but reported an incorrect position, which resulted in radio silence.

Heated arguments raged between us with respect to what should happen to both us and the vessel. This is how I would describe the scene:

The married fellows wanted to return to Kiel, but this was not possible due to the Allied orders and would have meant that we'd all be taken prisoners of war.

Those still single wanted to head to the Caribbean Islands or Hawaii, which was wishful thinking and would have also landed us in captivity.

The general and the colonel had Argentinian citizenship and suggested we sail to Buenos Aires and sell the boat to President Peron, thus allowing us to start all over again in a foreign country – a suggestion which was roundly rejected by nearly every officer. Much the same reaction was expressed with respect to travelling to Canada.

The Japanese requested we travel to Ireland, perhaps even Spain so that we wouldn't have to hand over our precious cargo to the Allies, which after all they had paid for in gold. That too was rejected.

That really left the commander with only one choice, which was to steer the boat into US waters and surrender to the Americans. Nobody objected to this decision, except for the Japanese, who had a horror of surrendering to the American enemies.

On 14 May our two Japanese friends took an overdose of Luminal and committed suicide behind their closed door, but we had sort of suspected this would happen. Nobody verbalised it as such, but from the beginning it was clear to us that suicide was the only available option for these two fabulous comrades. We didn't hear a sound coming from their cabin. After about two days we opened the door and found them dead, lying on their beds. We could still hear some rasping, very faintly, but they weren't conscious any more. We allowed them to die and our doctor didn't intervene. We were downcast – hardly anyone spoke.

Luminal was a strong sleeping pill which they carried on them for 'emergency situations'. The bushido, the moral code of the samurai, prefers death over captivity. With the USA and Japan still at war, the option of surrendering to the enemy voluntarily would have been unthinkable for these two Japanese men.

We wrapped them up in canvas sheets and stitched these up, but made sure to weigh them down with some iron and to include their samurai swords and documents. Burying them at sea with full military honours, my thoughts drifted to the pleasant hours I spent playing chess with Tomonaga during which he shared with me stories about his family and his country. Weeks or months later, Tomonaga would surely have realised that his suicide was just as meaningless as the war. But, of course, his decision to take his own life could not be reversed.

At lunch time we noticed signals on our Hohentwiel radar system and indeed a destroyer soon appeared. Red signal signs blinked their meanings: 'Boat?'

'U-234. Nationality?'

'US. Speed?'

'8nm.'

'Course 250', instructed the Americans.

'Okay.'

And that was it – nothing more and nothing less. With that we journeyed into captivity, short and painless. The US destroyer *Sutton* appeared alongside, all guns pointing at us. We felt crushed, utterly powerless, and it left me feeling literally dizzy.

It was a busy night on board, with everyone packing his most essential belongings into a self-made duffel bag or whatever other bag they could get their hands on. Secret documents and other materials were chucked overboard, with the most important items stored away in the minetubes. This included the uranium oxide 235, parts of the Me 262 jet aircraft, and my entire research into radar technology. The atmosphere vacillated between being very low to rather more positive as we recognised that the war was finally over after six years and we, compared to millions of others, were still alive. Our thoughts, nevertheless, kept returning to those two Japanese men whose deaths had moved us all. Packing up my briefcase and my flight kit, I tossed a bottle of cognac into my luggage – and that was me done. My *Flieger Kappmesser* [airman's cutting knife – used for cutting trapped parachutes from their rigging, cutting through harnesses or the hull, or for fighting] was dear to me, so I hid it inside the lining of my trouser leg.

On Tuesday, 15 May 1945 at 0800 hours the destroyer ordered us to stop and make way for the *Sutton* boarding party – it was exactly when I started my watch. It only took thirty minutes before an American officer climbed down the ladder along with a few of his marines, armed to the teeth, and headed to the commander's cabin. The soldiers then installed a telephone line reaching from the tower and through the boat, and we handed in our weapons and gathered in the officers' canteen. The boarding party officer read out Admiral King's statement declaring us prisoners of war of the American Navy based on the Allied regulations and that we had to obey their orders. It all took place in a very proper and polite tone of voice.

All the passengers and two-thirds of the boat's crew had to leave the boat and hastily pack their briefcases and bags. We were promised that we could collect the rest of our stuff, mostly private belongings, back at the port. Back on the bridge I realised that the destroyer was very close up to our boat and all the guns were still pointed in our direction. Once we had all gathered on the bridge, our crew took down the German war flag and, for the last time, we saluted by raising our hands and tipping the rim of our officers' caps. The Americans also saluted the flag – it was an impressive gesture. One of our mates took the flag, folded and hid it under his jacket before tossing it into the waters right in front of the destroyer – much to the Americans' annoyance, as they would have loved to bag this souvenir for themselves. They just went mad collecting such items. A little while later, while we were still on the boat, the American flag was hoisted.

Leaving our boat proved difficult as the destroyer's small motor boat twisted through the waves. The rough sea was making it almost impossible for us to jump – but jump we did, praying that we would land inside the boat. And then the whole spectacle repeated itself when we had to climb up the destroyer's rope ladder that swayed back and forth. The general and I wore our Luftwaffe officers' caps. We were barely on board

Closely observed by the boarding party from the US destroyer *Sutton*, the German crew take down the German flag.

before several machine guns were pointed at us and someone screamed, 'Hands up!' as cameras began whirring and clicking away.

But our general wouldn't have any of it. 'No, we don't do that – I wish to meet the captain,' he said. And that is indeed what happened. As we were shown to the rather comfortable day rooms and sleeping quarters, naturally under the watchful eyes of armed US sailors, three officers then greeted us, asked for our hand luggage, passports and money and with that I was parted from my diplomatic passport and 1,500 Swiss Francs, some Norwegian and Danish Kroner and German Reichsmarks.

We were then allowed to take a hot shower with some soap of a quality we hadn't experienced for years, along with white terry-cloth towels. The food was exceptionally tasty and, together with the cognac I had brought along, I must admit that these first days as prisoners of war were most agreeable. After the day's excitement we slept soundly, thankful to still be alive after nearly six years of fighting. It was not to be taken for granted.

The days between 16 and 19 May were spent on board the destroyer escort DE-771, with another warship, DE-770 *Muir* joining us. Eventually we all figured out a rather sensible way to 'collaborate'. The U-boat prisoners received Red Cross packages containing everyday clothing and washing things. Once we'd got rid of our beards, shaved and washed, we looked much more civilised. We were even given permission to take walks on deck with no guards to be seen anywhere. Those first talks with the American officers and sailors taught us a lot. It became obvious that, based on the American press and reporting, they had all assumed we were sub-human. We received US newspapers, heard our names mentioned on the radio and, a bit later, also got to read the *New York Times*.

Despite being considered 'sub-humans' we were given excellent meals and, for the first time in years enjoyed citrus fruit, golden-yellow butter, wheat bread and meat dishes. The only item missing was alcohol as it was not allowed to be served on any US ships. I was able to build an especially warm relationship with a young officer named Ensign T.I. Jones, hailing from Dallas in Texas, and we promised to visit each other, should an opportunity present itself, sometime in the future. We exchanged souvenirs, he gleefully accepted my sport shirt with the large printed image of the Luftwaffe eagle, and I was very happy with the officer jacket buttons he gave me. General Kessler had good chats with the commander, and we played Skat. Meanwhile the naval officers advised that we hand over to them all our precious belongings, such as our watches, rings, medals and memorabilia, assuring us that we'd get them sent to our home address. Back on land, they warned, we'd be treated quite differently than here on board. And they weren't wrong either.

Taken Prisoner

Our first days in captivity flew by, with us being treated most fairly. One got the impression that they, much like us, felt that we were soldiers, no more and no less, and that all we had done was our duty. It goes without saying that the *Sutton* crew was mightily proud to be able to travel home to the USA having taken possession of such coveted spoils of war – us. The Canadians from Halifax, however, felt frustrated as *Sutton* had blocked the radio communication between them and our boat.

20 May 1945 would forever be engraved in our memories. Four ships had surrounded our boat and a US aircraft circled above our heads shortly before we arrived at the Portsmouth navy yard in New Hampshire. But we didn't pull in directly at the quay and instead were first taken aboard *Argo*, a patrol boat. Before that we had taken leave of *Sutton*'s commander and his officers, and from our U-boat comrades as well, for in our position as 'guests' we needed to be separated from them.

We, the nine 'guests', were requested to sit on the cutter's long benches and place our hands on the table in front. We weren't allowed to speak and were filmed while armed soldiers pointed machine pistols at us. The cameramen were later joined by sketch artists, who created rather questionable 'gangster' illustrations to depict us with General Kessler sitting amongst us all, holding an English book in his hands with a title that read something like this: after the war, what now? Later, we had to descend from the boat in single file and were filmed in the process all over again while military police and spectators lined the gang plank. And then onto a bus which drove us into the prison courtyard.

The initial interrogation took place before an officers' commission. I obligingly answered the question 'Do you carry a weapon?' and drew from out of my three layers of long johns my flyer's cutting knife, still attached to its leather strap. As the sharp blade was locked into its handle, the colonel, with code name 'Alvarez', asked what kind of a weapon this was. He stood about 1 metre away from me. I pressed the release button, the blade jumped out, and the colonel got a fright.

'You'd have used that to kill Jews, right?' he sneered. I proceeded to describe how such a knife was used when a parachutist, attempting to land in strong winds, needed to cut himself free from his rigging so as not to be dragged by its suspension lines along the ground. This explanation seemed to do the trick and off I went to my cell.

After several hours all the guests were bussed to the airport, from where a two-engine transport aircraft, a C-47 Skytrain, flew us south. Our destination was Washington DC, with a stop-over at La Guardia airfield in New York. I will never forget this flight, as for the first time in ages I once again saw green fields. I also got a glimpse of these enormous American manufacturing plants, highways, skyscrapers and spaces. Goodness me! So much space! The sheer magnitude of it all was breathtaking. Looking around, I couldn't understand how it was at all possible that someone could even entertain the thought of waging war against a country such as this? Neither Hitler nor any of his 'paladins' had ever set foot in the USA. These criminals had sacrificed us to satisfy their delusional thirst for power, and it was now our people who were paying for it. These and similar thoughts went through my head even before landing in Washington DC.

In a closed bus guarded by soldiers, we drove through the city, listening to the noises of the traffic outside. We couldn't see any of what was happening outside until we finally arrived at the barracks. Here we were greeted by a Sergeant Koda, who spoke in a distinct Munich accent: '*Willkommen im Hotel.*' It was at least familiar, even if slightly unsettling.

After we had gone through the formalities and completed all the personal details, we had to strip down to nothing and hand in all our clothing, even our toiletries. The fear was obviously that we'd commit suicide with a razor blade. US army summer clothing was distributed and then everyone was led to a solitary cell equipped with a field cot, a wooden chair and a folding table. I was completely finished, physically and emotionally, but still glad to have remained alive. Sleep came to me instantly.

It was only the following morning that I became fully aware of the fact that I was stuck in prison. It was the famous P.O. Box 1142, a military intelligence camp, previously known as Fort Hunt, located between Alexandria and Mount Vernon on the Potomac river. The facility housed notable personalities and among the prisoners held here were Oshima, the Japanese ambassador to Berlin, as well as German scientists and high-ranking military personnel.

The cells were spartan, with light only dimly filtering through thickly frosted windows, with the lower glass panes rotating in order to air the room. We couldn't see the sky, not even when standing up tall – there was nothing in front of us other than a timber wall. The flooring was clad in large red and blue linoleum tiles and the walls and ceilings were papered in brown cardboard. One's eyes couldn't settle on anything – it was desolate.

Wake-up call was at 0600 hours, with a guard taking us to where we could shower and go to the toilet. It wasn't possible to shave as razors had been taken away from us, of course. Back in the cell, we could hear the breakfast trolley rumbling through the corridors and a tray was handed to me through the flap which could only be opened from the outside. On the tray, separated into indentations, were soft white bread, cornflakes, milk, butter, jam, an apple or an orange and a beaker filled with coffee. We were given thirty minutes, after which the tray was picked up. If you had to use the toilet, you pressed a button, but the guard wouldn't always appear.

Towards lunchtime the cell door was unlocked and an officer along with a priest asked me in German: *'Wie geht es Ihnen?'* (How are you?)

Why wouldn't I be doing well, seeing I was still alive? But after a few hours I got depressed, feeling like a trapped tiger.

The following day I was led to my first interrogation. Some years later, I asked to read the transcripts. Senior Lieutenant Kelly had judged that the POW-WG-1262 (my prisoner number) had 'lost the ground under his feet'.

And this indeed summed up my condition, on the one hand I was relieved to be alive, on the other hand I felt desperate and listless. I sort of didn't care any more.

Permission was given to walk around the prison courtyard for thirty minutes per day, alone and guarded by armed soldiers observing from the watchtower. Before going to sleep, I said my prayers out loud, and the light was switched off from the outside.

That following morning and much to my surprise, they handed me back my shaving stuff. Later, I was told that every cell was bugged and that the administration was under the impression that my prayers demonstrated I was not a suicide candidate.

The interrogations became much more frequent. I communicated to Kelly that I was prepared to cooperate and answer all their questions. I declared that, in my mind, all war was senseless and that I hoped Japan would also surrender soon.

Once I returned to my cell, my thoughts revolved around my own questions: are my loved ones in Germany still alive? What will my future career be? I was only twenty-four years old and wanted to work. But here I was, locked up, alone with my thoughts and doubts, and having absolutely nothing with which to occupy myself.

A few days later my morning routine changed somewhat and after a further few days I was asked whether there was anything I might be wanting. 'I would very much like to be among other people,' I ventured to suggest.

That same afternoon I, along with my camp bed, was moved from my room no. 18 to room no. 15, where I met up again with the engineer, Dr Heinz Schlicke [the inventor of infrared detection] who'd been with me on the U-boat. The moment the cell door had closed behind me, Schlicke decided to rubbish the Americans in a very loud and clear voice. Cabin fever, no doubt.

'These idiots think they are God themselves, treating us like criminals ... They have no clue about what has happened in Germany ... they don't have the faintest idea of what it means to live under a dictatorship!' he blustered.

We'd later find out that all our conversations were being taped and analysed. And in this way, based on these tape recordings, the Americans had information they wouldn't have gleaned from the official interrogations. But spending the day in your cell with someone else sure was preferable to being so isolated. Another reason for the two of us being locked in the same room was that Schlicke was a scientist and radar specialist with the navy, while I was considered a radar expert for the Luftwaffe.

We then received special prisoner of war writing paper to inform our family of our whereabouts and what had happened to us. The paper had been treated beforehand with lemon juice or urine to prevent us conveying sensitive or secret information that could have been deciphered upon receipt by applying heat. Looked like our old scout tricks were well known to the Americans. Despite being given permission to make contact with our loved ones, we remained convinced that the Americans only used this exercise to find out where we stood emotionally. They'd never post our letters, we kept saying to each other.

We received American newspapers, from which we found out, for the first time, that Germany had been divided into four zones, with the largest area, including my hometown, now occupied by the Russians. In the meantime, photographs of us were taken, perhaps for an album on 'criminals'? We weren't told. Fingerprints followed – one would think we were planning to rob a bank …

Schlicke and I had made it quite clear that we were prepared to collaborate with the US specialists and even give lectures at the Pentagon. It wasn't long before a sealed car picked us up and drove us to a large house, where we were taken to Apartment 9, a spacious and nicely furnished room with normal, albeit barred, windows. The view onto trees, bushes and grassy areas along with watching the branches bend in the wind and listening to the soft rustling of leaves filled us with a wonderful feeling. We were alive, and the barred window panes took nothing away from our excitement.

Because they had taken our watches away, we could only ever guess what time of day it was, working on the basis that a loud gunshot occurred at 0600 and at 1700 hours. And at 12 noon precisely they sounded an air-raid siren – a reminder of the dreadful times now behind us.

A surprise invitation to take a stroll along with Senior Lieutenant Kelly was yet another break from the routine, and we really enjoyed seeing for the first time the normal homes, cars and people. That evening, we received a bottle of 'Senate beer' from Washington.

On top of that, we were able to go to the camp's cinema, where they once screened *Tarzan and the Amazons*.

Eventually, it also became easier for me to communicate in English. I spent time writing my POW letters, addressing them to my cousin Gladys in Milwaukee, the Malchow family in Munich, my parents and of course to Ruth. Sadly, I was to find out later that these letters had never been mailed.

By and by, bits of information along with photographs about the German concentration camps were published in the USA. We usually received copies of newspapers describing the atrocities committed and we had to sign a form confirming that we had read the articles. They refused to believe me when I assured them that I never knew about any of these horrendous acts. And this was true for many Germans. They had kept their crimes secret as far as possible and, for that matter, front-line soldiers like us had been cut off from information.

After a while we were moved, this time to room no. 1, where we came across a desperate Colonel von Sandrart, who was visibly delighted to meet up and be able to speak to people, much like I had been before.

By this time, we were being allowed to go to the cinema every Friday, but were kept apart from the rest of the audience. The camp library was also open to us.

A tropical heat had set in, some 30 degrees Celsius alongside an unbelievable humidity of 90 per cent, and it really affected us.

I fondly remember a trip to Alexandria, a suburb of Washington, where we were driven through the town much like any other American and we truly felt 'normal'. The *Washington Post*, which we received daily, informed us about world affairs and specifically about the war between the USA and Japan. Among ourselves we discussed our future. Would we be able to stay on in America? With our hatred for our previous government in Germany growing by the day, we had come to realise that that criminal regime had lied to us and shamelessly deceived and betrayed us.

On 9 July, but with Colonel von Sandrart not included, we were transported to a cabin situated in dense forest, equipped with a shower and washing facilities. We had to give our word of honour not to escape and not to contact any of the other prisoners. A small truck would deliver us meals consisting of eggs, steaks, peanut butter or fruit, and after six lean years of war, we suddenly seemed to be treated as if in a spa. Apart from one aspect: we received no news from home, which demoralised and destabilised us. Our thoughts kept travelling to our families and we simply hoped that they were all alive and well.

In the meantime, Schlicke and I wrote our reports on our mission to Japan and our experiences in radar and high-frequency technology. At the same time, I also worked as Schlicke's assistant, preparing his forthcoming lectures for the Pentagon. On 19 July they brought us our own civilian suits, shoes and underwear (which they had retrieved from our luggage) and then off we went in an open convertible to Washington to deliver our first lecture. We drove by the Jefferson Monument, the White House, the Memorial Hall, the university and finally arrived at the Pentagon. Led to a room with air conditioning, which was totally novel for us, our lecture was about to start. The goal was to assist the Americans with our know-how and help them bring the war with Japan to an end. Our first lectures were held in German, aided by a translator, but later we managed to address them in English, which on some level was easier for us, as we could prepare more thoroughly. It was rather curious suddenly to be considered useful and appreciated once again. After the event was over, we went to the La Salle du Bois restaurant together with two officers and it felt like we were sleep-walking … they had poured us a Manhattan, a drink combining whisky, sweet vermouth and a maraschino cherry. It had been a while since we had seen such well-dressed people, and to dine in these 'ice-cold' rooms was very pleasant indeed. Afterwards, we were allowed to take a stroll through the streets before the car drove us back to Camp 1142 and Mr Menzel returned to being a POW.

The lectures and debates continued until 31 July with us being driven to Washington daily. In our cabin we were being looked after by an officer who spoke impeccable German and was, it turned out, charged with finding out more about our characters and inner make-up. Those discussions were deep and frank and usually ended with his final comment: 'But you lost the war, and Germany has to be punished!'

In the meantime, they had also returned my harmonica. I took to playing in the evenings, either in the cabin or climbing up into a tree – I could easily do that. At dusk one time, from somewhere in the forest, I could suddenly hear others whistling my German tunes. Moving slowly between bushes and trees, with Schlicke keeping an eye on the entrance to our lodgings, I was curious to find out what this was all about. And then, who should stand just before me but Robert Schumann, my friend, and next to him General Kessler. We talked and it was interesting, but unfortunately Robert knew nothing about my family and couldn't tell me whether they were all still alive. We certainly wanted to keep up our forest meetings, but couldn't chance being discovered. We found out that more illustrious people were housed in similar cabins nearby, for example two professors from Strasbourg, and they too were working for the Americans as 'deported foreign labourers'.

On 6 August 1945 the first atom bomb exploded over Hiroshima and in barely a few seconds nearly 100,000 people were killed. The Soviet Union declared war on Japan two days later, despite the neutrality pact concluded between them in 1941, and occupied Manchuria, the South Sakhalin, the Kuril Islands and northern Korea. Another B-29 Superfortress detonated the second atom bomb over Nagasaki, resulting in 40,000 dead and over 60,000 wounded. Besides that, Japanese cities suffered relentless and heavy bombardment inflicting severe damage and loss of life.

As of 11 August, we once again had access to our own radio and were thus immediately and directly informed about the world news. Despite having to listen to devastating news broadcasts, we also tuned into performances by the London Symphony Orchestra under the baton of Arturo Toscanini, which not only relaxed us, but also gave us emotional support, seeing as we were worried stiff as to what the Allies were going to do with this divided Germany.

On 14 August 1945 President Truman announced the unconditional surrender of Japan, who had accepted the Potsdam Agreement. This was obviously celebrated throughout the USA, with us lot glad that the carnage had ended – a total of over 60 million people had been killed over the years.

Over these days and weeks we heard more details about what was going on in our home. Germany had been divided into four zones: East Germany came under Russian occupation, Southern Germany was under American administration, Western Germany under the French, and Northern Germany was under British authority. All the details had been outlined in the Potsdam Conference between Truman, Churchill – later Atlee – and Stalin.

Then in October the UN was founded in San Francisco. We listened to a radio report informing us of the formal signing of Japan's surrender and heard General McArthur and Admiral Nimitz speak with Mr Truman, justifying the decision to drop the atomic bomb. This, he claimed, had saved the lives of tens of thousands American soldiers who were thus spared from having to occupy Japan.

After so many years of barbarity and horror, it now appeared that at long last world peace was beginning to establish itself, though our small

181

group of men were still doubtful. We could see signs of the forthcoming East–West conflict brewing. On 2 September the Americans celebrated the so-called Victory Day with the Eroica and with Beethoven's Fifth Symphony being played after the solemn addresses. In our forest, that very night, I climbed the tallest tree, perched on a thick branch and looked up into the star-bedecked sky, studying the constellations with the help of my star card that I had pulled out of my rucksack, trying to find some solace.

Schlicke and I accepted a dinner invitation for 20 August in Washington's Hotel Willard. There, accompanied by music performed by the Trade Winds (an American pop group), we felt young and free, though it was only for a moment. After enjoying the midnight show and an unusually mixed Manhattan which we hadn't tasted before, I fell into a deep and dreamless sleep. The next morning then brought memories of the silver wedding anniversary celebrated by my parents last year, and thoughts about my Ruth returned. I still hadn't heard from them.

In October they handed us some winter clothing picked out from US army stock, and we got to read many books borrowed from the camp library. During one such visit to the reading room, I chanced upon a book with the stamp of a German U-boat that had landed in Argentina and then been extradited with its entire crew to the USA.

Then in November, and much to our delight, we were housed in an apartment which had separate bed and living rooms. Rudi Bree had already moved in. He had been responsible for the development of the V1 flying bomb and the V2 rocket – he was accountable to the Ministry of Aviation and attached to General Milch's staff [Milch was the Luftwaffe Field Marshal]. He was an exceptionally empathetic person and managed to lift me out of my depression. My long conversations with him filled me with renewed confidence and hope.

Port Washington on Long Island

Towards the end of October, we were informed that we'd be permitted to leave the camp and meet up with those German scientists who had been working for the Americans. We were flown out of the navy airport in

Washington DC and reached New York via Baltimore and Philadelphia. A navy vehicle took us from there to Port Washington, with Colonel Hilbert part of our group.

A castle-like building constructed in English Tudor style with thick walls of granite and limestone, parapets atop the façade and punctuated by a tall tower welcomed us. The Guggenheim Estate (Hempstead House) was one of the most opulent manor houses I had ever come across and was set within an enormous estate. It boasted its own stables, a beach stretching over 3 km, a huge number of grand rooms once extravagantly furnished, and a long foyer with vaulted ceilings. In 1942 Mrs Guggenheim donated 162 acres of the estate to the Institute of Aeronautical Sciences, but in 1946 the US Navy purchased the property for the Naval Training Device Centre. At that point a luxurious entrance hall was added along with a water fountain and library. We were allocated a large, airy room with a bathroom, complete with gilded taps. We partook of elegant meals, which we enjoyed alongside navy reserve officers who turned out to be polite companions and Larry Hess, an architect by profession, was their exceptionally likeable commander. We made the acquaintance of Professor Wagner and his assistants Lahde and Hell, who had been 'imported' into the USA from Austria. Wagner had designed the remotely controlled Henschel 293 glide bomb, for which I had also worked on the research when I was still in Germany. This bomb could precisely attack and sink warships while controlled remotely from the aircraft. Schlicke, Bree and I were the only POWs of the navy – they didn't take any other prisoners of war apart from us, and instead handed them over to the army.

Looking in from the outside, we had literally been plonked into paradise, but because we were still out of touch with Germany and our American relatives as well, it felt like being in a gilded cage. Each weekday, we received a salary of 80 cents, and for Sunday it was 60 cents. During the next few weeks, the following engineers joined us: doctor of engineering Schedling and Dr Walker from Vienna, and doctor of engineering Schaper from Berlin. All of us continued working on our previous projects, such as the 'guided missiles' and counter-measures that had already been the subject of Professor Wagner's research studies back home. We were supervised by a Czech engineer who, quite honestly, didn't have a clue, but fancied himself the boss.

Max Coreth, originally from Austria but who had defected to the Americans along with his wife, liaised between the navy officers who didn't speak any German, and after some initial rough patches, we collaborated quite nicely with him, and he often looked out for us. To keep fit, we went for a daily swim in the sea until temperatures fell to below 10 degrees. After breakfast we had an hour to ourselves when we listened to music or the news, with the broadcast sponsored by the Henry Ford company. Work followed on a covered veranda with a view onto the sea. Yes, our circumstances were most favourable, as you can imagine, with the house offering us every imaginable comfort, heated by warm air pumped up from the cellar and travelling through the walls.

Shortly before Christmas we were permitted, accompanied by Coreth, to visit Port Washington's English Evangelical Lutheran Church where Henry von Schlichen served as a pastor. We were introduced to some of the congregation's leaders, who had seemingly heard about our POW existence at the Guggenheim palace. They supported us not only by meeting some of our physical needs, such as providing us with city suits or winter coats, but emotionally as well. The pastor especially looked after me with respect to the distress I was experiencing, since I still hadn't had any word from my relatives.

At times, we were allowed to visit New York, dressed in civvies and accompanied by Coreth. At each of our outings, I couldn't help feeling what a pity it was that none of our German government officials had ever been to that city. But here I was, a POW during Christmas-time, which at that point had lost all its meaning for me. On 25 December a party was held with high-ranking US officers and their wives, who were dying to meet those 'crazy' Germans seeing as they had heard our names mentioned in news reports about the U-boats. Some girls attached to the WACS, the Women Auxiliary Corps, also paid us a visit and we were even allowed to have a cocktail with them, though the 'no fraternisation' policy was strictly enforced, turning our conversations into superficial chat. The event ended with Father Christmas distributing small presents donated by the officers and the church community. It was only thanks to the alcohol, to which none of us had yet become used, that our spirits were lifted.

New Year's Eve was a small affair with only us, Max and Charlotte Coreth, and Mr and Mrs Dull from the church congregation, gathered to sing German and American songs, with my harmonica-playing adding to a somewhat festive atmosphere.

At the beginning of January we had some unexpected visitors drop in on us: Herr Sturm from the Strassfurter Licht und Kraftwerke AG [during World War II it developed radio control receivers for targeting air-to-surface missiles] and Hans Widmann from Eching, near Munich. Neither of them spoke a word of English and were completely in the dark as to why they had been brought to the USA. From then on, Mr Coreth gave us English lessons.

On 21 January I was allowed to write a letter to my friend Malchow in Munich and only much later did I find out that this was the first letter posted by me which had reached Germany.

Six days later it was my twenty-fifth birthday and, being the youngest of this group, they decided on a wake-up call at 0015 with a loud alarm bell ringing in my ears. Above my bed shone the words 'Happy Birthday' in neon lights and there were ten bars of chocolate. The other German guys had also got up – we recited poetry, drank whisky from water glasses and were in a fabulous mood. The US officers living in the same building barricaded themselves in as they thought a mutiny had broken out. After the fracas had ended in my room we dragged some guys along the corridors to their respective lodgings, causing further commotion, with peace and quiet returning as late as 0400 or 0500 hours.

Rudi Bree, who had consumed less, took it upon himself to explain to the US officers the reason for the disturbances during the night, with the result that the day was declared a 'holiday'. That afternoon some members from the church arrived, bringing a large cake with twenty-five candles and some small gifts.

To bring some change to our routine and a break from my desk work, I organised a football match and everyone was thrilled with the idea. Dr Schlicke's team lost nearly every game, with his uncontrolled attempts at kicking a goal mostly ending up off the pitch. It certainly didn't take away from the general enjoyment. In the evenings we played bridge with Professor Wagner, Rudi Bree and Dr Walter and sometimes Commander Hess would join us. We were less enthralled with the American films they showed as they tended to portray the Germans as criminal idiots.

Twice I had to go to the navy hospital in St Albans; the first time was for a prescription for new glasses, and getting these helped me enormously. Until then my astigmatism hadn't been diagnosed. My second visit involved two of my wisdom teeth being pulled out and a hygienist appointment. I had a further scare when I had what I thought was an inflamed appendix, but my pain quickly subsided and I was once again able to swim in the sea, just as before with, of course, weather permitting. As for receiving any news from home, there was still nothing. We, that is Professor Wagner, Theo Sturm, Peter Schaper, Dr Knausenberg, Hans Widmann and I, gathered to have a drink to celebrate Ruth's birthday on 6 April, and they all wrote a short message in my diary. It was jolly enough, but I remained wistful and reminded of the English poem 'Should You Go First …' (by Albert Rowswell, an American poet and broadcaster).

At Easter 1946 we were requested to vacate the castle as the navy required it for other purposes, and we were moved to the 'Quonset Huts' (prefabricated structures made mostly of corrugated iron) in the park, which was certainly quite a step down in terms of the luxury we had enjoyed so far. The lodgings consisted of several huts, one served as a day lounge, one as a bedroom, one as an office and one accommodated the washing facilities. While we, the front-line soldiers, were okay with the limited space, our civilians proved slightly more difficult.

The day I received my first letter from Ruth must count as one of the happiest days of my life. It was 30 April 1946 and I finally heard that my parents were alive, my siblings as well and even my friends. I could hardly believe my ears and my comrades were thrilled for me. Once again life had a purpose. More letters arrived over the following days, from my parents and from Thea in Remscheid. As a result of American officers having visited and interrogated them, the mail embargo had obviously been lifted. What an unbelievable relief!

Rumours about us being returned to Germany were flying around in May and June. We were assured that this was the case and were also given the option that should we wish to return one day, we'd receive a work visa for America. Schlicke was keen to accept this offer as he wished to bring his family to the States. Rudi Bree and I chose to decline. We wished to remain in Germany.

In the meantime, some young girls aged between twenty-one and twenty-five from the Women Auxiliary Corps were also housed in the park's huts. One of them, Joan Alloway Fox from Princetown, Mississippi, fell in love with me, without me having noticed it. Rudi Bree had noticed this even before I did as he was much more attuned to such matters. She gave me books to read and often shared with me the poetry and art she loved. She certainly was a very pretty and highly intelligent girl who was convinced that we Germans were way ahead of the US lads, both intellectually as well as generally – for example how we seemed to approach life. She suggested that I remain in America, marry her and pursue my studies. We had long and meaningful discussions during which I kept explaining to her that I loved my Ruth and that we had promised each other that, should we survive, we'd get married straight after the war. I was, admittedly, seriously tempted by her proposition, because she was an exceptionally lovable and clever young woman and very beautiful as well. As it turned out, she was also extremely determined.

My Return Journey to Germany

On 24 June we received the order to depart for Germany. Our farewell party was a grandiose affair in which we were joined by our comrades and all the friends we had made in America. I had packed two large duffle bags and left all my personal documents, such as my diplomatic passport and all my certificates and official documents in the trusty hands of Commander Larry Hess, who promised to return them to me at the next opportunity – he kept his word.

My last swim in the sea, then on to receiving my POW clothes, which consisted of a black US shirt and black trousers with the POW lettering on the back. After that we were driven to Camp Shanks – the largest US army port of embarkation from which thousands of prisoners were waiting for their transfer. And wouldn't you know it, I came across my friend Robert Schumann as well as Bringewald and Ruff, the two Messerschmitt engineers who'd been with me on the U-boat. To ensure that the six of us would reach Germany safely, a US navy captain was assigned to accompany us. On 28 June we boarded a ferry which was supposed to take us to a Liberty ship with the daunting name *Sea Devil*. At precisely 1000 hours the boat disembarked and we travelled one last time past the Statue of Liberty. Naturally, we were deep in thought. What would freedom offer us? What had imprisonment taught us? One thing was certain in our minds: as far as we were concerned, American imprisonment could have turned out a lot worse. What with having met people who had cared about and for us, it was difficult now to imagine a life in a world we didn't know and which, we feared, would surely be chaotic.

The good Neptune proved gracious, the waters were not too rough and we were spared the dreaded seasickness. Apart from some minor incidents, our crossing was pleasant enough and the food was fine. The Austrian prisoners had signs stuck on their shirts with 'Austria' printed on them, so they could be told apart from the Germans.

We reached Le Havre early one morning and my small group was the last one to disembark. From there, we were driven by truck to the Bolbec transit camp. We'd continue our journey the following day, we were told, and four trucks would take us to Frankfurt am Main. This was certainly not the case for thousands of other prisoners who were handed over to the French and, though contrary to the Geneva Convention, forced into hard labour in French mines for years to come.

Oberursel – It Was All a Mistake

We travelled in open trucks on a warm summer afternoon in August 1946, passing through Rouen, Soissons and Reims as we headed towards Luxembourg. Many houses still lay in ruins and only upon reaching Luxembourg did we see a town that was still intact. Close to 1700 hours we crossed the border, looking dishevelled and filthy. A large sign saying 'no fraternising permitted' spoke volumes about the Americans' priorities. Then we went past Trier and up and along the Hunsrück hills, followed by a very tiring drive through the night, passing Bingen and Kreuznach. Finally, towards 0500 we reached the Rhine river and entered the US zone. At 0600 we arrived at the Oberursel camp, where we were shoved into cells with two flat beds and immediately fell asleep.

It's unlikely we'll ever forget the four weeks from 9 July to 8 August 1946. We were put up in camps that were once used for imprisoned Allied air force officers and squeezed into one-man cells, which now had to accommodate two men and their luggage. Thankfully my friend Rudi and I managed to stick together and shared Cell D.

Food was in short supply. We received a watery soup in the morning with a piece of bread and some coffee substitute, while lunch and dinner consisted of another watery soup, a chunk of bread and a few potatoes. Twice a week we got some slivers of meat – all in all we were on a hunger ration. In this brief period alone, I lost twenty pounds.

A kind sergeant of the guard crew would sometimes donate a bit from his own rations, as he admitted that he felt sorry for us. It wasn't long before the doors of the cells were no longer locked, which at least allowed us to chat freely with the American comrades who, much like us, waited day after day to be set free. Our navy captain came to visit us twice, explaining the difficulties they experienced in pushing through our release, and the whole situation had the hallmark of a fight between army, navy and the US troops stationed in Germany, with no connections at all to the outside. During the evenings we were permitted to get some fresh air in the compound for an hour and a half. Why were we treated like serious criminals? No wonder that tensions ran high.

Return to Eislingen

On the morning of 8 August the chap who had accompanied our transfer to Germany, the US navy captain, appeared in our cell accompanied by the camp commander. Here is what he said: 'It's all been a mistake, grab your belongings, you're free to go. We'll take you home to Eislingen.'

Goodness! Our hearts started beating faster and we instantly got extremely nervous. We took a shower, put on the new US-issued clothes that were handed out to us, only this time they had nothing printed on the back, and packed our stuff. Never had I gathered all my belongings in so short a time, and I made particularly sure that neither my leather officer's coat nor my boots were left behind, packed along with several cartons of American cigarettes, chocolate, my civvies and the presents I had received from the church congregation in Port Washington. Importantly, I had a whole file of documents confirming my release, that I was not a Nazi and that I had worked for the US navy. And then there was the official US permit for me to study in the States. I had to sign papers confirming that I would not enter the Russian zone where my parents lived and that I would check in regularly with the CIC. And that was that.

After a quick goodbye from friends, mainly from Bree, Schumann and Hertz and an exchange of our respective addresses, I mounted a US jeep while the young driver loaded my luggage. I was deliriously happy and couldn't believe my luck as I relaxed in the seat next to him. The sun was shining.

Since the highway and bridges leading to Stuttgart had been destroyed and were still not repaired, we took the country roads. The only thought on my mind was that I was free and at long last able to return to my Ruth. Early that afternoon we entered the Eislingen factory, where people gathered and just stared at us. I enquired of Herr Mäusner, the factory's master locksmith, whether he knew where the Meister family lived, and while in conversation I handed him a pack of cigarettes. It did the trick – he trusted me and got in touch with Hannsjochen Meister, who then took me to his parents. They, together with Ruth and Hannsjochen, lived in part of a large workshop, with a living room, separate bedrooms for Ruth and her parents, and a room up in the loft for Hannsjochen. They had access to a bath and the workshop kitchen area, while the rest of the workshop belonged to Lucie Lemppenau, widow of the erstwhile owner of the textile factory.

When I got there Ruth was out, as she had taken a job as a secretary with the Tausch glass and porcelain wholesalers in Göppingen, but her parents gave me a warm welcome. They were eager to tell me about their past and how traumatic their escape from Radebeul had been … but I was more immediately preoccupied with the idea that Hannsjochen should drive as quickly as possible to Göppingen and fetch my Ruth. Words cannot describe the emotions, the joy when the two of us finally met up.

Another surprise was yet to come. Ruth had organised for me a separate room opposite hers at the far end of their corridor, complete with a bed, cupboard, chair and table. The window opened up to a slanted roof. My instant reaction when I entered was: 'from here I can easily escape over the roof', and it truly shocked her. My fear of being abducted, seeing I was a radar specialist, was foremost on my mind. Our conversations lasted till the early hours, when, at 5 o'clock we tumbled into bed, totally exhausted. Ruth's father suggested that we all address each other with the more familiar German '*Du*' [as opposed to the more formal '*Sie*'] – and with that, I was part of the family. To thank them for their kindness I liberally shared with them (they were all notorious smokers) my American cigarettes.

Germany in 1946

Yes, I had returned to Germany, but the old Germany had disappeared. It had been divided into four zones following the Potsdam Conference between 17 July and 2 August 1945 with Stalin, Truman, de Gaulle and Churchill. One could only cross over from one zone into the other under strict conditions. East Prussia was split between Russia and Poland, most of Silesia became part of Poland, a small strip west of the Oder–Neisse line that had belonged to Silesia became part of East Germany, and Alsace Lorraine was returned to France.

All Germans from these areas were expelled or fled, with millions of refugees crowding the roads, train stations and camps, where they were living in dire circumstances.

As of 1946 a fair degree of order and normality had once again returned to the German government institutions, albeit now under Allied command. But the general situation was dismal. Hunger was rampant, production of goods drastically reduced, and one could only buy food with the allotted food stamps. People resorted to hoarding food, with trade on the black-market burgeoning. Though the Reichsmark was the official currency, nobody was able to purchase anything much and the so-called cigarette economy evolved, with cigarettes attaining full currency status. Hungry city-dwellers travelled to farms in the outskirts and traded in their valuables for essential supplies. These scenes of collapse and widespread misery went hand in hand with the expropriation of business owners, nationalisation of banks and insurance companies and a land reform aimed at reviving rural society but initially achieving little. Additionally, there was a brain-drain with German scientists forcibly removed and sent to Russia, France or America. While us lot had already realised during our imprisonment that the victorious powers would take vengeance, the devastation I encountered, above all in the bombed-out cities, was beyond anything I could have imagined.

And yet, I was full of hope and optimism despite Germany being laid to waste and facing an uncertain future. We would make it work, Ruth and I said to ourselves, first for the two of us and soon, we hoped, with a little one. Nonetheless, I couldn't help revisiting the past, reflecting on the years that had gone by, long and arduous years which had wrought havoc in the world and brought suffering, misery and death to mankind. It became quite clear to me how we had fallen victim to a cruel regime. But now Ruth and I wished for nothing more than to move forward, remain positive and focus on creating a family and for me to embark on my studies. We hoped that the future would be bright and peaceful.

Ruth and Erich Menzel
at their wedding in 1946.

My Youth: Beautiful, Simple and Sad

AN EYEWITNESS ACCOUNT BY ROSA ASSBÖCK

Thinking back to my early years spent with my brothers in a happy family on a farmstead at the edge of rural Chiemgau, the conditions were ideal for a blissful childhood. Anybody growing up in a small rustic homestead can call themselves fortunate. Nature was everywhere. In the twenties my father was able to acquire an Alpine hut on the Höslwang, idyllically located amid a lush meadow and surrounded by forests. In the summer the corn stalks swayed in the warm breeze, and we could ramble through the hilly landscape with picturesque views of valleys and mountains. Timber was of the utmost importance to our farmers, for construction as well as for storing as heating material for the winter, with the snow glistening outside and only the living room being warm to retreat to thanks to the green-tiled stove. When it wasn't enough to protect us against the penetrating cold, Father would hang a horse blanket across our front door.

Spring was especially wonderful. Vibrant yellow primroses bloomed in the gardens, and further afield meadows beckoned, carpeted by a thick layer of dandelions and tiny blue gentians dotted around and in between. Glorious! The fragrance of the fruit trees' white blossoms filled the air, their apples and pears bringing us a regular income. They would be turned into liqueur, much enjoyed by the farmers, but of course were also used in the kitchen, where they were stewed, made into jam or compote. At one point a moonshiner offered me a small bottle of fruit brandy while warning me to use the stuff only to rub into the skin, and not to enjoy it as a drink. I had to smile.

Penhamer Lake, embedded in the oldest nature reserve in Bavaria, attracted people from all around for a peaceful swim. In the summer, we used to run to the beach barefoot, as we children only wore shoes during the colder months. A narrow stream flowed alongside our house, with its clear water running into the lake further on. The call of the cuckoo, crickets chirping and frogs croaking ... all of it the delightful music at

This is the home which belonged to my mother, Rosina Wagner.

the foothills of the Alps. Smelling the spicy aroma of the birch trees and watching bats flit across the sky at dusk was calming.

We could have enjoyed living in this paradisiacal setting for many years, without a worry in the world, if it hadn't been for the dreadful reign of the Nazi regime, if it hadn't been for the horrendous war, a war that would cut short my carefree childhood. My father never returned from Russia where he laboured as a POW. Schorschl, my older brother, was shot dead, and three of my mother's brothers fell in battle, along with two of my father's brothers who were killed in Stalingrad. [Schorsch is a German nickname for Georg, based on the French and English pronunciation of the name, the diminutive is Schorschl.]

My younger brother Bartl was born in 1930, but I can't remember those first years of his life. Hitler came to power in 1933 and Father was unemployed. He resorted to taking on work helping other farmers with cutting peat, making hay, harvesting the crops or chopping wood in the winter. It was a hard slog and was badly paid to boot, with 50 Pfennig for an entire day's labour. But he needed to put food on the table, and he'd also often be paid in kind. I can't honestly remember us ever going hungry. Just before Christmas a pig was slaughtered, the meat was smoked, fruit dried and our hens, of course, laid lots of eggs. Father planted potatoes in our plot of land and Mother baked her bread in an oven that had been set up in the fruit orchard. In other words, despite the miserable economic conditions, our family was doing fairly well. That said, we were by nature quite frugal folks and didn't need lots of money in order to be happy.

One day new neighbours arrived. A schoolfriend of my mother had bought a house next to ours which she shared with her husband, Schorsch Mittermaier from Lower Bavaria. Anni, Mother's friend, was always very pleasant and an amusing woman, while her husband was always subdued, with a sad look in his eyes. At some point Mother confided in me. Herr Mittermaier's father had been imprisoned for murder. He had killed his wife by intentionally driving his horse and cart down a slope with the cart toppling over and burying his wife underneath. His motive? He had a young female lover, whom he of course couldn't marry after being convicted because he was incarcerated. When Hitler carried out his euthanasia programme, Herr Mittelmaier was killed [the systematic killing programme included patients deemed criminally insane or those committed on criminal grounds].

His son subsequently left the large family farm in southern Bavaria and moved into our neck of the woods to avoid his name being blackened by the 'mark of Cain'. He too was called up to the army later on and returned relatively unscathed.

A further three farms were situated only ten minutes away from us, but one could only reach them by travelling along some dirt tracks. The owner of the largest farm was a family with twelve children, all honest youngsters whom we soon befriended. Their mother had to work incredibly hard, required to look after the stables and homestead, and who also helped with the home 'football team'. The older siblings mucked in, as anything else would not only have been unacceptable around those parts, but also because the burden on Annie would have simply been impossible for her to shoulder otherwise. Their father was an enthusiastic Hitler supporter, but he didn't strike me as a bad man. In his role as a *Ortsgruppenleiter* [local group leader], he was charged with giving propaganda speeches at our school, though I honestly can't remember what they were all about since I had little interest in that kind of thing. They praised the party and Hitler and invariably these speeches contained horrible diatribes against the Jews, who apparently were the cause of all the world's ills.

My own mother didn't appreciate this sort of politics and the labourers, busy with digging turf on our land, were not particularly keen on the National Socialist ideology either. Why would one suddenly have to greet each other with '*Heil Hitler*'? It didn't make much sense to us and besides, we all felt that this ideology stood in stark contrast to our strict Catholic belief. This, above all, struck us as suspicious, as we were faithful and religious folk who regularly attended church services.

One of our neighbours was a member of the Sturmabteilung [SA, Storm Troopers] and wore a brown shirt with a leather shoulder strap, an armband with the swastika on it and breeches. He tried to convince my father to read *Mein Kampf* but my father never read any books and this man's efforts proved in vain.

My mother with me and my
brothers, Bartl and Georg
(Schorschl), 1939.

My brothers were two rude and impertinent lads. One morning, on our way to school, Schorschl, who was two years my senior, greeted a neighbour with *'Heil Gratter'* [a derogative Bavarian term for a poor travelling pedlar]. When Father got wind of this encounter, he grabbed the boy and gave him a proper dressing-down. 'I wanted to say *"Heil Hitler"*,' Schorschl defended himself valiantly, 'but couldn't think of the name.' Well, that went down rather well, and Father moved on.

The family of our *Ortsgruppenleiter* seemed cursed. The mother died young, having written a long letter to her children before she passed away which was read out at her funeral with the family, thus doing away with the sermon at the grave. One of the twelve children succumbed to cancer shortly thereafter and most of the others also died from this disease.

In the mid-thirties our circumstances deteriorated; food was running low everywhere, to say nothing of other life essentials. Bread was scarce, and with us children always having a healthy appetite Father decided to enquire of other farmers whether he could help them cut peat. They all shook their heads. The pig in the sty also needed to be fed. And so my father went out to beg, often staying away for a whole week with us missing him terribly. But upon his return it was always the same story: all he brought home were some pieces of hard bread and a few Pfennig. Too little to live on and too much to die from.

It was our Uncle Sepp who had urged Father to join him when he'd go begging, as Sepp had for a long time managed to fight through the depression by doing just that. Father finally yielded to Uncle's pressure, though Mother disapproved. She was as embarrassed about this as indeed Father was, fearing nothing more than being recognised. After all, his father had been mayor of Bachmehring (a municipality in Bavaria). To disguise himself, mother gave him a long black cloak and a wide-brimmed hat, and he blackened his face.

'I refuse to go to the Wasserburger area [the town of Wasserburg is situated north-west of Bachmehring], because I don't want anybody to recognise my face.'

Rain was pouring down when the two of them left our house on foot, as Sepp couldn't ride a bike, but then, of course, he didn't own one. When they still hadn't returned after a week, Mother got anxious. 'I hope the farm dogs haven't attacked them if they decided to sleep in the haystacks,' she worried.

Schorschl tried to calm Mother down. 'Sepp carries a sharp switchblade and a *Hakenstecken* [a walking stick with a crooked handle and a metal spike at the bottom] – he can kill any dog he wants, but he might also be able to catch some fish with it!' he added, hoping to instil some optimism. She continued to fret, constantly throwing nervous glances out of the lounge window. Then, finally, after eight days, the two dragged themselves into our house, dirty, unwashed and despondent. They had gone as far as Ebersberg, with a kind farmer wife occasionally giving them some hot milk and bread, sometimes even an 'ox-eye', a sweet tart with a dot of jam in the middle. But then there were times a guard dog had chased them away from the property. They felt well protected, what with carrying the knife and the stick; they always escaped unharmed and they never failed to blacken their faces using the soot they found in outdoor ovens, trying to keep under cover, so to speak.

My brothers and I listened to the two, open-mouthed and curious about the big wide world, as we hadn't ever moved beyond the confines of our hamlet. This, however, was the end of their escapade and Father fell asleep on the couch, with Sepp opting for the haystack.

Whenever Father carved yet another *Hakenstecken*, mother asked him to explain his reasoning. 'It will come in handy when I go on treks, when I get involved in fights, smash stuff in the pub, go fishing or defend myself against dogs.'

The result of this 'world tour' yielded nothing more than some stone-hard bread and a bit of loose change. That evening we soaked the bread in a large pot of milk.

The fact was that at the time there were simply too many beggars on the road as times were very hard, not only for my father but for all the unemployed men.

Uncle Sepp, who hailed from Aberg, was single. He didn't know how to write and had difficulty reading as he had never properly attended school. Basically, he skipped classes as he had always been a little scoundrel. When he was younger, he'd occasionally get hired as a farmhand, but these stints were short lived as he'd soon lose interest. He sometimes caught himself a chicken and roasted it over an open fire, and when he was hungry or thirsty, he'd go from house to house knocking on doors. He was of no fixed abode and today would be considered a homeless person sleeping rough. He didn't require a bed as he'd find himself a haystack to sleep in, he looked unkempt and had long hair growing out of deep indents on his scalp caused by the blows he'd receive when involved in pub brawls. The fact that he no longer had any teeth either gives you the picture of a dirty and neglected man, down at heel.

But Sepp often helped Father with the wood chopping, cutting logs into wedges or spreading dung. When the weather was miserable, the two often played cards inside our house or sorted out the fodder for the cows. Sepp didn't ever ask for much, never wanting to add to our costs. He didn't bother with personal hygiene or cleanliness: he washed his feet in the river and it was my brother who'd cut his hair. He'd also take care of Sepp's toenails, which could only be cut by using pliers as they were too hard and normal nail clippers simply weren't up to the job. We children were always rather happy when Sepp arrived at our home. He wasn't allowed to sleep on the couch as he'd wet himself during the night if he had drunk too much. And because he had no teeth, Mother usually gave him a bowl of milk in the evening, into which he'd drop the pieces of bread that he had scrounged during the day.

And that's how Sepp got through life, for better or for worse.

Sometimes my brothers and Sepp fished illegally (in Bavaria the law requires you to have a fishing licence in order to be able to fish). And at times he'd use a sling to catch a deer, which he'd roast in the shed where we kept an old hob with an oven.

'But, Sepp,' my mother scolded, 'that's not proper.' But she then joined in the meal. When Sepp was unlucky with his poaching, he'd try and catch a cat and he was quite successful with that. The cat was slaughtered and roasted. Once he gave me some meat to eat, but I found it too sour as he had poured too much vinegar into the sauce and, anyway, Mother didn't want me to take part in these meals, as poaching was a crime. However, it wasn't considered dishonourable among us poor rural folks and Uncle Sepp knew not to get caught.

Life for those living like Sepp often ends tragically. And there was a time when he no longer dropped by. We found out that he had fractured his upper thigh, and it would never heal. He was put up in the Franziskanerwerk in Schönbrunn near Dachau [the Franziskanerwerk was a facility for mentally disabled people founded by the Franciscan order. Between 1940 and 1943, as part of the Aktion T4 programme, several hundred men, women and children classified as 'unworthy of life' were transported from there to the Hartheim killing centre and murdered by poison gas]. He once sent us a letter that a carer had written for him.

'I'm so very homesick,' we read, 'I miss Höslwang, your farm, I miss the children. How are you all, especially the three children?'

One day he turned up at our home, peering through the living-room window. Supported by two crutches, he hobbled in.

'Goodness, Sepp, so here you are! Will you stay with us?'

'I can't continue,' he sighed deeply and wistfully, 'I just can't.' Tears were running down his cheeks and I was upset for many days after his visit, I felt so very sorry for him. After a few hours he had to return to his care facility, all paid for by the community. We'd never see him again, but I often thought about him.

Over the years we noticed Mother getting increasingly unwell, becoming more depressive and melancholy as time went on. Though the doctor visited her three times a week, he was unable to help. She had tablets stored away in her cabinet which she was meant to take, and once my little brother got a hold of them. We found him quietly sucking a few of them and he promptly fell into a deep sleep. Fortunately, nothing more than that happened.

Our neighbour who helped us with our housework would often get angry at our mother, insisting that she was putting it on. Mother was then hospitalised in a mental home. We children got very anxious as we'd heard that children of mentally sick patients, patients with inherited diseases and Jews were 'lebensunwert' [unworthy of life] and might be murdered.

Mother was only thirty-three years old when she suddenly lost a lot of weight and suffered a nervous breakdown. Fortunately, she recovered quite quickly, returned home, once again had a healthy complexion and everything was like it had been before. That winter we were all together and at home, as during Mother's illness we had been taken to different relatives' places and weren't walking to school together. My route led through a forest, and one day an older man who had hidden behind some bushes called out to me to come over: 'Right over to where I stand, gal, there are plenty of berries for you to pick here!' I ran away as fast as I could and know today that I had had a lucky escape.

Once a year a photographer came to school to take class pictures. It was during the time when some travellers had settled themselves down in the village, just underneath the main square's lime tree. They were considered and often treated like tramps who cause only trouble. The council would have none of it and allocated them a plot where they could park themselves and their metal trailer, with the inn owner looking after their horse in his stable and the children joining us at school. Each of these children carried with them a booklet in which the teacher noted down the lessons they attended.

The photographer lined up the children and it so happened that a girl who came from this traveller community stood directly next to my brother.

Her hair was crawling with lice, but, quite honestly, this could have happened to any of us. When my brother looked at the picture later on he wanted to burn it as the girl had stood next to him, but Mother told him off. 'Just calm down, will you, these people are not much different to us.'

After Mother's recovery, our family life returned to normal, but Father had become quite strict, sometimes erupting into a violent temper. If we had done something wrong, we'd be summoned into the living room and ordered to kneel on the edge of a triangular piece of wood and even say some prayers while doing so. But secretly we turned the smooth side upwards so it wouldn't hurt us so much.

Prayers were a traditional part of our day, with grace recited before every mealtime while kneeling on the floor. At the weekends we prayed the rosary followed by a long private family prayer. Nearly every day we also had to attend church before school started and, because our walk to school took over an hour, we didn't relish these religious services, especially not in winter. We sometimes skipped going to church, but were then at a loss as to where to go and petrified of being found out – kneeling on the piece of wood would have been the least of our punishments.

In 1937 the NSDAP gained in influence and its ideology spread to our area, remote as it might have been. They railed against church and religion, the greeting of '*Heil Hitler*' with outstretched arm replaced the traditional '*Grüss Gott*' and we often had to sing the 'Deutschlandlied' [the official national anthem from 1922 to 1945]. It actually hurt my arm when we had to hold our arm outstretched throughout all the verses. In our gymnastic lessons marching music was played and we had to march in time. Youngsters were urged to join the Hitlerjugend or the Bund deutscher Mädel [the Association of German Girls, the female branch of the Hitlerjugend (HJ)]. And if the parents objected, it was their children who'd have to pay. Poems in praise of the flag were recited at every occasion, with Mother thinking that this was plain silly. Our priest was interrogated, and nobody was permitted to utter a critical word, neither with respect to the party nor the Führer. When our Pastor Greimel denounced the new regime in one of his sermons, he was arrested a few days later and taken to prison. Thanks to the local farmers who paid to have him released, he was then set free.

In August 1939 we came to realise that the situation had deteriorated and that our peaceful lives had well and truly come to an end. Herr Stübl, our neighbour, a fat man who also had diabetes, came rushing into our house. 'Rosl,' he blustered, 'they mobilised last night – war has broken out! Our son Bertl has been called up – he's gone!'

At first, I didn't have a clue what was happening. 'What a relief', Mother responded, turning to me after the man was out of earshot, 'that Father is thirty-nine and can't be enlisted. And the boys are still at school.' Old man Stübl, who had served in World War I, thought that either it would all end quickly, or last for a very long time.

Manoeuvres began taking place in our area and, because heavy weapons were being used, we children would often gather up the bullets strewn across the fields. A friend of my brother's, Alfons Bauer from Stacherting, found such a bullet and showed it to him. We knew him well as he was often around our farm and would come in to visit.

'Just hit it with a hammer, and it will blow up!' he explained as if he was an expert. When his parents were busy harvesting in the fields, he was true to his word. The blow from his hammer caused a massive explosion. Alfons turned around and blood was streaming from his eyes. He was taken to a clinic and despite an operation he could never see properly again and was only able to distinguish between light and dark. He returned to cut peat the following spring along with all the neighbours, but his eyes, we were told, had been perforated, and he couldn't come without a companion. It saddened us children.

'Alfons, do you want to play something on the accordion?' we begged him when he had arrived after being guided to our house. He had a good ear and was very musical, but near-blind. 'I have to attend a school for the blind,' he muttered sadly, 'in Munich.' He was homesick there but was able to study music and became a very well-known musician whom we could listen to on radio and television and who always performed wearing sunglasses [Alfons Bauer became a popular composer and famous zither player].

But Father couldn't avoid the army, and when he was called up in autumn 1940, he was deployed to the Luftwaffe as part of the ground personnel in Neubiberg near Munich. By then, many young men had

Me and Susi Bauer (left), winter 1941.

already been killed and this impacted heavily on the soldiers' families left behind. Along with my father, the Sonnering inn owner was also enlisted. And naturally, my father was extremely upset to leave my mother behind along with us three children.

Every morning at school, we had to listen to the *Wehrmachtsbericht* [the army news report], which in turn cut down on the lessons, with our teachers ostensibly enthusiastic about the political situation. Was it because the Nazis exercised pressure on them? However, Herr Nickl, our teacher, was anxious and couldn't hide it from us.

The first fellow from our community to be killed was Nickl Kober from Almertsham, a fine young man, and I was sad. Father wrote to us every day. The '*Heldensgottesdienste*' [services dedicated to the heroes] at church increased month by month. At school we were requested to listen to the Führer's speeches which bellowed out from the radio set up in Herr Nickl's own living room, as he was the main teacher. During the speeches we had to remain standing and anyone fidgeting or in the slightest way disruptive would be slapped across the face – tensions with Herr Nickl ran very high. I once got caught and I was slapped with such force that I couldn't hear anything in that ear for an entire week.

Boys were wearing the HJ uniform after assembly at the end of the school day but with my parents having to save money, my brothers and I went without. The girls were meant to wear a dark skirt with two front pleats and a white blouse, and I happened to own both. The brown leather ring gathering the black kerchief in a knot completed the outfit. A badge was sewn onto the sleeve of the blouse with the letters BdM – Bund deutscher Mädel.

Along with two other girls, I was asked to attend some short courses which would train us to become leaders and take the *'Appelle'* [roll-calls during which service instructions were passed on]. I was even given a card with my picture attached to it which we had to pick up in person in Endorf. At our meetings we sang songs, played games or did some crafting or knitting for the soldiers. But they couldn't convince us to give up on religion and we continued to go to church on a regular basis. Our life was shaped by the motto *'Sparen für den Sieg'* [economise for the war].

The Hitlerjugend, referred to as *'Pimpfe'* [pimps – a colloquial and derogatory term for little boys] were meant to be *'flink wie Windhunde, zäh wie Leder und hart wie Kruppstahl'* (nimble as greyhounds, tough as leather and hard as Krupp steel), a phrase taken from one of Hitler's speeches and one of the many slogans used. Mothers of more than four children were awarded the *Mutterkreuz* (Mother's Cross) in bronze. If she had six or seven children, she'd get the same thing in silver and mothers with more than eight children received the order in gold. The highest goal in life for women to strive for, according to the indoctrination instilled in us, was to give the Führer his soldiers, and yet the mere fact that this order was pejoratively called a *Karnickelkreuz* (rabbit cross) proved that not all people shared this belief, and there were others who were critical toward National Socialism or had absolutely no interest in anything to do with politics. Because of the entirely new educational system, aimed at withdrawing us from our parents' influence, we always got home very late. Mother was really cross about that as she needed us to help her with her chores. Many of our neighbours were also very much opposed to National Socialism but dared not show it, with the sword of Damocles hovering over us at all times: Dachau. One wasn't allowed to be Jewish nor come from a Jewish family, one had to be free of any inherited disease, nervous illness and not suffer from any disability or be homosexual – otherwise you'd run the risk of being murdered. Mother, in fact, forbade us to even speak about any of these topics. And then, when it came to elections, we all knew that they had been manipulated.

Clothing – but more importantly food – rationing was in place right at the very beginning of the war years, and you could only buy these things with coupons. Even shoes. Everywhere, women were labouring in the fields as, of course, men had been called up from the age of seventeen, which had a huge impact on the female rural population. To support them with their farm work, they'd be allocated French and Serbian prisoners of war, whose labour was also used in factories. Every day, the prisoners had to return to their camp. Here, 'our' prisoners were housed in the Höslwang inn and were always guarded by German soldiers. We were forbidden to have any close contact with them and they were excluded from any festivals or music events, which, of course, meant that they couldn't go to the barn dances that were put on.

A few forced labourers came from Poland, the Ukraine or Russia – both men and women – and they had to mark their clothing with a 'P' or 'East'. These were, in my mind, very lovely and hard-working folk, for whom it was surely very difficult to be so far from their homeland. One Ukrainian lady I remember particularly as she stayed with our neighbours and was exceptionally good at knitting and weaving. Her name was Hela, and though she didn't speak any German, she did gradually learn how to communicate with us.

Father was still attending a war school during 1941 and wore a dark-grey uniform, but when he was on leave, which would last for a few days, he wore civvies. After completing his training, he was deployed to Landau, along the Isar. After that he was stationed for a while in Strasbourg, from where he sent us postcards showing the cathedral. That was thrilling for us children who knew nothing about the big wide world. One day he sent a small parcel containing face cream, several tubes of

Rosa, Bartl and Schorschl.

toothpaste and some fabric. I carefully placed everything in my drawer, feeling extremely excited as there was so little one could buy at the time.

When my older brother was called up, I gave him one of the toothpastes to take with him, and I often knitted him this or that – a jumper, for example, and a headband – which I sent off to him. It gave me a lot of pleasure as these were the last presents from me. He cried on the day he left us to report to the army and I felt deeply sorry for him.

My mother's brother, also called Uncle Sepp, was deployed in Poland. When on leave, he visited us on our farm. He was a dear and very musical man who'd often write to me, and I'd always write back. Once he told me that while in Poland, he had come across a wristwatch which he wanted to give me. But then he was killed before he could ever fulfil his promise.

Because our cities were being bombed as early as 1941, it happened that summer guests often chose to visit Amerang, where they hoped to spend time surrounded by nature and our peaceful landscape, thus escaping the air raids for a few weeks. When, occasionally, Amerang's guesthouses were full, travellers would end up staying with us at our farm.

One day, an older couple walked past our house and got chatting to my mother. They hailed from Königswinter near Bonn and enquired whether they could take up lodgings with us for a few days, an idea Mother quite fancied. She made sure, however, to let the couple know that we didn't have any spare mattresses and could only offer them straw mattresses. 'No problem,' they said, and assured her that they were well used to such mattresses from their childhood years. Their priority was to survive.

So, Mother changed the sheets and offered them a jug of skimmed milk for breakfast, which she placed on the bench outside, near where she washed the laundry. I watched the couple humbly drinking their milk, and for lunch they visited the inn in Amerang. They so obviously enjoyed the milk as normally they could only have obtained one-quarter of a litre each per day on the ration card they had been allocated. 'At long last we can sit here in peace,' they sighed gratefully, 'and not in the air-raid shelter.'

They would have preferred to stay on with us, but after two weeks they had to return to their home. One day we got a letter from them saying that they had chanced upon the grave of one of our local boys, Michi Winkler, when visiting the soldiers' cemetery in Königswinter. Michi's stepmother, who had raised him, immediately travelled to Königswinter and when she was back told us how terribly lonely and sad she had felt standing at his grave. She had taken him into care when he was six years old and had loved him dearly. She now had to come to terms with the fact that he had been killed at the tender age of nineteen.

When the fourth year of war rolled along, conditions had deteriorated to an all-time low, with food supplies dropping to rock-bottom and, tragically, the number of soldiers killed rapidly rising. Families suffered tremendously, we couldn't even avail ourselves of wool and were only provided with some in our craft sessions at school, as we were meant to knit items for the soldiers at the front.

In the summer we were sent out into the fields to collect herbs, which we then dried in order that they could be sent to Russia for soldiers to make tea with. Fräulein Bindl, our teacher, allowed us to transport the herbs by cart to the school, where they were laid out in the loft for drying before being packed into sacks and picked up for transport.

In this dire situation, Father, much like many others, had bought a sheep, which we had to shear regularly. The washed wool was spun and this enabled us to knit stockings and jumpers. As we also ran low on wood for heating, these warm pieces of clothing really came in handy.

In school everyone was asked whether their families could take in a child from the Ruhr area or from Westphalia. This was in line with the *Kinderlandverschickung*, whereby children were evacuated from cities threatened by air raids and brought to the countryside where they could feel safe and also finally lead a life outside their shelters. I volunteered with Mother's permission as I was really hoping to have a girl share my life at home.

Then the Tuesday came when it was all going to happen! All the families who had put their names down were asked to pick up their child in Halfing. We crossed the wood, wondering anxiously what the girl who'd come to our farm would look like. A train rumbled into the station and children descended, all wearing a label strung around their neck. But oh dear! What a disappointment! The child bearing a carton with our name written on it was a boy. His name was Gerhard and he came from Gelsenkirchen and, my goodness, did he look pitiful. He couldn't understand a word as we spoke in a thick Bavarian dialect and could only speak *Hochdeutsch*. We all made a great effort though and he soon relaxed, even gradually learning to laugh again.

Mother had to look after three boys now, as Father was away at the Eastern Front. We walked to school together with Gerhard, a sharp little boy who was good at maths. He was obedient and often helped my mother with her chores; however, this got my brothers' backs up and they often ended up in fistfights. Gerhard stayed with us for half a year and when it was time for him to leave, we were disappointed and sad and all the quarrels were quickly forgotten.

In the meantime, 1943 had begun, and many young soldiers were reported to have lost their lives. Our family didn't remain unscathed. My uncle Matthias had been killed in Stalingrad and Ignaz, my stepbrother, as well. We mourned these deaths deeply, especially Mother. Meals were skimpy and those horrible air raids reached as far as our countryside, with the shrill sound of the sirens disrupting our school lessons. Judging by the many women who'd travel by train from towns to our remote villages, where they went around begging for food or to exchange their valuables for edible stuff, we could well imagine the horrendous situation they had fled. We called these people 'hamsters'.

The day I finished my school year – it was April 1943 – I came home to find a letter from Father. He asked whether I had considered a career as a nurse. It turned out that when he had written that letter in Stalingrad, the winter was particularly brutal, with temperatures sinking as low as -40 degrees. When the 6th Army surrendered, Father was in Donetsk in the Ukraine and was permitted leave for a few days to come home. As presents, he brought us a small can of sunflower oil and photos of the tiny farms he had come across during his deployment. He hold us how poor people were living there and they may have only owned one or, at most, two cows. He'd occasionally meet up with an older woman who spoke German and that obviously was of great comfort to him. His descriptions, including the one about how an entire family would sleep above a large stove that stood in the middle of the living room, were riveting. Toddlers were wrapped into blankets that were twisted into a cradle and then hung from the ceiling – it was warmer at the top of the room. He had been transferred to a transport squad charged with supplying reinforcements to the troops at the front, above all food supplies. He told us about the very many soldiers who had suffered frostbite, lost limbs or were taken prisoner of war. Such news deeply depressed us, of course, with the horrendous loss of life at the Eastern Front a profound tragedy for us all. After a few short days, Father had to return to the front, leaving us with the fervent hope that we'd see him again.

Later on we learnt from Father that he'd been sent to the army hospital located in Rendsburg in Schleswig-Holstein because of a kidney infection and in his letters he continually pleaded for Mother to visit him. But she simply didn't have the courage to do so, seeing that it was far away and travelling had become increasingly dangerous, what with the incessant aerial attacks that didn't only affect the large cities. Even where we lived out in the countryside, it was no longer possible to move around freely as you'd always be startled by low-flying enemy aircraft who'd shoot at anything and anybody. But Mother did go to great lengths in

My father, Bartl (front, right), who died in Russian captivity.

responding to each and every one of his letters. Meanwhile we listened to her memories of how she had met and befriended Father and of their carefree times going on bicycle rides.

The year was 1944 and once again we were urged to open our homes to refugees from the east. First, a woman from East Prussia along with her son were assigned to us. She cooked some of her local dishes for us, Königsberg dumplings and sorrel soup, but they didn't stay all that long. Afterwards we had the Fett family lodging with us, a woman and her two daughters, with the husband fighting at the front, of course. We put two furnished rooms at their disposal, as they had brought nothing with them apart from a bag with some clothing. The two girls were quite lovely, and we got on very well with each other and they stayed for two whole years. When they left for the Rhineland we were upset and missed their company.

Meanwhile, the war had entered its fifth year and circumstances went from bad to worse. My brothers no longer owned any shoes, but luckily my mother managed to obtain some from the shoe shop in Halfing; these were wooden clogs with a leather strap at the back. We were ridiculed at school, but never once missed a day.

I was a rather resourceful young girl and knew how to tune into the radio and listen to the enemy broadcasts – something strictly forbidden, of course – and I had all the information I needed to know: where the front lines were drawn and how high our losses were. With that, I drew myself a map, highlighting the various locations where our soldiers were embroiled in battle. I knew that what I was doing could be punished by death, and Mother, who naturally was terribly frightened, had our dog stand guard outside, and he'd bark if anybody approached the house.

The neighbours were trustworthy. In fact, they'd ask Mother if I could please note down the names of any soldiers from our village who had been killed and to let them know when there might be a funeral service for them. Notices of those killed in action grew in number. There was no longer a printing company that could have printed the images of the soldiers along with their dates, and all crosses had been removed in our school. The ruling that crosses should also disappear in Hölswang was scuppered as the local woman in charge, a feisty and courageous woman, was having none of it, and the crosses remained where they were.

It could be said that the more the German Luftwaffe disintegrated, the more the enemy aerial attacks hounded us. Low-flying aircraft caused immense damage quite close to our home. Cows grazing near Almertsham were targeted and many animals were either killed or seriously injured. Calves could be seen hanging from the bellys of pregnant cows. These were dreadful times.

Young though we were, these horrendous atrocities affected us children profoundly. High-explosives and incendiary bombs demolished acres of land, but others which didn't detonate were found by the Dachau KZ (Konzentrationslager, concentration camp) inmates and defused – a suicide mission in every sense! A farmer's wife volunteered to provide these people with a snack but was prohibited.

I was able to show some kindness, though, towards a few foreign labourers from Poland and Ukraine on at least one occasion. They had asked Mother if it would be possible that I play something on my harmonica for them on a Sunday. So, one Sunday I got together with them up at a hut where they had gathered, sitting on balconies and wheelbarrows. I played folk music, waltzes and other songs I had picked up from the radio. They all joined in and when I played the Volga, they listened to the lyrics 'Hear me, oh, hear me and answer my plea! Send an angel to earth to comfort me' with tears in their eyes. I was so pleased to be able to offer these people a bit of comfort.

In late autumn 1944, Father came for another short visit from Russia. He had lost a lot of weight and was exceptionally tense. He was extremely upset that his mother, my grandmother, had passed away in the meantime and when he was told about her passing he burst into tears and sobbed for a long while. I hadn't ever seen him like this and got frightened. He immediately took his bike to ride to the cemetery, whispering: 'My dear, good mother'.

His days of leave passed quickly and we were all deep in sad thoughts when we accompanied him to the train station in Amerang. Before boarding the train he began to cry again – something we children will never forget. Until the train was out of sight, he stood at the window waving to us, with Mother having gone completely quiet. A bit later she said: 'He'll never return.'

It was as if she had sensed what was coming, Father too. We received a few more letters which Father penned with what must have been a trembling hand, and we knew he wasn't doing well. We never saw him again.

Aerial attacks became more frequent by the week. We saw entire enemy squadrons streaking through the sky above us. We could hear from afar the dull drone and then roaring noises of planes approaching, never failing to send a shock of fear through our bodies. We heard that the railway station in Munich had largely been destroyed, the one in Rosenheim had been hit by several shells. At least the station had air-raid shelters to which people could run when the siren went off. Each alarm was eventually followed by an all-clear signal, with people crawling out of their hiding spaces and shelters and inspecting the devastation, watching houses burn to ruins and ashes. But if the shelter had been bombed, many mothers and children would not return home. Us girls were ordered to run to the picture gallery, which was fortunately never hit.

The more the war progressed, the harder life became for us. With the war situation worsening, the Nazi terror against its own population grew to an unimaginable extent. Even as late as February civilians were court-martialled if they were caught listening to enemy broadcasts or suspected of 'other activities which endangered Germany's fighting strength or its resolve'. But, secretly, people started whispering that the war was lost.

Pregnant foreign labourers were not allowed to keep their babies after they were born in the hospital, with the women returning to the farm deeply embarrassed and taciturn. Hela, who laboured on our neighbour's farm, was one of them, and I truly pitied her. She was a very hard-working young woman.

The war was coming to an end, with people growing ever more tense. The Nazi followers especially had become visibly more fearful, with nobody knowing what the future would bring. And yet … so many people persisted in obeying the rules of the brown-shirts to the tiniest detail. One time, I was just about to buy some rolls in a bakery and must have not greeted the owner properly upon entering the shop. 'We use the *Heil Hitler* greeting around here!' someone barked at me.

The news bulletins I listened to on the prohibited English radio station spoke about the war soon being over, commenting that resources for the Wehrmacht had come to a halt and that the civilian population could no longer be fed. And it was true, as we had to bring our own ingredients to school, where we then had to decide what we'd cook out of them [still today, it is not common for primary or secondary schools to serve meals, as children often return home for lunch]. The windows of our classrooms were boarded up and there was a ghostly feeling all around.

At some point I had no shoes. My last pair had completely fallen apart and could no longer be repaired. It was winter and yet I still had to leave the house every day, of course. At that time, buying shoes was not possible – the shops simply had no stock. Amalie, a good friend of my mother's, wanted to be helpful and as she often travelled to Munich for work, she offered to come up with something. One day she appeared at our door, holding two strong men's shoes in her hand, and though they were different sizes and the toes of the shoes stuck up, I was over the moon. I immediately put them on and they turned out to do the job, keeping my feet dry and warm. In order not to slip out of them, I wore a pair of socks I had knitted myself out of sheep's wool, and the difference in size no longer bothered me.

We hadn't received any mail from Father, and he had given no sign of life. Mother was distraught and anxious at the same time. What if one day she received the notification of his death? Whenever the postman came by, she'd literally tear the mail out of his hands, and this went on for two months.

'Let's pray to the holy Thaddeus,' Mother encouraged us, hoping this might help [Thaddeus is the patron saint of desperate and lost causes]. And so we prayed every day. During those times, since it was bitter cold and we had almost run out of firewood for our stove, we dragged our beds into the living room, huddling together for warmth.

We then received news via a letter from Father that he been able to smuggle out from a POW camp. So this is where he was – we finally knew that he had been taken prisoner. He had only written a few short lines; his writing was wonky and they told us nothing about his actual whereabouts. Many boys from our neighbourhood had been killed in action – all nice lads who had often been to our farm and played with my brothers. I still see their laughing faces before me – and I will never see them again.

The hustle and bustle in the homes of our area had gone quiet. So many parents, wives and girlfriends sat in mourning, grieving over these men buried somewhere far away.

Hitler's regime was collapsing, and though Mother had stopped singing long ago, she was still holding on to a thread of hope. But then came 16 February 1945, the day my mother and I would never forget, and which has become imprinted into our memory forever.

It was, in fact, a calm wintery day, grey and overcast. The countryside was flecked with some patches of snow and the mood in our house was low, as it had been for some time. There were just too many deaths to mourn, so many young lads who'd been destined to take over the family farm had been killed. In the face of defeat, the Nazis called on the last remaining reserves, with the losses mounting sky-high. Nobody knew how this would continue, and who would return. The only ones left living in our house were Mother and me. We got on with our work, ate our meals, spoke little. For several weeks I had taken to sleeping on the first floor in Father's bed and my mother slept in the small room next to it.

215

That night, 16 February, there was a deathly silence – no rush of wind nor fall of snow. We turned off the light in the living room, lit a candle and went upstairs (we only had electricity on the ground floor). I sank into a deep sleep and probably so did my mother as well. But suddenly Mother came bursting into my room, shook me by the shoulders and screamed: 'Rosa, Father has called us! He called my name Rosl, three times! Loud and clear! He's here, right at the door!'

She lit a candle, took the house keys, tied them to a long piece of rope which she then dropped down out of the open window. That's how she always did it when Father returned late from the inn. But there was no sound and no movement – it was completely still. Mother went downstairs, holding her candle and unlocked the house door. 'Bartl, are you there?!' she shouted.

There was no response. It remained still. Mother stood at the threshold for some time, cocking her ears, then locked the door and returned upstairs with the candle.

'I definitely heard his voice', she whispered. 'I definitely heard him call me three times … by my name. I heard "Rosl" three times, quite clearly. It was definitely your father I heard.' She went back to the window, opened it and called again: 'Bartl, are you here?'

She didn't get an answer. We finally went to bed, but Mother was much too agitated to fall back to sleep.

'Surely you just imagined things, Mother,' I kept telling her afterwards to calm her down, but neither of us could explain what had happened that night.

It was only when some months later a comrade of my father came to the farm and informed us that Father, struck by hunger and disease, had passed away on exactly that day, 16 February at 3.30 in the morning, that it dawned on us what had actually happened. Father had by then only weighed 80 pounds but was conscious until the end. He was buried in a mass grave near Schachty in Petrovka oblast.

That same comrade, who had travelled all the way from Deggendorf in Lower Bavaria to share with us the news in person, was suffering from tuberculosis and succumbed to the illness shortly after visiting us. He had more news. When Father lay dying, he told us, he had shouted out several times 'Rosl' and spoke softly about his children, but barely audibly, as he was fast deteriorating. Mother walked over to the calendar and saw her note marked below 16 February: 'Father called!'

But let me return to the last months of the war. Of course, we all knew that the war was lost and all of us tried our hardest to make the best of the situation. How can I, how can *we* move forward? This was the question on everybody's mind, and yet nobody knew what the answer was. What would the future bring?

It was a busy time at our farm as life continued, with turf needing to be cut. There was nothing we could buy, however, as shops had nothing to sell. Fortunately, where we lived, it was possible for farmers to exchange goods among themselves. We still had many foreign labourers working in the area, as well as two Russians who had defected to our side. They had served in the German Wehrmacht and spoke German well. I seem to remember that they were officers. Soldiers who defected faced certain death if they fell into the hands of the Allies. Alexander and Peter kept a low profile and slept in our haystacks. In the evening they set out searching for a field of potatoes or just anything they could lay their hands on. Mother gave them some skimmed milk every day and then one day we saw them hiding their *Wehrpässe* [military service books for men who were conscripted and listing personal details such as birth, address etc.] in bottles and burying them underneath the turf.

Many years later Sepp Geisler from Amerang, who had cut the turf at the time, arrived at our home with these two bottles and the *Wehrpässe*. The two men had just disappeared and, though they seemed decent chaps, the younger of the two bothered me. He kept wanting to touch me up when we crossed the woods, but the older guy told him off in Russian. Fortunately, nothing happened.

My older brother Schorschl was drafted to the Luftwaffe as late as January 1945. Even though the war had nearly ended, he was forced to join. But where was he now? The war was finished and yet we had heard nothing from him.

It was May and the Americans were approaching from the west, pushing into our area, and it was only the totally mad Nazis who decided to put up a resistance.

My brother Schorschl (back row, right) in 1944 after his physical examination prior to his military service.

Schorschl, we had been informed, had been dismissed from the army at the beginning of May. He was supposed to have travelled along with nine other young comrades from Munich towards Traunstein. Thinking back, all he would have had to do was jump from the train when it was moving slowly and then walk on foot to reach home. But he didn't do that, and for some reason remained on the train all the way to Traunstein. Why? It was a question I kept asking myself over several decades. Whatever the reason – it had fateful consequences.

When those young recruits arrived in Traunstein, the Waffen-SS collected them and drove them to Siegsdorf. Thursday 3 May was a turbulent day, with the Americans advancing from the west and inhabitants swiftly going about to hang white sheets from their windows. At the same time some fanatics insisted on an armed resistance. Some SS men, perhaps an anti-tank unit, mounted 8.8-cm naval guns to stall the American advance. When the ten young soldiers with my brother among them arrived on site, they were ordered to blow up the bridge across the

Traun to make the crossing impossible. 'Total madness,' the ten men retorted in one voice, 'we should surrender!'

The Waffen-SS soldiers, fanatics the lot of them, had these ten young lads line up and killed each and every one of them, the first shot to their forehead, the second to the heart.

The mayor of our town, Herr Linner, came to our farm two weeks later to bring the news of Schorschl's death. He had been a hard-working mechanical engineer apprentice and at the time of his first physical examination he had been dispensed from duty due to working in an industry considered essential for the war economy.

The news shocked us profoundly. We were heartbroken, couldn't eat anything for days and Mother was practically paralysed, unable to lift a finger. I had to go on my bike to the surrounding villages where our relatives lived and bring them the news of my brother's death and ask for a church service to be organised. My eyes kept welling up with tears.

The gravedigger, Andreas Nieder from Siegsdorf, called us on the telephone and confirmed that, based on the documents they had retrieved, it was definitely my brother. But because of the many deaths at the time, there weren't sufficient coffins available and he'd just been put into a wooden box. Toni Kistler, a builder from our village, volunteered to fetch the box and transport it home, but when it arrived, we couldn't bring ourselves to open it to look at our dear Schorschl one last time. We had a quiet burial for him in our Höslwang cemetery.

Yes, the war was officially over but we still felt the repercussions. Three weeks after the war had ended, a vehicle drove up to our farm late at night. Mother went downstairs, unlocked the door and I could hear whispers in hushed voices. Mother then returned to her room, and I asked her what that was all about.

'We're forbidden to tell anybody.'

Much later I found out what had gone on. The owner of the Eggstätter factory had fled to us under the cover of night because forced labourers who had worked in his place were now after him, trying to kill him. They had, apparently, already murdered someone else. He was in a right panic and hid in our haystack. And that's where he remained for several weeks, covering himself with a blanket during the night. I noticed Mother tying a can of milk to a rope every day, and that same evening the can was empty. I learnt only after it was all over that someone had stayed with us but then left. Fortunately he survived.

And most fortunately, we survived all the madness, at least I did, along with my mother and my younger brother. In my thoughts, however, I always revisited the past, especially with respect to my father and my brother Schorschl, who so tragically went to his death at the very end of the war – such a senseless death. Why on earth didn't he just jump off the train?

Whoever survived this horrendous war will never be able to erase the memories. And when I pass the old oak close to our house, I often ask myself what this venerable tree might think, having looked down on all these atrocious events. Human beings are insane, when you think about it. They kill one another, and then what? The world moves on. But our mountains don't change, nor do our splendid lakes, nor our wondrous woods. The trees live on, they remain firm and are calmly rooted into our landscape. Perhaps they might shake their leafy heads above us, witnessing the madness below. But, sadly, we don't pay any attention.